Y0-BEA-269

THE CHRISTIAN RENAISSANCE

By the same Author

MYTH AND MIRACLE:

An Essay on the Mystic Symbolism of Shakespeare's Final Plays. Burrow & Co., 43-47 Kingsway, London .... 50c.

THE WHEEL OF FIRE:

Essays in interpretation of Shakespeare's Sombre Plays. Oxford University Press.. $3.75

THE IMPERIAL THEME:

Further interpretations of Shakespeare's tragedies, including the Roman Plays. Oxford University Press $3.75

THE SHAKESPEARIAN TEMPEST:

Oxford University Press............................ $3.75

The Christian Renaissance

With Interpretations of

Dante, Shakespeare and Goethe

And a Note on

T. S. Eliot

by

G. WILSON KNIGHT

Chancellors' Professor of English, Trinity College, Toronto

TORONTO: THE MACMILLAN COMPANY OF CANADA LIMITED, AT ST. MARTIN'S HOUSE
1933

Printed in Canada

PRESS OF THE HUNTER-ROSE CO., LIMITED, TORONTO

Thou hast conquered, O pale Galilean, the
world has grown grey with thy breath;
We have drunken of things Lethean, and
fed on the fulness of death.

'Tis life, whereof our nerves are scant,
Oh life, not death, for which we pant;
More life, and fuller, that I want.

I am come that men might have life and might have it
more abundantly.

CONTENTS

Introduction

PREFACE

I wish to make clear at the start that my criticisms in this book of post-Renaissance Christianity are wide and general, and directed against no particular sections of belief or practice. I have reason to be very grateful to the editors of Church periodicals of various denominations: and indeed my acknowledgments are here due to *The Hibbert Journal* and *The Canadian Journal of Religious Thought* where certain passages in the following pages originally appeared.

Though the ideas in this sort of writing usually come as discoveries, this is partly deceptive. My book thus owes a profound debt to those modern tendencies which are its context. Especially I would name here the writings and general influence of Mr. T. S. Eliot, Mr. Aldous Huxley, and Mr. Middleton Murry: I refer to Mr. Murry's less recent writings. Also these books: Mr. I. G. Bartholomew's *The Cause of Evil*, M. Henri Bergson's *Creative Evolution,* Mr. G. K. Chesterton's *The Everlasting Man,* William James' *The Varieties of Religious Experience,* Mr. Max Plowman's study of Blake, Prof. Saurat's *Literature and Occult Tradition,* Mr. Colin Still's *Shakespeare's Mystery Play,* Canon Streeter's *Reality,* Prof. A. N. Whitehead's *Science and the Modern World,* and Oscar Wilde's *De Profundis.* I owe certain details to Miss C. F. Spurgeon's work on Shakespeare's imagery, and a valuable quotation, and perhaps more than that, to Prof. Herbert Read's *Wordsworth.*

I wish to record also my gratitude to Dr. F. T. H. Fletcher, formerly of Trinity College, whose sympathy and insight did much to fertilize my own thinking during the initial stages of my work; to Prof. C. Lewis of Trinity College for reading my interpretation of *Faust,* and lending me the encouragement of his approval; to the Rev. W. Lyndon Smith for casting a professional eye over my two interpretative essays on the New Testament; and to Prof. C. A. Ashley for reading the whole book in proof. Finally, I am greatly indebted to Miss Eayrs of the Macmillan Company of Canada for her care in helping to settle details of typography, and also for her generous assistance in checking my references.

These references are drawn mainly from Dr. Moffat's translation of the Bible, the Globe Shakespeare, Cary's Dante; and also Prof. Latham's excellent version of *Faust* in the Everyman series, to which I have had to be content with giving page references only. Prof. Latham's notes have been helpful to me; and so have those in both Cary's Dante and the edition of the *Divina Commedia* published in the Temple Classics. I hope my readers will forgive my quoting throughout from translations: I confess to having small Greek, less Italian, and no German or Hebrew.

G. W. K.

Toronto, March, 1933.

For
my Mother

Preliminary Notice:—

It is suggested that any reader who is likely to find parts of this book difficult might do well to read first, in order, the following chapters: I, VI, VIII, IX, XI, XII, XIII.

I. THE PROPHETIC IMAGINATION

IN this book I extend my work beyond Shakespearian interpretation, discussing other great poets and their relation to the New Testament. A somewhat fresh reading of the New Testament and Christianity emerges, as well as a new view of poetry in general. It has, of course, been evident that my interpretations of Shakespeare must, sooner or later, necessarily have something to say about Christianity. Either a great poet means nothing definite at all: or he means something of vast importance. Shakespeare and the other poets I inspect in the following pages cannot henceforward be kept without the pale of our religious consciousness. They are the prophets of the modern world. It is true that a profound poetic understanding inevitably reveals the New Testament to be the most consummate vision of any: but unless we first focus the imaginative richness of pure poetry we shall scarcely be able to receive the yet greater richness of revelation. Now in that they aim to reveal the relation of poetry to Christianity and to expose certain riches in both that are generally neglected, the following chapters themselves lay claim to prophetic validity and significance. And I know that to prophesy, as they do, a Christian and poetic renaissance in the near future, is, to-day, an ambitious act in the world of letters. But it is as well to make quite clear at the outset that such is the direction I take and such the position to which I arrive.

It is, unfortunately, inevitable that any new approach to things which are old should result in misunderstanding and misrepresentation. And since this book follows logically from my works on Shakespeare, I devote its preliminary chapters to the theory implicit in my imaginative interpretations. A method that has produced misunderstanding when applied to Shakespeare is scarcely likely to meet a more universal sympathy when applied to the New Testament. But I do not refer only to adverse criticism. It sometimes happens that a generous attempt to meet my point of view only the more clearly reveals a wide divergency in standpoint. For I am not offering yet another variation of critical 'belles-lettres' as is usually supposed: I rather work at a new science of poetic interpretation.

We are to-day lost in a pseudo-intellectualism which, by claiming a final authority and logical clarity that it in no sense possesses, has made a positive—or rather a negative—chaos in the world of thought. The criticisms levelled at my Shakespearian interpretations may be regarded as typical of a wider context; and my references here to my own work are introduced mainly to illuminate this general situation. A usual complaint asserts that I do not consider Shakespeare in relation to his time, or his personal intentions. But why should I? It is poetry, not history or biography, that I wish to interpret. And with the greater writers we instinctively make what minor historical allowances may be necessary. Moreover, the critics who say this invariably try to judge my book on its merits. They make no allowances for the strange time in which we live, nor for my own more personal experiences. And they are right not to do so. Similarly, I regard any great work that has survived the centuries as something independent of its own generation. It is, indeed, exactly this independence which is the condition of literary greatness:

since we habitually and naturally consider as less significant those works which the race is content to forget. Wordsworth's Preface to the *Lyrical Ballads* has to be read in relation to the eighteenth century critical theories and poetic practice from which he reacts, and, when so understood, is seen to be important. But it is far less important than Shelley's *Defence of Poetry* which needs no such allowances. Similarly, Ben Jonson needs far more archæological commentary than Shakespeare. But it is not really the Elizabethan Shakespeare at all to which my critics would recall me. It is they who lack the power to see imaginative work objectively. Thus Victorian criticism tended to make Shakespeare a nineteenth century novelist, and that was followed by the modern attempt to see him as a twentieth century dramatist. In actual fact, he is like neither: he is much nearer the Elizabethans. I find 'symbolic' qualities in Shakespeare, and am told that that is unreasonable. But what of the medieval miracle and morality plays from which Elizabethan drama developed? What of *Everyman,* with its personification of Death and other abstractions, and the *Interlude of the Four Elements,* a metaphysical argument in dramatic form? Or of Lyly with his clustering divinities, allegories, and symbols? What of Death and Revenge as personified in plays attributed to Kyd, and the highly symbolical and theological structure of Marlowe's *Faustus?*—or Spenser and his extravagant use of symbolism, allegory, and metaphysical speculation? This is the soil of Shakespearian drama. That Shakespeare more perfectly than other writers projected these essences into living and convincing figures is an additional merit: that is all. I use these arguments merely to show that, if the point is raised, it is I, not my critics, who see the Elizabethan Shakespeare objectively. But it is by no means my aim to see Shakespeare primarily in terms of the Elizabethan age: it is merely a necessary consequence of seeing him imaginatively. The Elizabethan was a poetical age, and it is the poetry—which includes the richly symbolical effects I emphasize—that has endued Shakespeare's work with so extraordinary a power, and which vitalizes my own interpretations. Now this is one instance, a symptom, of a universal and dangerous disease in the modern mind: we mask, under a veneer of realism, intellectualism, and objectivity, a completely unfettered subjectivity leading to intellectual chaos; whereas loyalty to the imagination will ever lead to a convincing intellectual coherence. Here the process of false reasoning is very clear. The Elizabethan period was intensely poetical and symbolical; whereas we live in a peculiarly unimaginative age. We have not seen the symbolisms in Shakespeare, and, when pointed out, we say, paying no regard whatsoever to the evidence, that they are incompatible with the period of their creation. What we mean is that they are incompatible with the period of our own criticism. And very much the same has happened with our attitude to the Christian Religion.

Intellect is a good servant but, when allowed to assume autonomous rights, a most inefficient master. Immediately it lets the passions run riot, lending them unwittingly its own authority. By putting primary faith in the imagination, however, we endue our intellectual activities with a power they cannot elsewise possess. Now imagination is certainly not purely emotional, nor intellectual: it results from a blending of emotion with intellect, the two creating a faculty which mysteriously controls both. Though difficult to explain in theory, it is not necessarily hard to practise, at all events when contemplating the poets. There is, however, one necessity: we must sincerely desire—trying alone is no use—to receive the message for which we are looking. There is an element of love in all imaginative apprehension. But the critical faculty with a host of false associations is only too ready to prevent our focussing a fact in the imaginative world: and in an excessively intellectual age like the present it seldom fails. I therefore emphasize the need to-day of imaginative understanding: first of the prophets and poets, next of life itself.

For not only must we try to see symbolic literature with a truly imaginative apprehension if we are to find its more objective significance, but poetry and religious symbolism in general is itself a more objective approach to reality than other less richly inlaid methods of expression; since it reports not facts abstracted from their vital context but facts fused with a proper passionate significance. Moreover, being thus closely in touch with reality, poetry is automatically set outside the swiftly-changing superficialities which currently pass for exact truth. It is significant, and 'significance' inevitably and always points to the future. Therefore, though great literature may be unpopular during the age of its birth, and might be called, in a sense, subjective and fanciful within those limits, it is yet highly objective in terms of the unlimited future. And it is especially this futurity about high poetry that I wish to emphasize. All great work, in literature or life, is prophetic, and exists not in the past from which it arises but in the future to which it points and which it helps to create.

But to-day many minds refuse to grant the

imagination the sovereignty to which its claim is hereditary. And I reply that not only in matters of religion and poetry, but even in excessively intellectual pursuits, no primary excellence can be attained without something which quite transcends the ratiocinative process. I quote an example from chess which will be most fertile to our inspection. Now most moderate chess players, like myself, try to analyse at every turn the diverging ramifications of the next few moves. 'If I do this, he will do that, or perhaps that, and then I . . . Or if I do that, then he . . .' and so on. Clearly the complications become swiftly infinite, and the baffled mind eventually makes a move in despair. But a player of a much higher order, Mr. H. P. Parsbo of Cheltenham, tells me that he sees a whole movement simultaneously outrolled and leading to an ideal mate. He does not think in terms of a process, but rather visualizes what he names a 'pattern' spread out immediately in space and time, or rather in space-time, and rejects moves that do not fit this pattern. This clearly is an aesthetic and creative, rather than an intellectual and analytic, method. He admits there are no words by which it can be explained exactly how such a mind-activity is possible: it seems, however, a simple and direct faculty to the possessor. The good player, therefore, tries not so much to play the game right as to prevent its playing itself wrong. Implicit in the laws of chess is always at any moment an ideal continuance: and this must be allowed to unfurl itself. But there is an important fact to be noted. Though he may thus select his move by a purely imaginative faculty, Mr. Parsbo tells me, as, of course, one must expect, that he could at any time give exact reasons, if asked, for his decision, playing out alternative variations step by step and demonstrating to a weaker player like myself the faults in those he has rejected. Thus the imagination here includes, but does not depend on, the intellect. I confess that this method, applied to chess, is quite beyond my understanding. But this is certainly the true chess faculty: it is what M. Alekhine must mean when he says that he sees the pieces as 'lines of force'. And when one considers the amazing feats a chess-master can accomplish, playing numerous simultaneous games blindfold, it is clear that no intellectual analysis of the normal kind could possibly be adequate.

But though I find imaginative chess of this order beyond my intellectual comprehension, as indeed it must be, even to the possessor, or he could explain it in intellectual terms, I see clearly that it is only a single instance of a more general law governing the relative powers of the analytic intellect and synthetic imagination in any field. I once taught mathematics to a pupil of intense mathematical ability who could see the answer to a most complicated problem about trains by immediate intuition: he then swiftly showed that it was correct, doing the sum backwards. Having myself arrived at a different answer by the soundest and most laborious of methods three times in succession, it was scarcely possible, when there was no room for doubt as to who was right, for me to point out that his method was inadvisable. That the finest mathematical faculty is intuitive rather than intellectual is also evidenced by M. Poincare's well-known description in *Science and Method* of the way in which a long-sought solution seems to be worked out in the unconscious mind, the whole combination rising to consciousness when the pattern is perfected: which corresponds to the chess-player's rejection of unsuitable moves. Now if a super-intellectual faculty is needed for the highest skill in chess and mathematics, it is scarcely likely that the intellect, as usually understood, can by itself grapple with the intricacies of poetry and religion.

Consider the primary qualities of this faculty as shown by my examples. It is immediate, and either visual or best expressed in visual terms; hence Mr. Parsbo's word 'pattern'. It may have something to do with both the conscious and unconscious mind, as shown by M. Poincare's description. It is an aesthetic faculty, and may thus be supposed to contain an emotional element. For it space and time may cease to exist as such, otherwise it would be impossible to see chess-variations both spreading across the board in space and developing move by move in time as a single pattern: which pattern, since it clearly contains elements both spatial and temporal, must be allowed to exist in some space-time continuum difficult to define. Such an imagination acts successfully and with consummate ease where the labouring intellect is quite at a loss, yet it can at any moment, if called on to do so, prove its own rightness on any one point in intellectual terms. But it may be quite impossible for the adept to explain the secret of his method to those not naturally initiated. To him, the thing is simple and eminently practical, a simple sight, but there are no words by which he may explain it to anyone wandering darkly in the world of the theorizing intellect.

Now in my interpretative work I find myself in a somewhat similar position. Interpretation is, indeed, simple. One of my most hostile critics generously compares my book *The Imperial Theme* to the 'infinitely painstaking work in Eastern mosaics' and suggests that 'it would be harsh not to feel a kind of numbed reverence on account of the amount of human energy expended'. That reverence is misplaced. Except when actually at work on an essay I have kept no notes save what can be written at the back of my Shakespeare. My interpretations are the result of a perfectly simple and direct view of the plays. They follow automatically from an attitude instinctively adopted. It is true that, until written out, the patterns they describe have not been clearly visualized, but it is also true that my work has seemed to develop inevitably along lines vaguely seen, though not always understood, from the outset. Long before I knew exactly how to do it or had any direct evidence that it could systematically be done, I asserted that a true interpretation would everywhere attend to the 'flesh and blood' of poetry rather than the skeleton which is the logical content. Similarly, it was clear to me, however overpowering might seem the reasons against it, that Shakespeare's final plays must necessarily be regarded as immortality visions: but not till now have I fully worked out the defence against such reasonings. Sometimes I have definitely asserted, with very little evidence in my conscious mind, that such and such an imaginative association would be found throughout Shakespeare, only afterwards collecting suitable passages—of whose presence I knew in a way I cannot explain—when proof appeared to be necessary: and thus, though I have for long stressed the supreme importance of the 'tempest' symbol in Shakespeare, it was not till I collected the material quoted in *The Shakespearian Tempest* that I was actually aware of its extent. My interpretations have unfurled by themselves, with little effort on my part and certainly no hard thinking. I conclude that the faculty I employ is imaginative rather than strictly intellectual. But that does not mean it is the less trustworthy. On the contrary, imagination ever reveals facts in the poetic world, whereas intellect involves itself in theories. Our chess analogy is helpful. However I may think my reasoning the safer with all its 'ifs' and suppositions, the imaginative player, seeing the ideal pattern as a single reality, wins. You cannot get beyond that. Similarly, by disregarding inimical theories, we can all focus hitherto neglected facts in the Shakespearian world. Seeing an already existent reality, we shall know that the fullest intellectual support can be relied on at any moment when defence is necessary: but intellectual reasonings will scarcely themselves help to break new ground. They can consolidate a position, but cannot win it. Yet when properly subordinated to an imaginative purpose, the intellect is, certainly, of inestimable importance. Moreover, an intuition that cannot defend itself in terms of intellect is of doubtful value. I tend to lose confidence at once in my chess expert's space-time pattern if he cannot, if asked, at any point in his play demonstrate the dangers attending the move I should myself have chosen.

Poetic interpretation, moreover, is also concerned with 'patterns'. I have urged that we see the pattern of a Shakespearian play outrolled 'in space as well as time'. An easy play to visualize like this is *Timon*: on the one side a glittering world, rich garments, feasting, luxury and love; on the other, nakedness and hatred, a desert-cave, and the muffled thunder of the breaking seas. It is surely not hard to visualize these, as a single contrast, two areas of human experience. And yet some minds find it all but impossible: they cannot see such effects till they know whether Shakespeare intended them. And how can we possibly tell them? And would they believe us if we did? Sometimes a critic is more definitely hostile: as though you were to show a man a view from a hill-top and, after gazing at it for a while, he were to turn round and say fiercely: 'I don't agree'. Therefore, when I point out the vivid importance of the child-symbolism in *Macbeth,* the same critic I have already quoted answers that 'in our experience of the play babies and their symbolic meaning matter hardly in the slightest'. I ask the reader to compare this statement with my *Macbeth* quotation in Chapter III; and, remembering that traditional commentary regards the second child-apparition, his 'baby-brow' bound with gold, as merely representing Malcolm, a young man of about twenty, to consider which interpretation does least violence to the facts. To those who can adopt the imaginative view—and fortunately there are many —it is ever remarkably simple; to others, mysterious with the mystery that clouds the obvious. It is, at all events, both practical and fruitful: so that, after starting from the patterns in single plays, and what I have called the Shakespearian Progress in the plays of Shakespeare's later years, it has been possible next to see the whole work of Shakespeare as a pattern of 'tempests' and 'music'; and in this book I similarly attempt to visualize in outline the course of European poetic literature as a whole since the New Testament, in a way that covers in its suggestion territories quite beyond my actual reading, and clearly also suggests the course our poetry should take in the future. Imagination continually thus unrolls the future, seeing it implicit in the present. And it should be clear that none of this is necessarily difficult; that it may be, to many minds at least, quite simple and obvious.

Such interpretations seem, therefore, in both the manner of their creation and the vision they expose to exhibit certain characteristics similar to the intuitive methods I have reviewed in chess and mathematics. We may next suggest that the work they analyse is itself a product owing its existence to some such faculty. I have often shown that the Shakespearian play is compact of many inter-tissued suggestions in thought and imagery besides its more outstanding symbolisms, its action, and the vital human persons who tread its stage. Now it is evident that no amount of thought alone could possibly spin out the myriad of detailed perfections which are revealed to an intellectual interpretation. I say 'intellectual' since interpretation is clearly a degree nearer the intellectual mode than poetry. Moreover, the Shakespearian play has often been submitted, with similar results, to quite different interpretations from mine. It replies with equal ease to quite incompatible advances from critics of widely different schools. There is some mystery about all this, especially to those who are able to focus Shakespeare's infinite and all but miraculous delicacy in symbolic suggestion. I conclude that the original creative faculty in the poet need not be thought to have covered all the ground explored by these varying interpretations: but that we, who interpret, see an original simplicity in terms of our own labouring intelligence. I believe the writing of *Antony and Cleopatra* was to Shakespeare at least as simple and spontaneous as my interpretations are to me; that he used a faculty similar to that of the chess adept, a faculty which cuts directly across the numerous difficulties we foolishly suppose to have been laboriously overcome.

I have often demonstrated that the Shakespearian play is to be regarded 'spatially' as well as 'temporally': that we must be prepared to see it as a whole, presenting a massed area of corresponding units intermeshed with each other in close texture to build a system which is directly related to the story in which these units are also necessary event links. Put more simply, each imaginative suggestion has a part to play in the story and a duty to fulfil to the 'atmosphere' as well. This sounds all very complicated, but that is due entirely to the failure of our intellects to express a very simple thing. I have often urged that both these elements are abstractions from the one unity, and that fully to possess the play we must, in a sense, see both at once in a single view. This can come only after long acquaintance with a particular work, though my interpretations aim to expedite the process. I cannot say how such a space-time image is possible, but it clearly exists. Shakespeare's plays are space-time visions conceived simply, but expressed through numerous mind-pictures and concepts relating a simple sight to the complexities of our intellectual world. Shakespeare saw *Macbeth* first in some space-time continuum of the imagination, and the sight was simple, since space-time vision must not be thought to involve all the complexities of a space-vision fused with a time-vision: it overlooks them from above, resolving them into simplicities. It is reported that Mozart saw, or heard, a complete work as a single whole unfurled to his immediate awareness before setting it down in the time-sequence of composition, and it is reasonable to suppose that *King Lear* was created in some such fashion. Nor does it matter whether we regard the original 'seeing' as unconscious, since that is only another way of saying it was not intellectual or perceptive in the ordinary sense, the 'unconscious mind' being a paradoxical concept, an unknown quantity, the 'x' of our whole equation. My own work has unrolled without my purposive direction, yet with a continual assurance that I was writing from a centre which could not lead me astray. And in this sense Shakespeare himself regards the 'soul' as 'prophetic' in many passages, which 'soul' is often, with him, to be equated with the original creative force, the mysterious 'nothing', the unconscious purpose, to be incarnated in material shapes by the artist's technique. A passage I have often referred to in *Richard II* illustrates admirably this sort of growth: Shakespeare makes his imprisoned hero, in meditative mood, create a dream-world of the imagination similar to Shakespeare's own world of drama. Richard's thought-sequence next remarkably forecasts the progress of Shakespeare's greater plays at that time unwritten, unconceived. And this is not really strange. The one does not follow from the other: but both unfurl from the same origin, they are small and great circles outrippling from the same centre, the centre of life and creation. That the space-time or creative reality should often be directly prophetic in temporal terms is, indeed, inevitable: but only in temporal terms is it at all miraculous.

All this is very close to the chess-expert's ability to see intuitively the potentialities in a complicated position, seeing, however, not the myriad complexities which are to be rejected so much as the one simplicity to be adopted; instinctively ruling out at any one point all those moves which do not fit the simple pattern outrolling towards the ideal mate. I am myself conscious not so much of thinking out ideas as of receiving thoughts that come either from within or without, in meditation or conversation. The heading of this chapter was known to be necessary and therefore fixed before I had planned what I should say. Just before starting it, I had the conversation on chess which was immediately recognized as significant and has given me my main direction: and that is my normal way of progression. I accept what fits, and reject what does not fit, my sense of significance. Shakespeare likewise may be considered at every turn not so much to have thought out his effects as to have rejected those that did not fit his ideal pattern. He may not have been aware that his *Antony and Cleopatra* is full of vivid life-suggestions, but an impression of loathly disease or starvation—and there are many in Plutarch—would have immediately stimulated his sense of incongruity.

These faculties are all, in their way, prophetic: they see in full or twilight consciousness the future necessity already thrusting up from the soil of the present, creatively flowering; and reject all that hinders this necessary growth. And they are most naturally expressed in visual terms: 'intuition' and 'imagination' each, by derivation, suggesting 'sight'. They should be considered not as a 'thinking out', the laborious and faulty process usually employed by unskilful workmen, but as a conscious 'rejection' of effects incompatible with the creative ideal in the soul, or unconscious mind, or imaginative intuition. We remember M. Poincare's description of how the mathematical problem sorts itself out in unconsciousness, rising to consciousness only when complete: which is another way of saying exactly the same thing. Poetry rises to the mind in a similar fashion. The conscious intellect, indeed, cannot create: it can only reject. Art is largely the rejection of incompatibilities whilst having regard to an ideal recognized first in terms of what it is not and realized after by the expression of what it is. And therefore the truly creative mind will be distinguished not so much by its memory but rather by its sieve-like power to forget, to reject, all that does not fit its creative purpose. To compare small things with great: there were days when I tried hard to stock my memory with Elizabethan archaeology. The attempt was as unnatural and as futile for my mind as it has proved instinctive and of world-wide importance with Sir Edmund Chambers. We are all bound to the patterns of our own natures.

All poetry flowers from this 'second sight'. The poet is a 'seer' and a prophet, because he 'sees' something in the space-time world. But this 'seeing' is not ordinary space-sight. It often appears to be independent of sight as usually understood, a mental reality only: it is significant that the chess-expert can usually play blindfold with a facility not far beneath that of his usual play. Imaginative sight is truly mysterious. It is not sight in the ordinary sense, yet can only be expressed in visual—or aural—terms. Hence poetic imagery is ever most important. But we must regard images not in static isolation, but rather in their succession and interrelation. In the space-time world all pictures are dynamic. We must see a poem first as a rapid series of complex pictures; next, keeping the whole in our memory, try to possess all separate images in one extensive view without forgetting the series. Our aim in receiving the poet's vision should be to hold all his pictures in our mind simultaneously whilst not forgetting the order of their sequence.

The more richly we can do this, the more perfectly we shall recreate the original vision or experience to which the poem directs us. The infinite subtleties in Dante's *Paradiso* flower from a simple and immediate sight. Poetry is a spectroscope refracting the one beam into a whole heirarchy of tints; or a sea whose ripples split the sun's light into a myriad sparkles. The original vision in all great literature is difficult, but vastly important: it is sight of life itself in the space-time, that is, the creative, dimension. The poet is thus the seer and prophet of creation and life.

By life I mean the whole concrete reality. Habitually we abstract from it, making two worlds, the inward and the outward. If we are emotionalists, we try to see the outer world as our instincts desire it; if we are intellectualists, we try to see it objectively, without reference to our own desires. Both methods are liable to create pitiful abstractions from the real. The emotionalist, however, by allegiance to a certain pattern, aesthetically conceived in himself, may well succeed in releasing a vital force, for good or ill. His pattern is a creative thing within a limited field. The intellectualist is more liable to fall into a rather pallid blamelessness such as Dante relegates to Limbo. But the yet greater life is created by a continual allegiance to the inward desire and a simultaneous surrender of the intellect to the wider world. The two inevitably clash with most of us, but these tragedies are necessary and creative, if not positively, at least negatively: where many fail one may succeed. There is thus a middle and difficult path for us. We must preserve loyalty to our own more emotional intuitions, however they may appear to be denied: and this is what Dante means when he tells us to act creatively from immediate communion with the life-source rather than derive morality from any 'created good' in the objective world. Yet clearly we cannot, unless at our peril, forget the facts of life. We have therefore to act in accordance with our own inward pattern of ideal beauty, while never forgetting the evil present or apparent in the world around us. In so far as we can blend these two we do something of the greatest importance. Our ideal pattern is extended and becomes richer and richer; and our knowledge of the world becomes more and more profound.

The greatest prophets, like the greatest poets, seem to have attained a high degree of correspondence between these two, the inward and outward. It is as though the world they see reflects the pattern in their own souls. Hence their tremendous assurance, and Jesus' assertion that the great God is a God of Love. The world is as they would have it be: they see it, and see that it is good. And yet they seem not to deduce their actions or teaching logically from an inspection of their world, but rather to reject certain patent facts which would destroy their belief. Yet Jesus' pattern of action certainly included a uniquely full awareness of evil and pain: he is the eternal prototype of sympathy. While his mind accepts and sanctions the evil, his acts persistently create the good. Though his imagination certainly played with profound understanding over good and evil phenomena, his acts were clearly dictated by an intuition that seems to us to have rejected all evidence persuading him that his trust was vain. The result, certainly, was a life more purely creative than any in history. This is unquestionable: he has no rival in respect to creative response from future generations. And it is not hard to see how this came about, how his acts could unswervingly obey an intuition to us not at all deducible from his world and indeed definitely conflicting with it, yet clearly taking it into account.

Remember our chess-expert and see Jesus playing with the white pieces of life against the black forces of death. The present position is the mental and political state of Judaea and the Roman World. Now the pattern he instinctively visualizes is not only the space-pattern of his own place and day. He rather sees—by nature he cannot help it—a quite different position outrolled simultaneously in present space and future time. Neither space nor time are here distinct, and in the space-time world both are quite transfigured. So his pattern is still and solid, not subject to flux and variations, yet composed entirely of them, itself dynamic, prophetic, and creative. He does not think out his actions nor his words, but intuitively rejects those that do not fit the unwavering creative design on which his eyes are fixed. Hence the unerring precision of his life. Now, seeing not indeed the unwritten history of the future as an indefinite time-sequence with all its manifold possibilities and contingencies, all the things that may or may not happen, attended by the fears and doubts to which such thinking must give rise, he yet visualizes futurity as co-existent with the present, implicit in it, out-flowering from it, and makes every time the move that fits into this universal solidity. Like the chess-expert he makes sacrifices which to the less skilful seem disastrous. At the last, he sacrifices even the queen of his life, only next moment to queen the pawn of his death. So he lets his creative play unfurl itself with an inviolable artistic symmetry towards that ideal mate and final cause to which life itself is moving. For his words and actions are ever direct and lucid expressions of that central creative power which is moulding the future of his world: they therefore both foresee and help to create that future.

Jesus' life continually suggests that his consciousness is directly comparable to that 'prophetic imagination' I have been discussing. Whatever he knows intuitively he can defend intellectually. And this is not so much because he is skilled to think out intellectual answers as that he can see the fallacies in all intellectual attacks. This is not 'cleverness': he is on a height where intellectual difficulties are puerile, and refutation is therefore easy. He is never liable to be caught off his guard, because his adversaries' weapons are of straw. Yet he certainly finds the same exasperating difficulty, as anyone must who works from an imaginative centre, in explaining his message to those whose minds work differently. That is why the simple rather than the lettered are his disciples; since it is not ignorance but rather a deceptive knowledge that shuts man from the imaginative sight. I find exactly the same in my own limited field: a young pupil whose mind is unhampered by the litter of false scholarship can, if shown, see the Shakespearian world far more objectively than many recognized experts. It is with reluctance that I quote such an instance in this context, but the point is important. I may be forgiven when I say that I lay no claim whatsoever to the authentic vision of life, any more than to that of chess: in poetry only do I claim such a sight, where the greater part of the work has already been done by the poet. That is, I claim only to be a reader of understanding.

To return to the life of Jesus. We must recognize always that he, seeing a simplicity in which present and future, fact and creative significance, are not distinct, must often express himself in terms which baffle us. He knows he has tremendous authority and that his justification is certain: this he may image in terms of his second coming, and if he appears to place this in the near future, we may say that his justification certainly started within a generation, at the birth of the Christian Church. What to him was an immediate reality is later unfurled in history. But he will not himself think in purely historical terms: since his mind works in a dimension from which history is a partial abstraction only. We can always interpret such words in terms of evolution: but interpretation must never limit its original. The second coming will have other meanings too. At root, the difficulty is always the same. Jesus is expressing a very simple thing in terms of a very complicated machine: the human intellect. He 'sees' something himself, and continually urges men to 'see' with him, complaining that they have eyes but do not see, ears but do not hear. Necessarily, he speaks often as a poet, poetry being the authentic language of the space-time vision. He thus expresses his sight in images of the birds, the lily, the vine-yard and fig-tree, harvests, and the marriage-banquet. These are in some sort visual correlatives to his own knowledge. He uses a picture-language richly suggesting creation and growth, love and life: a dynamic and living imagery. All these are symbols, blending the space-world of sense-perception with the time-world of significant growth. His parables are stories: yet more than stories. They are works of art where the spatial quality of the whole is as important as the time-sequence of events. It will be seen that I variously regard the relative parts played by space and time in poetry. It does not matter: neither are finally real, they are abstractions and figments of our own minds. I merely try to show how these varied appearances are by poetry re-integrated into a higher reality. So Jesus expresses his sight in creative imagery and a still more concrete poetry of direct example. He is less a teacher than a poet and an exemplar, creating the one pattern equally in his mind-pictures and the picture-drama of his life.

To him, men's difficulties are self-made. To men death is an enigma, and immortality an impossible dream. Therefore 'let the dead bury their dead . . .' Again, questioned about death, he says: 'God is the God of the living, not the dead', adding, 'You are far wrong'. How exquisite that last phrase! And how simple his answer, so simple that even yet we cannot understand it. Death is a delusion. No one ever yet was dead. A dead man is no longer a man and therefore cannot be even a dead man. It is very simple: the gravedigger in *Hamlet* knows it, but it is beyond Hamlet himself, beyond most of us. There are no dead. Jesus knows the answers to all these queries immediately because the questions are meaningless: that is, his answer sets itself only to sweep away the rubbish which constitutes the question, and leave people free to see what is before their eyes. And certainly, in the space-time vision, death cannot in any case be real: since imagination appears to take little thought of the dead past, and there is never any rigid distinction between the living present and the future. The future is implicit in the present, the present lives yet in the future: and all extension is not in time nor in space, but in the space-time continuum. Thus death cannot be real: a space-time reality cannot be slain by time alone, since that would make the part more powerful than the whole. And this is another way of saying that Jesus sees man, not as body or soul, but in a body-soul continuum. All dualisms are at root the same figments of the abstracting intellect. And if we are to explain his miracles in terms of the intellect that denies them, we shall say then that facts happen in the material order; whereas miracles happen in the real world, made of body and soul, wherein, however, neither are what we usually think them. Physical science traces the causality of disease in the material order alone; psychology does the same with the soul. No science, however, understands the body-soul complex, wherein alone is there any real causal-chain. Suppose a man sees the shadow of a newly invented machine he has not met before laid out flat. The machine is started and he watches the play of shadows. What chance has he of reconstructing the original or explaining the interlinked causality of its working? A few outlines, that is all, may be hazarded. And medical science regards only such a shadow, its cause-sequence is in the shadow-world only. Hence its purely tentative action, its provisional assurance. But Jesus speaks, and works, in terms of the real machine of life. Miracles are simple facts in the world of reality.

Everywhere, in such imaginative matters, the problem is the same. How can the expert explain when there is nothing to explain? All he can do is to point out facts and to try to sweep away the false reasoning which clouds the sight. In my own experience, the most simple things have been the hardest to demonstrate. My critics reason in a direction exactly contrary to my own process. They complain that they do not see the picture to which they have turned their backs. I see facts in the poetic world and explain their significance; they cannot even see a fact until its cause, necessity and significance in their own false sequence is proved. For example, I point out that 'tempests' occur often in Shakespeare in tragic contexts, and that I therefore regard them as symbols of tragedy. I am perhaps told in answer that tempests will be found in many writers in similar contexts, and that my contention is unsound. Now observe the nature of this reasoning: 'Tempests are common, therefore they are uninteresting. What is uninteresting cannot be important. Symbols, however, are generally considered important. Therefore tempests are not symbols'. Yet tempests occur in nearly every Shakespearian play, in tragic contexts: nothing can alter that. The imaginative apprehension sees a simple concrete reality and no theorizing can make it waver. Hence the confidence of those who wield it. But it is almost impossible to convince the sceptical intellect, since there is no possible way of proving that a fact is a fact. We are down to rock bottom, and no arguments can dig deeper. Any one train of false reasoning can, it is true, be beaten down easily; but another will rise in its stead. I am reminded of Dives in Hell, who asks that he may revisit his brother to warn him; and is told that if his brother has not heard the prophets, he will not believe, even though one rose from the dead. And it is profoundly true.

Or again, I make an essay interpreting a play or poem, and in that I collect 'crown' references, pointing out that they suggest 'kingship'. Now a critic will object to one certain reference, arguing that it clearly has no special symbolic meaning. But he utterly mistakes my method. I can only explain it in terms of his way of thinking by saying that I follow the laws of imaginative chess and artistic creation in general in that, once I am on a certain train of imagery, I do not so much select suitable examples as reject unsuitable ones. If I find a reference to a ship I shall not consider it suitable for my list of crowns. But whenever I find a crown reference, it clearly does not deserve rejection. It may be absolutely necessitated by the story, apart from all symbolic suggestion: that has nothing to do with it. For I have already half-consciously sensed a blaze of crowns in the play and am to put down in cold print all quotations that support this. Imaginative work is thus always positive in the sense that to search questioningly for anything is negative, implying a probability of absence. Thus, if I am wanting crowns, I expect them everywhere and am disappointed wherever I do not find them. We remember how the chess-expert does not search for the right move but rather rejects the wrong ones: for imagination has the ideal positive pattern already in the mind. In the same way, the producer of a play may have received suggestions from numerous people; all the best ideas may have been given him by others. Yet the whole production may be as much to his credit as any art can be, for if he has been given ten most valuable ideas that suit his pattern, he has probably rejected at least fifty worthless ones that conflict with it.

This book likewise claims to derive from the prophetic imagination. Its ideas and interpretations are valuable, if at all, for two primary reasons. First, its pieces fit together into a cohering whole. For some months I have been, I suppose, rejecting unsuitable ideas, and this book is the residue. Second, it is positive, not negative; it points ahead, not back. I destroy nothing, but ask only that the visionary literature we possess be properly regarded, its own prophetic life be fulfilled in us. In our analogy from chess and our short inspection of the life of Jesus we have seen how the imagination exists in terms of the present and future. Given a position, no chess-expert worries about the past moves: the position, to him, only exists in terms of its further evolution. To the imagination all things treasure their most glorious future within their present existence; they are 'lines of force' directed and co-ordinated towards victory. Imagination sees all life unfurling into futurity, and watches within the closed bud the yet invisible birth, the fiery and perfumed rose that is to be. Imagination is, indeed, always prophetic. It is prophetic because it is creative; and it is creative because one of its parents is love.

PART I

GENERAL THEORY

II. SYMBOLISM

I PASS to analyse poetry from a slightly different view. Already we have seen it as 'expressing' a 'vision' of a 'space-time' world. Now a vision without expression, either in art or life, being scarcely our concern, the 'expression' is necessarily very important: and as my arguments develop, its importance will be seen to grow. Poetry may be said to blend the arts of music and painting: to fuse the spiritual and material. These indeed may often be considered to correspond in some sort to our 'space' and 'time' elements, though 'space' and 'time' must be allowed to correspond respectively either to 'spirit' or 'matter' according to the argument. All these dualisms are unreal, and poetry, which resolves them, creates always something much nearer to reality; and therefore our thinking in these provisional terms—in terms of dualisms—though necessary, must be elastic. In my next few chapters, then, I analyse the poetic product rather than any vision, and see it as the result of a marriage of elements. From this marriage of the spiritual and material results the specific poetic 'incarnation'. And thence we shall begin to see poetry as a rounded whole, concrete, solid. My theoretical chapters conclude eventually with a return to our starting point: the discussion bringing us back to the essentially prophetic nature of all great literature. In this chapter I discuss the term symbolism, a word whose true meaning will point direct to a sound and comprehensive aesthetic theory.

The word indicates, by derivation, a 'throwing together', and hence it was used to mean an agreement between two or more people as to the significance of an object. But, if we regard the symbol in isolation, this agreement between outsiders as to its significance will be reflected into a 'throwing together' of elements in the symbol itself. Now we may usually distinguish such elemental parts as 'material fact' and 'emotional significance'. In my following chapters I shall use the word 'fact' to denote an event drained of any strong emotional content: which will be quite different from the 'facts' I have observed in the space-time world. Consider the Union Jack. It is, first, a rectangular piece of bunting, rather inartistically coloured. But, bound together with these facts we recognize a whole category of emotional associations. The history and future of Great Britain, the question of imperial right, the present state of English and, indeed, world politics—all these attend the modern mind contemplating this flag. They are natural and therefore reasonable associations. A symbol is thus a passionate thing radiating dynamic ideas. And yet it is, too, remote and cold. Do we attach our own emotions to it? Yes, partly. But it is a symbol only by reason of the original fusion binding an infinite and romantic association with a limited and practical fact. The fact is, as it were, the shape given to a chaos of fleeting intuitions and psychic forces generally, lending them focus and location. It shapes their significance and channels their direction. It is cold and remote with that remoteness that may often characterize the leader of men: but it contains a unique power to liberate and employ the fires in those minds to which it is addressed. And yet this power is only potential. It is not simply in the symbol, or the contemplating mind, but is manifest only in a secondary fusion of both. So, in any art, the form will be still and cold, yet potentially is it alive with ever-new universes of meaning.

Thus a symbol is more full of meaning than any ordinary statement can possibly be. I mean, the Christian Trinity is not only more true, but true in a completely different and more potent fashion, than any logically formulated philosophy of religion. A symbol may in all simplicity speak volumes. The Christian Cross does this. We may regard a logical statement as flat, two-dimensional: whereas symbolic utterance, or rather creation, is solid, rounded. And here we can see a very clear development of our symbol world in poetry. Words may be symbols: in so far as they are poetic, that is creative, they have been born of a fusion of passion with fact and are thus exactly symbolic. All imaginative writing is to be regarded as obeying the laws of symbolic creation: it is first a living reality, only secondly a statement. It contains an infinity of possible statements. Shelley writes well of Dante:

> His very words are instinct with spirit; each is as a spark, a burning atom of inextinguishable thought; and many yet lie covered in the ashes of their birth, and pregnant with a lightning which has yet found no conductor. All high poetry is infinite; it is as the first acorn, which contained all oaks potentially. Veil after veil may be undrawn, and the inmost naked beauty of the meaning never exposed. A great poem is a fountain for ever overflowing with the waters of wisdom and delight; and after one person and one age has exhausted all its divine effluence which their peculiar relations enable them to share, another and yet another succeeds, and new relations are ever developed, the source of an unforeseen and an unconceived delight.

That is one of our grandest passages of aesthetic philosophy. I know of none more universally true, none more important. Symbolic language, as Shelley says, is indeed inexhaustible. But its riches

—the riches of any symbol—will never be truly apparent while we regard symbolism as a secondary sort of expression. And when I say, here or elsewhere, that A is symbolical of B, I do not mean that A stands instead of B; rather that suggestion of B is inbound in A. Discursive reasoning is the handmaid of poetry and prophecy, not their master. So, also, metaphoric speech is not the fanciful and insecure thing it is usually considered, but rather the truest flower of verbal art.

'Only a metaphor'. And therefore the less true? Rather, I should say, the more true. A metaphor is a very perfect example of the symbolic process. Consider the lines:

> Such an act
> That blurs the blush and grace of modesty,
> Calls virtue hypocrite, takes off the rose
> From the fair forehead of an innocent love
> And sets a blister there, makes marriage vows
> As false as dicers' oaths.
>
> (*Hamlet*, III, iv, 40)

We have a complex woven of passionate thinking and visual apprehension. As Hamlet regards the Queen his mind contrasts the blushes of innocence, the rose, and marriage vows with blurring ugliness, a 'blister', 'dicers' oaths'. This is, we may say, the primary impression in his mind. Also the abstract words 'virtue' and 'hypocrite' are contrasted. But it is dangerous to say that the impressionistic contrast is used merely in order to express the conceptual contrast of virtue and hypocrisy, since in such passages the former is the very stuff of poetry, and may often pre-exist the poet's conscious thinking. So the rose-blister contrast is a richer expression of Hamlet's mind than the other. And it is clearly the more obviously symbolic—at first sight, anyway—since the rose is an image impregnated with the poet's passion to create a powerful metaphor. It is, indeed, better to say that the virtue-hypocrite contrast is introduced to illustrate the impressionistic contrast, the visual image, the word rich in sense-impressions, being primary.

Metaphors are always so created: a concrete image is fused with a spiritual vitality, and the completed result is specifically poetic. A simile is merely an extension of the same process. But metaphoric language, as usually understood, is not an essential. Or we may say that all language is, when powerfully used, metaphoric; and, if so used, it will hold variations of meaning quite beyond the usual common-sense content, though this is there too. Poetry might be defined as words inflated by mind, if we allow 'mind' to cover emotion and thought alike. Nor must we ever too arbitrarily distinguish between emotion and thought. It might even be argued that our virtue-hypocrite contrast, in this passionate context, draws on as powerful a passion as the more pictorial impression. Poetic utterance may thus result from a blending of emotion and thought in one abstract noun, or a blending of either, or both, with a more concrete image. The one primary process is all we need to remember: a fusion of the subjective mind with words to create a potent and living utterance. But with these reservations we may certainly say that the poetic result is usually rich in sensory impressions and emotional associations. These are inwoven with thought processes and logical statement. The resulting whole is poetry, words inflated by mind, symbolic speech; and this result contains meanings which may usually be best approached by regarding first the more striking sense-impressions.

Literary art is thus always creation: there is a

marriage of elements and a new birth. It is neither expression alone, nor imitation, but a mingling of the two; neither subjective nor objective, but both. In Shakespeare there are two passages which very clearly illustrate this. Here is one:

> I have been studying how I may compare
> This prison where I live unto the world:
> And for because the world is populous
> And here is not a creature but myself,
> I cannot do it. Yet I'll hammer it out.
> My brain I'll prove the female to my soul,
> My soul the father. And these two beget
> A generation of still-breeding thoughts.
> And these same thoughts people this little world
> In humours like the people of this world,
> For no thought is contented . . (*Richard II*, V, v, 1)

Elsewhere I have shown how Richard's following thoughts do actually pursue the rhythm of Shakespeare's later creative work. We can therefore clearly regard Richard here as a lonely poet creating a dream-world comparable with Shakespeare's. And this creation comes about by a marriage of 'brain' with 'soul'. Brain is the more material faculty, covering intellect perhaps, certainly sense-impressions; soul is the mysterious spiritual force, incapable of definition. From this marriage of the sense-world, the memory-world, with the soul we have something like poetic creation. It is a marriage of the material and the spiritual.

To this our other passage is a valuable complement. I refer to Theseus' words in *A Midsummer Night's Dream:*

> The poet's eye in a fine frenzy rolling
> Doth glance from heaven to earth, from earth to heaven;
> And, as imagination bodies forth
> The forms of things unknown, the poet's pen
> Turns them to shapes, and gives to airy nothing
> A local habitation and a name. (V, i, 12)

Poetic art thus incarnates in 'shapes' the vague 'forms' of the spiritual world. These shapes are earthly things, they are images, sensory impressions, words of any kind: the 'forms' are indefinable, spiritual realities. Thus the poet is said to glance 'from earth to heaven': his work includes both and by blending the heavenly or spiritual with the earthly he accomplishes the newly incarnated birth of poetry. We see here that the spiritual alone is a 'nothing'—a usual Shakespearian word for the 'spiritual'—it has no place, no meaning, no value until given its body. This thought is implicit widely both in Christianity and Shakespeare's work, extending beyond aesthetic theory. 'Nothing' in this sense is not, however, wholly derogatory in Shakespeare. It represents often the dark, abysmal, mysterious world of spirit. As such it is powerful, for good or evil. Alone, it will be dangerous to man: but mated to shapes, it is the vitalizing heart, the inspired breath that makes words or actions to glow with divine life. From such harmonious marriage of elements is made the music of poetic creation and creative life.

Poetic or symbolic creation is but a microcosm of the larger creation. Human birth in Shakespeare is conditional on the same marriage of elements:

> Why rail'st thou on thy birth, on heaven, and earth,
> Since birth and heaven and earth all three do meet
> In thee at once?
>
> (*Romeo and Juliet,* III, iii, 119)

Birth is here synchronized with a marriage of 'heaven' and 'earth'. Elsewhere there is clearly expressed the idea that at birth an immortal spirit is encased in a fleshly home (*Twelfth Night,* V, i, 243; *The Merchant of Venice,* V, i, 63). Conversely, murder is shown as the severance of body and spirit. Romeo addresses Tybalt:

> for Mercutio's soul
> Is but a little way above our heads,
> Staying for thine to keep him company.
> (*Romeo and Juliet,* III, i, 131)

So, too, Bolingbroke speaks to Mowbray:

> By this time, had the king permitted us,
> One of our souls had wander'd in the air,
> Banish'd this frail sepulchre of our flesh . . .
> (*Richard II,* I, iii, 194)

The colourings are various. Creation in Genesis is similarly imagined, as a union of the 'abyss', the waters, that is, chaos, with the 'spirit of God' (i, 1); and later God 'moulded man from the dust of the ground, breathing into his nostrils the breath of life' (ii,7). Now life in Shakespeare is often elsewhere suggested to exist in terms of a body-soul dualism. When these are in harmony, there is reality, life: when severed, unreality and death. In terms of these we see life, as we know it, and death; creation, and destruction. Symbolic creation is but a variation of the larger processes of life.

Now I have suggested that the created symbol, or symbolic language, may be regarded as solid, whereas un-poetic language, or poetic language regarded only from its logical and ratiocinative aspect, is flat. By this analogy we may view the richness in meaning which Shelley claims to be a quality inherent in poetry. For a solid object presents different aspects as we change our view point. A Union Jack, for example, does not make a statement. It does not say, 'England is a great nation'. To an Englishman it may mean this, or something of the sort. But suppose a Russian Communist to be regarding the flag. It might well stimulate his hatred of

British Imperialism. Thus a symbol may often have two almost contradictory aspects; and for this reason religious truth can seldom be housed in direct statement. Any simple assertion is, as a rule, to be complemented by its opposite to create any universal truth: paradox and symbolism being thus closely related. Poetry is usually both paradoxical and symbolic: symbolic as I have shown already, and paradoxical since often the thought-content may be contradicted by the associations, a process very clear in mournful poetry where the beauty of the language interpenetrates the pessimism of the thought. Now a symbol may often change its significance from age to age, may turn a new facet of its meaning to a new generation. Consider the Virgin Birth in Christianity. It has for long been an advertisement for asceticism, and has appeared to exert a frowning disapproval of the sex instinct. That has, very likely, been providential: we usually see in a symbol what we most need to draw from it. But to-day we may find a very different meaning here. In this book I prefer to talk of the Divine or Sacred Birth; which will rather suggest the divinity of birth and creation generally. It thus will be seen to elevate, rather than cast any aspersion on, the processes of sex and procreation. Nor is this, finally, quite irreconcilable with the older view, for to hold up virginity as an ideal is merely to raise sex to an infinite value. In this way there are easy answers to all these apparent contradictions.

But it may be said that if symbols are so rich in meanings they must be valueless: to mean anything whatsoever is to mean nothing. The answer is that symbols do not mean anything whatsoever: there is always a certain fixed boundary in their suggestion. The Union Jack is always to be related to the

British Empire. Within this limit, it has various meanings. It says an infinite number of powerful things about the Empire to which it is related. Similarly, the Divine Birth says an infinite number of things about the divinity of a certain human birth. A symbol is thus mysteriously both finite and infinite. It results from a fusing of some shape—I use the word for its material and visual suggestion —with a myriad complex instincts and impressions. It is a channel, rendering dynamic those ideas and passions which, like a river breaking down its banks, would, without some lateral impediment, cease their swift course onward and spread their vitality to waste in every direction. Symbolism results in the impressure of a certain mysterious form on emotions and ideas. It incarnates them in shapes, in word, or image. It is thus creation, and creative. And here we may directly relate it to morality.

Art and morality necessarily appear at first to conflict, and it is very dangerous to attempt any too facile equation. The more instinctive and dangerous emotions—love, ambition, hate—find continual expression in Shakespeare and are, indeed, the very substance of his tragic work. From these originates much of his power. We can, of course, argue that the great plays serve a moral purpose in that the moral order is ever closely regarded: Macbeth and Antony are shown as ruining themselves by their actions. But good people are often ruined, too, in Shakespeare and in life. Moreover, we see that a good character is usually subsidiary, a foil to the protagonist, no more: such are Kent in *Lear,* Horatio in *Hamlet,* Osborne in *Journey's End,* a play in the Shakespearian tradition. It is, indeed, exactly the breaking free of passionate instincts in the protagonist that gives the poet his chance. The moral lessons usually drawn from high art being subsidiary, not primary. We will therefore consider a single poetic line: no theory that does not cover such an instance will prove finally satisfying. I select one from *Timon of Athens:*

> Hate all, curse all, show charity to none.

No one, living in a Christian community, will call that a moral statement in the ordinary sense. Yet it is a gem of poetry. The poet has married words to a powerful emotion: or we may say that he has 'incarnated' his emotion in words: and in this very marriage and incarnation consists the only true morality of art. Moreover, if we consider this line as a unit, we see that the poet has subdued his emotion to a limited number of words; in which surrendering of instinctive and unlimited power to a confining purpose we shall find an analogy to the moral life. For goodness is always an incarnation: that is, it is creative. The word 'virtue' holds—or used to hold—many suggestions, many echoes, of the idea of 'power', creative power. The process is this: the invisible and infinite passion is married to a limited and concrete expression—the limit is always necessary—and from this is born an art-form. Here it is a single line: it might be a single word, scene, play, novel, paragraph. The morality of art is in its essential creativeness, which implies incarnation and limitation.

Wherever we have a satisfactory artistic whole, we may apply this same reasoning. There is usually a sense of power compressed. Consider Wordsworth's lines on Newton's statue:

> The marble index of a mind for ever
> Voyaging through strange seas of thought, alone.

The limiting quality of the line-unit is very evident

here. It charges each word—not very exciting words themselves in the second line—and as we read the charge is liberated, exploded, a pistol shot reverberating into the infinite. So always in poetry thoughts and passions are married to words and images, actions or persons, to create a new whole the more powerful for the compression and sacrifice necessary to subdue vast psychic forces to the limits of the particular medium. The new whole is an art-form of some kind. Even a word is a miniature art-form, bottling so much power: language used artistically tends always towards the symbolic, being born of a marriage between author and dictionary. Art is thus a mastery of instincts, and the poet may be said to catch fleeting emotional or intellectual essences on the wing and put them in a glass case: his work is a butterfly collection of bright or dark winged aspirations. So the artist must ever control his instincts for an artistic end, surrendering them to marriage with the material of his expression. Thus the highest literary creation is essentially incarnation, a descent of the spiritual to the material. That is, the original impulse has to burn through some hard, often intransigent, material: either realistic events or some close analytic thought. The fancy is not free to play as it will. Dante's philosophic and historic references and Shakespeare's continual faithfulness to his originals are enough to illustrate this. And Goethe's *Faust,* perhaps, suffers a little from this very lack: in the second part there is little outside authority to fetter his intuition. Nevertheless, his expression is, in all other ways, very concrete and impersonal. Without this impersonal element, this limiting material, there is no creation.

The artist works in terms of repressed and sublimated instincts. Were human existence as perfectly harmonized as the instinctive and disciplined life of animals, there would be less need for art; nor, indeed, much scope for thought or language even, which all derive mainly from a disparity and tension between desire and realization. Human consciousness as we know it functions most often in terms of insufficiency; and art seems not only to derive from this very insufficiency but to exist primarily in order to remedy it. It will appear, then, that in so far as the artist satiates his desires, he can dispense with art; in so far as he is forced to repress and sacrifice those desires, he will tend to liberate them by artistic expression, surrendering them to marriage with words, images, stories. Whether in art or life, submission and control are necessary: technique is the morality of art, just as morality is the technique of life. Nor can we argue from particular biographies of artists that art is, if not immoral, certainly unmoral. Many poets have lived immoral lives. But then their desires may have been excessive, and their art results not from the satisfaction but rather the dissatisfaction of such desires. The lovely patterns of art thus reflect the patterns continually graved on the mind by its pain and frustration. What we enjoy, we enjoy, and there is an end of it. What we hunger for and cannot find, this we possess in another sense, stored with eternal things. Art is an earnest of heavenly riches. And it is highly moral. For art is the surrendering of instincts to a material medium and universal purpose, with all that that implies; and morality is the surrendering of instinct to an end sanctioned by a judgment which regards the future as well as the present, the community as well as the individual. A moral act thus expresses instincts in terms of the world beyond the individual, an immoral act is one whereby the individual carves for himself regardless or witless of the laws of the created world. Both art and morality are thus, in their different ways, a fusion, a marriage, of the subjective mind with an objective universe. Finally, the close relation of the moral and artistic modes is most evident from one further consideration. Morality seems to depend on the concept of 'will': now the further we pursue analysis of instinct and behaviour, the less reality can be attributed to 'the moral will'. At the extreme, the concept vanishes. It has no reality apart from the essences it orders: it is rather an aspect of those essences when harmonized. The artistic parallel is exact. Form without content is meaningless. Form is one aspect of essences in harmony: under close analysis, it is found to exist not here nor there but in and through the organic whole. The harmonies of art are thus born from and induce a harmony of being. Art and morality converge.

Thus the making of a symbol or of poetry is not only a fine way of expressing difficult things: it is a highly moral act. The only immoral art is bad art. Sentimentality in art, that is, uncontrolled emotion, emotion not properly surrendered to an artistic whole, is immoral as any lawless action in life: though, of course, we must remember always in art or life that poverty of spirit lends itself more readily to facile control than greatness of heart. And not only is poetic creation a moral act: it has a definitely moral result. It purges and purifies. Passions and desires are, it is true, raised: but no passions or desires are raised that are not in the same act satisfied. The harmony of the marriage of the elements that goes to the making of a symbol or a poem induces a corresponding harmony in the recipient.

Consider for a while our simplest instance of poetic creation, the making of some symbol by 'throwing together' in dynamic marriage some spiritual essence with a sense-impression. From this marriage results a harmony. Instead of conflicting and tempestuous forces there is blended the music of symbol. And, in that the symbol is as music, it induces in us a state akin to musical delight. And necessarily so. For our pains and troubles in this world seem ever to derive from our seeing a natural fact or facts without correspondingly being able to focus any dynamic significance therein pointing us onward or, conversely, from our feeling of passionate desire, unfitted to any shape, person, or line of action that may release and sanction our energy and urge to creative life. But whenever and wherever, for however short a space, we find these two worlds, the inward and outward, the human and the natural, woven in harmonious design, then is our peace, our sense of significance and purpose recaptured. And when these two fall apart, we are separated from our world, unhappy; seeing around us a barren and stony stare in the world of manifestation, a field strewn now with corpses of the late romantic joy, while within us burn unquenched fires of desire, Satan torments, conflicting, inwardly tempestuous. In this way, the symbol, in which significant emotions are blended with some concrete image, is potent to save. This is why Jesus spoke ever in parables. He is the great king of metaphoric speech. What is his teaching? We do wrong to abstract a superficial ethic from his words. Rather he points us to the lily, the birds of the air, the vine, the marriage-banquet. We are to let our instincts pursue the joy, the rhythms of growth, the creative luxuriance, the blessed peace of these. In symbol, he preaches the symbolic life. He would have us blend our life with the life around us, incarnate our instincts along the creative rhythms of nature. He would have us live our metaphors. The process which is at the heart of metaphor is exactly the most important thing in Christianity. The Incarnation is itself one gigantic metaphor whereby the divine Logos is married to a human form. And Jesus calls us to metaphoric action. He would have us realize a new harmony whereby the human and the natural are blended: and in this marriage we recognize the divine.

And yet, in the moment when, in art or any romantic joy such as love or mystic sight, a symbolic potency is achieved, we do not normally use the word symbol. From our lower consciousness it is a necessary term, denoting the two worlds that have been 'thrown-together'. Yet, when that marriage is actualized, we indeed forget that there were ever two worlds to be reconciled; indeed, we know then that they were never in reality distinct. What is a symbol to intellectual enquiry is a simple sight and fact to the romantic sight. The symbol exerts a power whereby we are brought to a state beyond the categories of analysis. It is of little interest to a man who is properly in love to say that he has correctly symbolized his sex-desires. Even philosophically we can explain this. For, when any two things are blended to produce a third, it is clear that that third will hold significance of its own quite apart from its constituent elements. A child has its own inviolable individuality, and Christ, the incarnate God, is at once more than man and more than God.

Such then will be our understanding of both poetry and religious symbolism. But it may be objected that by giving the word 'symbol' so wide a content, covering all poetic expression, I have robbed it of its specific and usual meaning. This is true. But then I show, here and elsewhere, that there actually is very much more to be found in our poets than has hitherto been supposed: that is, I have by interpretation extended the symbolic richness of the poetic world. But it is true too that I often select certain dominant symbols, abstract them from their setting and regard them as entities: and this may seem an arbitrary act. Certain elements, however, in any art-form will very clearly be more symbolically powerful than others: and to an intellectual analysis these will necessarily seem more important. Hence in my treatment here of Dante and Goethe I select impressions of the circle, the rose, of fire and water and mountains. The perfectly receptive reader would, of course, need no interpretation: but neither would the perfect scientist need any science. Moreover, it is natural in reading to miss important suggestions by limiting a particular poetic effect to its position as a link in the narrative. We should rather be prepared at any time to see any one piece of a poetic pattern as symbolic in its own right, radiating power over and beyond its place in the story, and if we do that we find riches unguessed in all our greater works. There is, however, a useful distinction to be drawn between elements which are natural to the story and pregnant to imaginative inspection as well, and those which are addressed more particularly to the romantic vision without appearing to make contact with the usual processes of the world. These latter I call 'direct symbolism'. For example, when in *Macbeth* Duncan's horses are said to have eaten each other, we have an event outside natural law. It serves a poetic but not a realistic purpose. And we will find in the New Testament many events which appear to be of a similar order. But there is scarcely a rigid bounding line. In imaginative writing direct symbolism seems to emerge from the symbolic world of its growth, rooted in that world and inseparable from it. And it is always most important for our understanding of the world it grows from.

My interpretations of Shakespeare bear the same relation to their original as does the science of Christian theology to the Bible. In both, dominant symbols are abstracted to further our understanding. From the one, I have taken the tempest-music opposition; from the other, theologians have created the Trinity. These tune our minds to understanding in a way otherwise impossible. So in this book I shall again often abstract from the created whole of an art-form certain persons, impressions, images, treating them as symbols, that is, as units poetically conceived and created, in order to channel the fine frenzies of poetry and prophecy to our use and raise our minds to a plane where they may the more fully receive the all but ineffable dreams of great art. And they, in turn, will next raise us to life itself. The Bible narrative is a new-created abstraction from life, just as the Church dogmas are abstractions from the Bible. By studying the Bible or the work of Shakespeare, or Dante, or Goethe, we raise our understanding beyond the complexities of prophecy and literature, history and revelation, and all their varied intricate symbolisms, to Life itself, or Immortality. The Trinity and the tempest-music opposition are not only direct intellectual introductions to the mysterious rhythms of existence, but, by pointing us to a wider view of the Bible and Shakespeare, they inspire our life. They and their originals are all conductors to that divine lightning which we await to flash its blaze across our death-shadowed consciousness.

III. THE SHAKESPERIAN ART-FORM

I NOW pass to analyse shortly the texture of the Shakespearian art-form. I have discussed already the Shakespearian aesthetic theory presented in terms of a heaven-earth or a soul-brain dualism. It will be found to illuminate the Shakespearian practice on a large scale. The process of poetic creation is repeated from step to step. It occurs in choice of a word, in the making of a scene, the creation of a whole work of art. Always two elements are blended. We can see very clearly in the plays two such elements in close texture. Elsewhere I have referred to the temporal and spatial elements in Shakespearian drama; we might, provisionally, call them the story and the imaginative design; or the plot and the philosophic significance; and so on. Exactitude is impossible, but we can clearly all agree that there is much thought and feeling inwoven with the tale in a Shakespearian play. The poet expresses every fact and event in his narrative together with its finer significances at every point. He entwines his own mind with the story he uses, incarnating his thoughts and feelings in the material before him. The soul and body are finally close-knit in poetic life.

Now, we can distinguish the Shakespearian artist from the newspaper reporter by saying that the latter presents only one of the two elements necessary to art. He tells us the facts, no more. Shakespeare is interested not only in facts but in their significance. The one gives us a series of memorised incidents; the other a dynamic and living experience. Therefore the Shakespearian play is not realistic in the usual sense. It is not like events we remember, and our knowledge of the world is almost entirely a matter of memory; rather it is like experience itself. The plays are vivid experiences, to be lived through and judged not as life-memories but as life itself, not as a distillation of experience but as experience itself. Hence Keats' phrase about 'burning through' *King Lear*. It will be seen that I sharply distinguish the memory-world from experience: and this is necessary. Our memory falsifies experience, abstracts from it. The unique and immediate actuality ever eludes us. Nothing is so mysterious as the actual, and all our poets and prophets work to draw the veil which shuts us from the life we live. We remember either the fact without its significance; that is what gives us science. Or we reason about the significance abstracted from any living fact; that is what gives us philosophy. These two worlds, the material and the spiritual, are unreal. The immediate reality, intractable to intellect, is made of both, transcends both. And the Shakespearian play, so finely welding fact with significance, earth with heaven, reintegrates, recreates, the actual world of experience, the reality of life.

It is true, however, that some writers, such as Tolstoy and Chaucer, have the magic gift of presenting fact or incident in all simplicity yet so washed, as it were, with some spiritual light, that they may claim to recreate the whole glory of the actual, even of actual experience, without so much trafficking with intellect. Tolstoy in his novels and short stories shows great mastery in this kind. They are not written like a newspaper report; yet they are not interwelded at every point with the author's profound thinking, or at least this does not appear. At its best, such writing is naively, childishly magical and actual at once. Contrast this with Dostoievsky's work, or Melville's. Melville suits well. Consider *Moby Dick* or *Pierre*. In *Moby Dick* there is a very obvious interweaving of a straightforward and realistic tale with a mass of philosophic speculation, the two perfectly married in the whale-symbol; for the White Whale is by far the more terrific as a symbol of natural enmity by reason of the meticulous and laborious descriptions which habituate us to whaling in general and all its ramifications. In this book the two elements are powerfully present and nobly blended: the speculative spirit is seen continually married to narrative. Now with Dante and Hardy we have something similar. But there is, or appears to be, a more static philosophy, not so modified at every turn by the action, a philosophy against which the action is silhouetted. Dante employs a Christian philosophy, Hardy a personal pessimistic intuition which was fairly consistent through his life. The Melvillian or Shakespearian writer, however, has scarcely any static philosophy: the thinking is so closely interwoven with each narrative in turn that you cannot readily tell whether it is being applied to the tale or suggested by it. We thus have three types of literary artist. The Dantesque, where philosophy and narrative seem fairly distinct, in the sense that a single philosophy appears to brood over the poet's whole work, changeless; the Chaucerian or Tolstoyan, where the one is so perfectly incarnated in the other that no process is evident, no distinction possible; and the Shakespearian, set between these two, where we watch, as it were, the process of marriage and resultant incarnation continually being acted on a large scale before us, where the philosophy appears ever to vary according to the work in hand. Now, considering that the two elements, fact and philosophy, are ultimately false abstractions from the real, it will at first seem that the Chaucerian writer is far the most valuable, directly introducing us to reality. But this is curiously misleading.

First, we must see that, whether we like it or not, there does exist a mass of philosophic lore; and, as individuals, we cannot help thinking things out, which thinking is a major part of a thoughtful man's life. Moreover, it is equally natural to us to abstract bare narrative facts, noting them in memory or in writing, facts robbed of peculiar spiritual significance. Indeed, this dualism is at the root of all evil in the world. It is a gaping wound in man. Now religion and poetry, all symbolic creation, is concerned with healing this very wound: which cannot well be done by neglecting it. The sick, not the healthy, need a physician, and a physician who understands sickness. So the most important work carefully and minutely reintegrates the two worlds that have fallen asunder. It deals in terms of the false abstractions by which we live. Nor does the Shakespearian artist at all cut out from his programme any opportunity that may present itself of writing in the Chaucerian way: there are clearly passages in Shakespeare where a naive simplicity is most beautifully employed. The sleep-walking scene in *Macbeth* is an example. Such simple mastery is usually most perfect not in poetry but in prose. But I doubt if the finest intensity in this kind could ever be accomplished without the context of such a play as *Macbeth,* with all its commentary and direct symbolism, its free use of all that may create a dynamic experience in our minds. Similarly, Jesus' parables would be less powerful if abstracted from their context. We may say that the Shakespearian artist deals in wholesale marriages which nevertheless often produce the most perfect forms of such naive incarnation; whereas the Tolstoyan, presenting the final simplicity direct, makes less contact with the labouring world of human thought, avoids the philosophic weight that the poet must lift if he is to be a redeemer to mankind. And the most perfect and intense examples of simplicity may be found continually in the words of the Shakespearian artist. They are generally the climax of his ascent; and because he first descends to the valleys of intellectual error and pain, he is enabled the more surely to take us with him to the height. In such works there is, as it were, a superhuman contest, an intellectual activity wrestling with the story—this very clear in *Macbeth* or *Moby Dick;* two vast forces, their Titan limbs enmeshed, and the naked muscles so swelling under the strain that in this antagonist activity both philosophy and story are finally presented in greater power and meaning, to us at all events in our present state of consciousness, than by any facile neglect of the more intransigent essences. After all, it is hard to distinguish a facile simplicity from supreme vision. We have outgrown our childhood and are not yet entered into Paradise. To wrestle with our God, or the God within us, is necessary. And having written our *Macbeth* we may advance to *Antony and Cleopatra,* a play of poetic intensity and intellectual profundity quite incommensurable with Chaucer's simplicity, yet one where the struggle is over, and a peace irradiates not any fierce contest, but the other reciprocity of love.

Now wherever we find these two elements in a great work of Shakespearian quality, we will find too that the final creation transcends both its parts and their sum, and exists not as spirit or materiality but in that spiritual-material continuum which alone is real. Both philosophy and story cease to exist, as such, in the result. This miracle is done before our eyes, in terms of what we know, our pain and frustration, our questions and pitiful abstractions. For example, though *Macbeth* on every level gives us a sense of conflict, the conflict is always being resolved in the music and power of the poetry. Thus we actually endure, experience, the change of being, take part in the process. The Shakespearian play is a created organism, yet ever active, ever in process of new creation and recreation, dependent on us to take part in its vital movement, its redeeming purpose. It is not a copy of experience, it is itself experience. We burn through it: it is purgatorial. Thus, superficially unrealistic, that is, not very close to the contours of life as we remember events a year, a week, a second past, it is yet most realistic as direct experience, its giant and inhuman figures blurred by nearness, by psychic currents, the actual impending event, by the terror or beauty of the immediate. A Tolstoyan novel is like a distant range of hills, rhythmic contours switch-backing against the sky; with *Moby Dick* or *Macbeth* we ourselves enter those dark ranges, lost in their circuits, climbing darkly up, unknowing, unseeing, dim giants around and above: but the reward awaiting our ascent is great, and the panoramic vision we expect of infinite value.

I have called the Shakespearian art-form an organism. Now organic life is characterized by this: every part of the organism, every aspect, presents a facet of the one controlling and infusing principle. I have shown how a spirit-matter marriage, or incarnation, is, in one way or other, at the heart of poetic creation, and, indeed, if we follow Shakespeare, creation generally. It will be next important to realize how this dualism is similarly reflected in the art-content as distinguished from the creative process. We shall see that art, being itself creation, has ever creation for its theme. But creation is always the ideal, the closing of the dualism. Destruction in some form will tend to make the action: creation to close it. Two worlds will be first separated, then joined. In regarding these elements, I shall neglect for the moment the fact that all dualisms are continually being resolved by the music of created poetry. For the present, I inspect the action only, the content as opposed to the form.

Our extreme example is *Macbeth.* Now, we have here a destruction-vision, a death-vision. There is therefore a rough disjointing of the spirit-world from the natural world. Here the spirit world is gloomy and satanic: we have Hecate and the Weird Sisters, Banquo's ghost, the air-drawn dagger, apparitions, dreams, miraculous portents. The play is crammed with spirit-essences. It is dark with impending death. At the extreme this death-reality is utterly dark, a nothing. 'Nothing is but what is not', says Macbeth. And this nothing may be linked to the 'nothing' to which the poet gives a 'local habitation and a name'. It is the 'nothing' of eternity toward which Timon moves. And Richard II, thrown back on the pure negations of inward mysticism, in his lonely despair feels that

> Nor I nor any man that but man is
> With nothing shall be pleased till he be eased
> By being nothing.

Richard is severed, like Timon, from all incarnate joy. There is the soul's 'nothing' in the Queen's foreboding earlier in the same play. A dark, abysmal, mysterious thing. It is eternity, abstracted from time, meaningless until incarnate: the mysterious 'mothers' in Goethe's *Faust*. When this severance takes place, both time and eternity are meaningless, unreal. In *Macbeth* the spirit-world is insubstantial, deceitful. And the world of nature, severed from its soul, its infusing principle, is now formless, inorganic. Nature's laws are upset: horses eat each other, the owl preys on the falcon, there is hideous tempest and the earth quakes. Thus we have our body-spirit dualism starkly apparent: the world of colour, shapes, life disorganized; that of naked spirit void and dark, unfettered; conflict, chaos and death. In Macbeth's person we likewise find an aspiring and ambitious spirit untuned to creative action in the world-order. All evil is to be related to such a severance, all good to the opposing harmony. Thus Shakespeare's usual expression of murder as a body-spirit severance may be extended on the planes of ethics, aesthetic and metaphysic, indeed, indefinitely. This is the way with Shakespeare: his words, his theory and practice of art, his plots and metaphysic, his thought and action as both dramatist and poet, all are one. They all obey the laws of destruction and creation; of death and life; of tempest and music. Hence the harmony, minute and massive, of Shakespeare's work.

This is not an idea arbitrarily applied to *Macbeth*. It is rooted in the play's texture. The play is a death-vision, where death-forces are seen embattled against life. All this is very evident to a careful inspection, especially important in the child-symbolism of the apparitions. And the death-life contest results in a body-spirit dualism. This, our most powerful destruction vision in Shakespeare, will be clearly the richest in spiritual phenomena and the most unrealistic generally. But similar patterns are found elsewhere. *Julius Caesar,* for example, is a close replica of *Macbeth* on a more optimistic plane. There is the same disjointing of spirit and nature, with similar results. Here 'spirit' is a thickly-scattered word, and its sense-equivalent is 'fire'. The spirit-world of *Macbeth* is murky, though shot with fire; but *Julius Caesar* is full of fire. Throughout our poets 'fire' and 'spirit' are roughly correspondent. Now wherever we have evil and destruction in Shakespeare, there is a laying bare of spirit in some form. We see the protagonist horribly aware of unincarnated spirit in *Hamlet.* Events so tear the superficial coverings of life from Hamlet's eyes; tear also the superficial consciousness from his mind; that they leave him a naked soul, confronting the naked soul of mankind. And all this is most exquisitely expressed from the start by the resurrection of his father's tormented soul, nakedly unincarnate, hideously immortal. So in this play, as full of Death as *Macbeth* but with less violent a contest, we again have a spirit-world contrasted with life, here the glitter and bustle of the Court. Or in *Lear,* deceptive appearance is agonizingly withdrawn, a deceptive consciousness dethroned, and Lear himself, accompanied by the naked Tom, reaches self-knowledge through the fantastic leaping devils of lunacy, knowledge of himself and of the world. In all these plays there is a lurid, extravagant, bizarre spirit-world hideously exposed, as the world of manifestation is stripped of its garments, and naked spirit revealed. Such is the wrenching apart of spirit and nature: but the action ever moves toward a recreation, a rebirth, a new harmony. In *Timon,* too, the tinsel glitter of civilization and humanism is torn down, leaving mankind naked to the imprecations of the naked Timon. 'Naked Spirit' is in Shakespeare all but correlevant to evil. Shakespeare is the great poet of incarnate life.

I do not mean, however, that there is no reference in Shakespeare to good spirits; angels, for example. All I say is that evil takes the form of a spirit-nature conflict; and there will be little in Shakespeare to prevent us calling him 'the great poet of incarnate life'. For example, *Macbeth* has many references to divine grace, and religious transcendentalism generally. We could argue that these are only called in to combat the supernatural evil, are dependent on it. And, indeed, religion is ever mainly dependent on evil. In Revelations we are told that the New Jerusalem will need no temple: which is self-evident. But everywhere, in Shakespeare and our own minds, expression of a belief in divine beings does not necessarily offer any disrespect to incarnate life. There is a place for good spirits, such as the gods in Shakespeare's final plays. They are, indeed, clearly a different order of being: they are not ghostly in any sense. We can thus have supernatural effects where there is no evil suggestion, but not any evil without supernatural effects.

Consider the upward progress from *Macbeth* to *Antony and Cleopatra* and thence to *Pericles*. In *Macbeth* spirit and nature are roughly disjointed; in *Antony and Cleopatra*, spirit infuses, inflates nature beyond natural boundaries till our natural world seems divine; in *Pericles*, we have a vision of Diana. Now *Antony and Cleopatra* gives us the most perfect vision in that it needs no religious symbolism beyond its paradisal humanism. There the two worlds are exquisitely blended and the one purely supernatural effect is the mysterious music in Act IV which may itself be taken to heighten our impression of this harmony. But the poet in his later work, less tense than this exquisite vision, allows himself gods and goddesses, showing their divine world ever in harmony with that of man. These thus symbolize the harmony existent between man and God, the nature-spirit harmony. In *The Tempest,* they are introduced as spirits in the Masque and there given slight autonomy. Prospero commands them at will. But what of Ariel? He is, indeed, very real and most important. And here we see how Prospero controls both Ariel and Caliban. The excessively spiritual and the excessively earthly both need to be rigidly schooled and controlled. The moral of this is obvious. The spirit-nature harmony is ever our ideal, but need not preclude the possibility of divine beings, who are conceived as pure self-sufficient personalities, not like ghosts which are merely hideous abstractions from the human. Shakespeare's later work shows first the conflict, then the blending, of these two elements.

There is one other play which, if we allow its fairies to correspond to the concept 'spirit', most admirably illustrates the regularity with which Shakespeare's patterns obey the law of incarnation. In *A Midsummer Night's Dream* we have fairies set against mortals. In the Bottom-Titania union we have a clear and vivid contrast. Moreover, the action shows disorder and tempest in terms of fairyland and humanity in disorganized contact. There is disorder among the fairies, due to their excessive aspirations toward mortal favour, and among mortals due to their excessive aspiration towards the fairy consciousness of love. Next, there is a complex and hazardous interthreading of fairy and mortal life. Finally, the two worlds appear to be satisfied symbolically by the extreme act of the Bottom-Titania union. The unruly desires are lifted, dissolved, or satisfied. There is concord, and the two worlds embrace to music on the bridal night where, in the lovers, spirit and body are in perfect harmony, and the fairies dance to music and song in Theseus' palace. Over all this action Theseus stands as a man in whom discords are resolved. He shares with Bottom and Oberon the dominance of the drama, but finally dominates both. For he is an unbeliever in all frenzied imaginations, whether of the lunatic, lover, or poet. His poetry is incarnated in life. He is thus a Christ-figure, possesses the Christ-harmony. So the essence of destruction in Shakespeare is a nature-spirit dislocation; the corresponding harmony is life and creation. All these thoughts lead us direct to Christianity. Shakespeare's *Henry VIII*, probably his last play, where there is a powerful Christian mysticism, might suggest that his own art led him in a similar direction. So man must make himself a channel, in Shakespeare, for the spirit-world to blend with the natural. If he fails to do this, to control his Ariel as well as his Caliban, the spirit-world itself will become a world of rampaging furies as in *Macbeth*.

I have examined the body-spirit dualism in the artistic process; also in the resultant vision. Next I narrow my subject to the dramatic protagonist in relation to his environment. At every level these plays present a dynamic interaction of two elements, either antagonized or shown to blend in marriage. I have called the plays 'experience': either of the poet's mind interacting with his world or in the reader who submits himself to them. Now experience itself involves ever a dualism. Indeed, I use the term primarily because it holds powerful suggestion of both a subject and an object; a mind, or spirit, and a material environment. It denotes that reality existent in the interaction, whether in opposition or harmony, of a conscious unit with some outer event, which can, if we like, be considered always material, in order to preserve our spirit-matter dualism the more neatly. It is quite legitimate to do this, since the material and spiritual must both be present and all the purely spiritual essences can be easily considered to exist in the subject's mind. Now it will be clear from our arguments hitherto that only in such experience can we expect any absolute reality to exist. No units are, by themselves, creative, nor real, nor indeed possible: hence the unique power of the Shakespearian writer, whose work so richly on every level partakes of the dual nature of experience. But we here come up against a curious but necessary inference. If experience alone be real, and neither the experiencer nor the experienced have complete reality, we see at once that reality is extra-human, super-personal; related to humanity and human action, but never limited to one person. The resultant from any organic mingling is something which transcends the constituent parts: hence human experience is ever more than human, indeed it becomes superhuman. In it we touch the divine. True, this rather makes of the divine an every-day affair: but so it is. All religions and all art are purposive towards awaking our sight to the miraculous life we live, that is, to experience, immediate experience. And this exists not in terms of matter or spirit but both; or rather in the matter-spirit continuum which transcends its elements, which continuum corresponds to the 'eternal life' of the Gospels.

The plays of Shakespeare continually show a hero placed in dynamic relation to his environment. In *Macbeth* there is a hideous disharmony between the protagonist and the state of Scotland. This relation is the essence of the play. But the hero and his world are not rigidly separate: they are interdependent, reciprocal. Disorder in the state and in the hero's mind balance each other, depend on each other. And the disjointing contact affects both, both suffer alike. The evil finally is in the disorganized relation, not in the hero. A murderous lion is not evil, lacking conscience. Macbeth's evil depends on Macbeth's consciousness of evil, thence on Banquo's, on Macduff's: it is this that forbids the murderer to enjoy the security that his kingly power would otherwise appear to make quite possible. Now this relation, the play's essence, is transmitted to us most purely by the imaginative effects in the style and particularly in the more direct symbolisms.

Consider, for example, the three apparitions that appear to Macbeth (*Macbeth,* IV, i). They are a microcosm of the play's statement, reflecting the contest of death and life. This is the first:

Thunder. First Apparition: an armed Head.

This shows us a hideous dislocation, a mockery of the human organism: yet it is iron-plated and menacing. It reflects the absurdity of Macbeth's evil course, his murderous acts. He is the head of the community, absurdly severed from the body, Scotland. Yet he is dangerous. But also this symbol throws forward to the end, where Macbeth's own head is to be severed from his body and brought before Malcolm. Thus ever a destructive force is finally self-destructive. Against this death-force, however, life is marshalling its champion:

Thunder. Second Apparition: a bloody Child.

From the bloody agony of death is born the other blood-agony of birth; from the soil of destruction springs the plant of creation. This apparition symbolizes the pangs of creative life, forcing to birth a saviour from out the bloody fields of death. And here is that saviour, that saving life:

Thunder. Third Apparition: a Child crowned with a tree in his hand.

This is the baby royalty of life, the Life-Child victorious, sceptred with the Tree of Life. So Macbeth addresses it:

> What is this
> That rises like the issue of a king,
> And wears upon his baby-brow the round
> And top of sovereignty? (IV, i, 86)

These apparitions all appear to thunder, this suggesting tempest and conflict; conflict of life and death. Now this miniature drama tells us more of the play's profound meaning than any psychological analysis of the protagonist. He is not all important. But his relation with his environment, his experience, is. That relation is one of a death-like conflict: and here we have it. It is most important to realize here that the direct symbolism reflects the total meaning in any art-form of Shakespearian quality. One might compare Tiresias in Mr. T. S. Eliot's *The Waste Land.* Many other examples from Shakespeare could be given: the animal references in *Lear,* the fiery spirits in *Julius Caesar,* and, of course, the continual tempests accompanying tragedy everywhere; the music in *Antony and Cleopatra;* also, in the later plays, the divine beings, Diana, Apollo's oracle, Jupiter. The essential experience at the heart of a play will be bodied into such symbolism, usually supernatural.

But we shall see next that the nearer a play approaches to a vision of good essences, life-themes, the less conflict there will be; the less jarring and nerve-racking the experience; and consequently the less of supernatural phenomena and direct symbolism generally—the two correspond. Direct symbolism serves to cement the gaping apart of the two worlds: the sharper the dualism, or conflict, the more direct symbolism is necessary. *Macbeth* is rich in such symbolism, presenting so violent a death-life contest: so is, necessarily, the New Testament. In *Lear* there is less. *Antony and Cleopatra* has none but the music I have already noted. The experience here is love, the reality is love, the protagonists are 'in love with' each other. The love-reality is reflected in the imagery of the play, but there is no powerful supernatural symbolism, except the music. The experience is intense, but there is no violent conflict, and this very fact is reflected in the symbolic music. The amount of such direct symbolism varies in these plays according to the violence of the conflict expressed. Clearly what is good is natural and needs no violent and unnatural effects, and so a love-play will be more quiet than a crime play. But drama depends largely on conflict, and *Antony and Cleopatra* is unique: a vision of action from a height, so to speak, where movement is static, tragedy joy, and all evil dissolved. You cannot have many plays like this: they would cease to have dramatic meaning and relevance. Therefore in the final plays there are divine symbols as in the New Testament. Evil is again present, if only to be quickly vanquished by harmony. Contact is thus more easily made with our everyday consciousness. *Antony and Cleopatra* gives, as it were, a sudden flash of sight: we cannot live in that world long, but fall back again on more natural implements of thought.

It has been my aim in this chapter to show that the Shakespearian tragedy can readily and profitably be considered a blending of two elements in creation; that the vision it exposes is a vision of life as itself composed of two such elements; and that the experience of the protagonist, like the experience of the poet or reader, is similarly to be regarded as of two-fold origin. Finally, I have stressed the importance of direct symbolism as binding the two worlds within the drama and pointing the meaning of the action. I now pass to apply a similar examination to the New Testament.

IV. THE NEW TESTAMENT AS AN ART-FORM

INCARNATION is a general principal of creation. But there are various degrees of incarnate life. Only by understanding this, shall we clarify our artistic and religious apprehensions. There is, for example, a sense in which a poet who puts his whole soul into a great work has incarnated his deepest instincts, and has thus performed a truly creative act. But we can also suggest not unreasonably that, to a final judgment, creative living is on a higher plane than creative art. A dissolute poet is, surely, a lesser order of being than a man who is greatly good. To deny this is to deny the ultimate value of the created world and put our faith in an abstract transcendentalism. A word is an incarnate instinct. Words bodied carefully and creatively into a fictional story are more perfectly incarnated. If the story is itself more or less true, or at least traditional, and the artist's instincts are also powerfully employed—this cuts out biography—the result is perhaps even more valuable, though this is questionable: yet we might again remember the great artist's reluctance to invent his plots. But the truly creative life is greater than any art abstracted from creative action: though art is, of course, itself a kind of creative action, and may often be seen as harmonious part of the wider context of the poet's creative life. This does not mean that great art is one whit the less valuable because the artist was dissolute: in such an instance we at all costs must keep our aesthetic intuition free from biographical associations. Nor does it mean that any dutiful parish priest is a greater than Byron. It might mean, however, that Charles Lamb was a greater than Byron in a final judgment: I assume here that Byron's work—extent, height and depth remembered—is very much the more valuable of the two. Goodness must come before poetry: incarnation in life before incarnation in words. And in this way, to compare giants with each other, we see that Jesus, if we are to believe the New Testament, is, to us, a greater than Shakespeare, whose life, however good or bad it may have been, is forgotten and therefore now irrelevant. Jesus lived the perfectly incarnate life; that is, the perfect life, since all evil is to be seen as an imperfect incarnation of instincts.

'If we are to believe the New Testament.' But why should we? Much of it certainly appears to be 'only symbolism' and fails to reach the nobility of factual narrative attained by the newspaper reporter. Certainly our only authority for believing in Jesus rests finally on the New Testament. And that we shall not, to-day, properly understand without a clear view of its specifically artistic qualities; though there are also in it some important divergences from art as well.

I have already suggested that poetry is an organic creation, born of a spirit-matter marriage in some form. Now, being organic, it presents, on every level, the same ruling principle of its life. This I have already partly demonstrated. But the subtleties are inexhaustible. For example, *Macbeth* is a play presenting a violent and unnatural evil: it thus is not only crammed with unnatural phenomena, but its very style is baffling, and at every point unanswered questions are being raised in our minds. Why does this or that happen? The play is itself full of questions, doubts, insecurities. Again, all poetry deals in creation on the analogy of life. Its main subject is ever life; and therefore also the antagonist to life, death. Life and death impressions are usually the first things to look for in inspecting a new work. Creative work thus automatically presents created life to us, and its dominant symbols are drawn from impressions of life and death, light and dark, the life-giving sun or obscuring cloud; the vegetation of earth, especially the vine and harvests generally; trees of all kinds; flowers, especially the rose, and so on; and, peculiarly important, the human symbols of the child and the lover. A good example is Wordsworth's Immortality Ode. It is a vivid life-vision, its style showing a more perfect incarnation in concrete poetic symbols than we usually have from this poet: and, rising from its impressions—of the kind just noted—is the dominant symbol, the child. Creation is both the theme and process of creative literature, life and death the ever-recurrent subjects of poetic life: such is the organic quality of poetry. Now consider the New Testament as an art-form. Its subject is the Incarnation of the mysterious Logos in human life. It is thus our supreme life-vision. It has a most powerful child symbolism in the Divine Birth, with the opposing death in the Massacre of the Innocents. Incarnation, birth, and life are its beginnings: and the personal life narrated shows a perfect incarnation of spirit in the world-order. The book announces a marriage of heaven and earth. Moreover, the general pattern or plan of the Gospels presents a very clear life-death contrast, as I show later. Such, then, being essences within, or at the heart of, the organism, we must expect the whole, like the Shakespearian art-form, also to present a process of incarnation. And by considering this process we shall tune our minds to resolve many difficulties.

Since there are degrees of incarnation, we can readily regard poetry itself as an abstraction from life; a more perfect, because more concrete, abstraction than factual narrative on the one side and philosophy on the other, but yet an abstraction. Moreover, history, being a highly selective and organized product of the world-memory, though less highly organized than poetry, is more real than a series of unrelated facts. Both poetry—or some religious orthodoxy—and history are, then, creative abstractions from the total reality. Neither by itself will be quite final: and therefore their fusion can give us a still more perfect literary reality. Now just as the Shakespearian philosophy is enmeshed in a Plutarchan story to give us poetic creation in *Antony and Cleopatra,* so some mysterious impersonal poetic quality has been fused on a yet higher plane with history to give us the New Testament. Its subject is incarnation: its technique is also incarnation. The world of poetry—that is, the divine Logos—blends with the world of history to create a whole greater than the work of any single poet: poetry being now not the completed product, but only one of the factors serving to produce the final result. Life events and their fullest significance are blended. We face essential life, only one degree below the actual.

The world of myth is close to that of poetry. Myths are more valuable than is usually supposed. In them, on the poetic plane, fact and value are reintegrated, and an immediate, unfalsified, reality created: that is why the child, in whom the breaking asunder of the two worlds has not properly begun, is directly responsive to fairy-tales. Now the New Testament has many correspondences with ancient myth. The sublimation of a hero is very usual in mythology: Hercules and Achilles in Greek legends, Rustum in Persian, and many others, are endued with all but divine qualities. The human-divine distinction is here not at all rigid. Conversely, we have gods taking the form of beasts or men, Jupiter as a bull, Dionysus a man. Norse legends pursue a similar direction. Ancestor worship in China is correspondent. The tendency of the child towards hero-worship is an analogy; so also is the tendency of early writers to believe implicitly what legends tell them, without exertion of criticism and discrimination. The mysterious semi-divine birth of Arthur reminds us of the Gospels; and Aeneas' mother was a goddess. All this represents an instinctive reaction to an immediate and unfalsified experience presented in terms of the fact-value integration. Fact and value correspond to the past and future respectively. Integrated, they create immediate experience: and only in such integration and immediacy can we know our own life, our immortality. Hence the truly creative mind in any field will tend to select past facts for attention with a view to their future significance, rejecting the rest as irrelevant. But it is often hard to do this. As we grow up, as civilization advances, the dualism opens, a yawning chasm. We cannot receive myths as true, since they are not historical facts; we find little help in history, since it has, by itself, no final significance for the future. Now we do not want to fall back to our childhood, as individuals or as a race; nor could we, if we wished it. There is necessity, indeed a tremendous purpose, in the dualism we endure. Nevertheless, the truth that life is a greater and more divinely ordered thing than our lower consciousness allows, the truth that all human experience is super-human, is reflected properly in these myths. Therefore a yet richer integration, childlike, but not childish, must be our hope: an integration yet incorporating in some way the purest poetry with a keen critical and historical faculty. Such an integration we may find in the New Testament.

For it holds analogies with poetry as well as myth. The story of Jesus is finely dramatic. To point this quality I shall notice shortly just one facet of the Shakespearian art-form, and regard its similarity with the Gospel narrative. Works of the Shakespearian kind vary considerably as to the details of their form: and yet they show a fairly consistent similarity at one point in their narrative progression. The Shakespearian tragedy itself often has some such rhythm as this: first, concord, feasting, music, or family love of some kind; next, the tempests and discords of tragedy; then, a short period of happy or resigned or pathetic calm and beauty, usually accompanied by music, generally broken or in some way interrupted, about the fourth act; and, finally, the concluding disaster. Two waves break, one about Act three, one in Act five. Here I especially draw attention to the hush that preludes the gathering strength of the last wave. There is a pause, a whispering stillness, like the sultry silence before typhoon.

Romeo, just before he hears news of Juliet's death, is meditating on a dream of a miraculous love-consummation beyond the grave; and Richard II, in his prison, meditates and hears music, just before he is murdered. In *Hamlet,* the gravedigger's songs and Hamlet's lyric prose over Yorick's skull build a short space of serene acceptance of death, a thought explicit in a later speech. So, too, a deathly sweetness, a serene peace of utter negation, breathes in the tortured silences of Lady Macbeth's sleep-walking. Brutus solaces his anguished mind with Lucius' music: a momentary peace shattered by the intruding Ghost of Caesar. In *Lear,* the music of love is serenely assured in the temporary reunion of Lear and Cordelia: a blessed peace, preluding the final agony. We have Desdemona's willow-song. In all these, there is a hint, a delicate suggestion, of some unutterable beauty. Even the inevitable and crashing conclusion is aureoled with some angelic sweetness cast ahead by these more blessed silences. And other writers share this intuition. There is Faustus' dialogue with the Scholars, in a lyric prose sweetness recalling Hamlet's, just before the end of Marlowe's *Faustus.* And in Webster's *Duchess of Malfi,* the over-glooming arch of tragedy drops its approaching shadow on the scene where Delio and Antonio listen to the ominous reports of the echo. They stand beside 'ancient ruins' with a 'reverend history', ancient religious ruins. So, too, another writer of Websterian quality sets the stage for his fourth-act at Stonehenge by relics of past religion. I refer to Hardy's *Tess,* and how Angel tells Tess that the ruins are Druidical remains and that she lies on an altar. She asks him if there are reunions beyond death; and he can give no answer. In both these sombre works there is a deathly peace before the peace of death; and the ruins suggest the eternal past, perhaps the infinite future. In both *Wuthering Heights* and *Moby Dick* the protagonist before the end unburdens his lonely soul to a companion; Heathcliff to Nelly, Ahab to Starbuck. But there is really no communion: the unutterable cannot be told. In *Moby Dick,* it is a calm morning, a still sea, and a summer breeze, inviting to sanity, and land, and home. But, after raising Starbuck's hopes,

Ahab again pursues his course towards the White Whale, and death. In these two books we see that the suffering may not be shared: yet in each, there is a great purpose, a direction, a necessity in the undeviating course the drama pursues.

Consider again our impressions: a communion with some eternal calm, yet submission to an unbending fate; a divine peace leading direct to a human death; the utter incommensurability of the hero's consciousness with that of his companions; the whole sometimes set on some historic ground that makes eternity a living presence in the drama. There is often a parting, of lovers or friends: with this we may compare the Last Supper. But the incidents I have observed recall rather the moments of lonely prayer spent by Jesus in communion with the eternal will the night that he was betrayed; his disciples wearied, sleeping, poor comrades to his purpose. So each of our tragic heroes in turn endures a miniature Gethsemane.

But here we may note in passing that in the Gospel narrative we see Jesus himself with full consciousness of all the implications that we ourselves find in the art-form, but which no one person in the poetic drama is supposed to share completely. I mean, we, but not Lear, may have a sense of approaching doom while he is reunited to Cordelia; Ahab never knows exactly why he must kill the White Whale; and so on. And this is a primary difference. Jesus, as a person, corresponds to the art-form of the poet. He is in himself the incarnation the poet accomplishes in art. He creates in his imagination his own poetry, and then acts it, making himself protagonist in his own drama. Many of Shakespeare's tragic heroes are to be, at certain points in their story, considered as figures of a

Christ-like endurance and martyrdom. Timon is in this way a Christ-figure, so is Richard II: the analogies being directly pointed in the text. Lear has been compared to the Christ, and the comparison is further suggested, perhaps, by his crown of flowers. But there is this difference. Shakespeare's heroes meet tragedy through a certain partiality in themselves: Jesus is complete. That is why Jesus is a purely moral figure, whereas the tragic protagonist is ever, in some degree, immoral. Morality is incarnation, and the poetic protagonist cannot be shown as himself possessing the full incarnation possessed only by the art-form. That is, the protagonist in a poet's work can be only partially moral, since the morality of art exists not in the persons, but in the whole drama. For a poet to create a work of Shakespearian power about a perfect man would be difficult; for, to control the whole action surrounding such a man, the poet himself would have to be a greater than that man. Any one protagonist is thus likely to represent a facet only of the poet's experience: he will therefore lack the rounded solidity of the good life. This difference in the protagonist, therefore, marks the extra dimension of incarnation which the New Testament possesses over the Shakespearian play.

Now, though Jesus may, as a person, be said in some sense to correspond to the art-form of a Shakespearian play, yet he does also remain protagonist in a wider context; which context we shall best regard as an art-form created by the Divine Artist. The New Testament is, as it were, a divine poetry. And it is this in that it blends the poetic world with the world's history, as the human poet blends his private philosophy with a narrative. I have demonstrated that the New Testament contains essences closely correspondent to those found in mythology and art. That some of it—I do not say all—is directly historical in the ordinary sense is self-evident. I shall next observe how these two elements may be considered to blend.

In the Shakespearian play we may distinguish three sorts of event. First, those which are necessary for story-links, but cannot be considered to hold any imaginative significance beyond this; as when, in the first scene of *Lear,* Lear asks if France and Burgundy are waiting outside. Next, we have direct symbolism, such as the extravagant behaviour, the lurid madness, and remarkably perfect acting of Edgar as poor Tom in the middle acts of *Lear.* And, thirdly, a blending of the imaginative and the natural in Lear's symbolic crown of weeds and flowers, which is quite in keeping with his actual madness. This is the kind of result we get from the interplay of Shakespeare's mind with the old play, *Leir,* on which he was working. Now in the New Testament, where the Divine imagination, or something similar, is interlocked with history, we must expect again three orders of event: some which are factually true, but imaginatively non-significant; some which are symbolical, but factually false; and many which are both true to fact and imaginatively and poetically cogent. But, though we can easily recognize that these three orders of event or idea are contained in either the Shakespearian play or the New Testament, it is very obvious that individual judgments will disagree in any careful allotment. I do not intend to make any dogmatic statement as to which events in the New Testament are impossible. Here are a few which have caused trouble to some minds: the Virgin Birth, the Voice of God from Heaven naming Jesus His Son, the

Temptations by the Devil, some of the more startling miracles, the bodily Resurrection of Jesus, the Ascension into Heaven. I suggest that some of these, at least, are unlikely to have occurred as facts: that is, a newspaper reporter would not have observed them. But a fact, as usually understood, is a pitiful abstraction from experience. We need not, therefore, deny that these may have been in some sense actualities: that is, immediately true to qualified recipients, then and now. We find, then, a fair sprinkling here of what I call direct symbolism, mostly of a kind, as in Shakespeare's final plays, suggesting an earth-heaven harmony, yet also to be closely related to the corresponding disharmony it opposes. The miracles are variously improbable as facts, pseudo-natural, or quite easy to understand. I am referring, however, all the time to the modern mind, which, in its sharp separation of facts and values creates a distinction which can hardly be finally valid. But since the New Testament has supreme meaning for us precisely because of, and in order to close, this very rift opened between Heaven and Earth, we may, indeed should, clearly think in terms both earthly and heavenly as freely as we choose; such elasticity and varied receptivity being the condition of understanding.

The New Testament thus shows us a convergence of two lines: the line of value and the line of fact, that of poetry and that of history. This does not mean that poetry and history never elsewhere correspond. All myth, all poetry, as I have already observed, aims at the reintegration of these two, the incarnation of the homeless God. But the New Testament differs in degree, if not in kind, from these. Here both elements, the historic and poetic, are of excessive importance and richness, beyond those of any other work. A maximum of valuable historic truth—because Jesus was so great a man—is married to a maximum of poetic splendour. Nor is it in any way surprising, nor does it in any way detract from the wonder of this Incarnate Logos, that some elements in our tale are purely symbolic, if you like, fictional. Consider again our image of two lines, crossing. It is that crossing, that interpenetration, that the book we are considering reveals. It does not show us only the point where they cross, nor two lines coinciding. We see the very process of incarnation, the crossing of the lines. And we cannot expect a crossing without a divergence: it would have, at this point in our argument, no meaning. Later on I shall regard the whole as a perfected fusion at every point. But first we must see it as a process, a vivid intersection of two worlds. Therefore our drama must be seen as often both historically true and symbolically significant; some of it will be historically true and symbolically comparatively unimportant; some of it symbolically true but historically, in the modern sense, false. We have therefore not a static picture of the incarnated Logos but rather a dynamic experience of incarnation, a sense of the world-order being interpenetrated by the divine. Every time a sensitive mind re-reads it, the book, so to speak, is recreating itself afresh. It is a silk, shot with dazzling colours as you turn it to the sun; it 'glistens', to use Goethe's word; it sparkles. It is dynamic, active, a living organism, and thus an inexhaustible well of life. Were every single event in the New Testament factually true, it would be of no use to us. It would be nearer the art of biography than poetic creation. 'The life and letters of the Christ': the very suggestion—partly owing to my use of one word with symbolic associations—sounds ludicrous, irreverent. Or it might, on the other hand, be purely poetical: it would then be no greater than *King Lear*. It would be, in a sense, too fanciful; we might say, too spiritual. And it would bear no relevance to history. We are given not a temporary dislocation of the world-order by the heavenly but an interpenetration of it. Its whole purpose is to blend the worlds of poetry and history. It presents both a divine reality and a bridge towards it, there is a relation, an interpenetration, a divine marriage, an incarnation. This principle of incarnation applies not only to the central figure of the organism, Jesus, but to the whole book: if it did not, the book would be less organic than a play of Shakespeare's. Thus the very truth of the living reality of the Incarnation, properly understood, may be said to be directly dependent on the historic falsity of some of its facts.

There is yet another aspect from which we may the more richly understand these varied and powerfully direct symbolisms. Remember what I have said about Jesus' morality as contrasted with that of the Shakespearian protagonist. The Shakespearian hero is immoral in that he aspires to a partial, exclusive ideal. Even Macbeth can be said to sin only through an improper direction and co-ordination of instincts themselves good: all crime is pathological. And consider the aspirations of other tragic heroes: Hamlet's excessive idealism, Angelo's excessive puritanism, Lear's selfish and sentimental love, Brutus' quest of absolute honour, Timon's more universal desire for an immediate paradise on earth, Coriolanus' pride, Cleopatra's consuming love for Antony. All these are, in their way, fine things. But we usually feel that in some sense these heroes have failed to incarnate their desires on the highest, that is, the most creative, level. Now Jesus seems to fulfil the required conditions. But can he be said to have incarnated his instincts in harmony with his environment? He is clearly shown as conflicting with his surroundings. To be too far beyond one's time may thus at first seem as immoral as to be behind it. But there is a fallacy here. The truly creative incarnation of instincts works in terms not only of the present but the future. It is creative in time as well as space. Creativeness, indeed, always points ahead. Therefore it is most important that Jesus' influence should be shown as pointing forwards. Strictly speaking, the Gospels alone leave us with a Jesus who is immoral. In the wider context only, a context including the Acts, Epistles, and Revelations, do we realize the pure creativeness of his life. We remember how, in our first chapter, we saw Jesus visualizing a whole pattern of which he himself was a part; and how his acts were calculated in terms of that pattern's present and future development.

Therefore we must not limit our primary attention to Jesus the man; nor even to the Gospels. Rather we must regard the whole New Testament as a single art-form of Shakespearian quality. We must always see Jesus in relation to the whole New Testament. Now we remember how dangerous it was to fix attention on the Shakespearian protagonist alone; how the play's essence is ever to be seen in the relation existent between the hero and his environment; and how this essence, something transcending any one individual, is necessarily reflected in direct symbolisms, usually supernatural. So Jesus is not to be regarded as a lonely God on earth: he is divine, the Christ, not in his own right as a person, but rather by right of his convictions, words, and actions together with the reaction to these of other men. Remember the symbol of the Divine Birth, the Voice from Heaven at Jesus' Baptism, the Transfiguration, the Resurrection and Ascension, and regard them in terms of Jesus' relation to his disciples, his meaning to them; remember, too, the interpretative and highly symbolical gospel of John; the coming of the Holy Spirit or, as I prefer to call it, the Sacred Life; the mystic experience of Paul and his later Herculean evangelism; the birth of the Church, and the intellectual visions of the Epistles; and, finally, the prophetic Book of Revelation pointing its shaft of light into the darkness. By considering these we shall understand how the New Testament is expressing the relation of Jesus to the present and future world of men, and how this is continually and necessarily being bodied into direct symbolism. This relation, rather than any one figure, is indeed, the Christ: hence the Christ is divine and exists potentially within the experience of all men. Now this smaller relation is an aspect of the great experience which makes the New Testament: the experience of the Divine Principle in terms of Jesus and his influence; the experience of the great God of Life in terms of man.

The New Testament compresses the very essence of life. There is no other book like it in the world. Nowhere else do art and history so combine to create a thing unique. The nearest thing to it is the Shakespearian play; and only by seeing it on the analogy of Shakespeare can we understand exactly how and in what sense it holds a truth and a power unparalleled elsewhere. There is no question now of belief or unbelief: the New Testament is a living reality. And this thought points us ahead to the theme of my next chapter.

I answer, however, one final objection. It might be argued that, however we may reason, yet the New Testament has not the minute poetic exactitude of the Shakespearian play, and that this lack in the work of the Divine Artist is, to say the least, curious. But the purpose of the book is different. The New Testament has to integrate the world of history and value in a sense hardly done by Shakespeare. Shakespeare's art is clearly close-twined with history very often. In the historical cycle he writes as a national poet, and in the Roman plays he revivifies the grandeur of the ancient world with striking success. There is a true blending of personal passion with historic fact to create a poetic result. But, even though we grant this, even though we remember, what is too often forgotten, that there is no very great difference in point of historicity between the work of Shakespeare and the Old Testament, yet the very fact that Shakespeare's book is the work of one man points its subjectivity, and lessens its final validity as history. It is primarily a poetic world in that it is a poet's world: in which it differs from the New Testament wherein the Logos, or poetic world, is incarnated in historical fact. Moreover, since the New Testament is composed by different authors, its harmonies, though clearly less minutely intercorrespondent throughout the book, will be the more evidently the result of some organic principle working in human terms yet transcending any single human person. Divergencies and contradictions will be a necessary part of this organism: hence the divergent accounts in the Gospels, and the surface differences in the philosophies, say, of St. John and St. Paul.

Browning adopted a similar technique as a road to the richest truth in *The Ring and the Book;* and indeed all drama does the same, in that its persons present and voice conflicting aspects of the dramatic theme. Only so can a superhuman truth be told in terms of man. The New Testament is always very human as well as divine: we may remember the very practical and business-like details that occur in the Epistles of St. Paul; and also how thought of the Roman Empire is entwined in the symbolism of Revelations, a book whose modern value and deeper purpose pierces very much farther than certain of its references might at first lead us to suppose. Hence, when we find the thought that the world-order is soon to come to an end, the word 'soon' needs an elastic understanding. God is not writing a book to drop from heaven so that man may have all his difficulties resolved: it is as though Life itself were travailling to create it in terms of the human mind.

I have tried to show that the New Testament is neither throughout poetry nor history, but a blending of the two. Often it reads like a work of art, yet we are simultaneously aware that actuality is so stamped on it that there can be no fiction. But we may also have jagged pieces, either crude fact or heightened symbolism, that at first appear to spoil its pattern either as art or history: and I have shown why and how these are necessary, indeed essential. But if we still do not like the more symbolical qualities, we may consider that, if a Divine Author is to make a book about Jesus, he is more likely to create in the style of the Shakespearian artist—surely as near to divine artistry as anything human we can conceive—than as a newspaper reporter. Or again, if we do not like the rough facts and discrepancies in the book, we might remember that the divine art-form will not necessarily conform to human ideas of neatness. We instinctively like our back gardens, their lawns and marbled pools; their arbours, flowers, and splaying fountains. This is nature narrowed down to human dimensions: and such is the work of Shakespeare. But the primeval forest, the volcano, the prairie, desert, and steppe, the mountain cataract and restless ocean, these obey different laws, and are part of a pattern whose exact artistry we cannot easily define.

V. CREATIVE NEWNESS

THE purpose of this chapter is to prove its title tautologous. I have already pointed out that poetry is to be thought of as 'creation'. It is too seldom recognized that 'expression' and 'imitation' are only facets, the poetic process being essentially creative. The word 'poet' means 'maker'. And, indeed, in the Middle Ages 'maker' was a very usual term for 'poet'. But though to regard poetry as 'creation' is not altogether new in theory, the implications which in practice follow are quite revolutionary. For consider what creation is. First, it is essentially new. Secondly, creation points ahead. Jesus' life, it will be recalled, was a pure creation in that it showed a perfect incarnation of spirit in the world-order; and therefore necessarily pointed beyond the world-order of his day, penetrating into the future, carving its way by its very nature into the thought and actions of the next generation, and then widening out in space and time. This is a very pure example of creativeness. And it will be remembered, too, how I have shown that any creation results from a marriage of two elements; and how destruction is to be regarded as a separation of these elements, a severing of spirit from body. Apply this to our poetic product, and we see at once how much past criticism—we might remember the word's derivation—has, by its continual attempt to reverse the poetic process, to resolve the poetry into its constituent elements, been essentially destructive. Conversely, to regard poetry as always new will lead to an essentially creative interpretation, pointing not to the past, but the future. In this chapter I cease to regard creation primarily as a process: I ask that we contemplate it rather as a product.

All creation is miraculous. That is, a completely new thing is formed that was not implicit in those elements whose marriage has led to its birth. And that is why it is so often necessary to call in categories of the divine and supernatural to explain the creative mystery. All human experience, we remember, was seen to be superhuman: it is only human from the subjective view of the experiencer. Experience is, in varying degrees, creative: and creation is ever excessively miraculous. I have already shown how in Shakespeare both human birth and poetic creation are seen in terms of an earth-heaven marriage. Next, I shall show how in Dante a similar line of thought is everywhere developed. In Shakespeare heaven is one of the marrying elements: it is so in Dante, but its personal and divine quality is here more powerfully emphasized. But however and wherever the divine element is stressed as an higher element than the material—and it is often not unreasonable to do this—it must not be forgotten that Christianity and poetry in general, including Dante, assert primarily the splendour of incarnation: that is, the created whole, not one of the parts. When separated, as in the action of *Macbeth*, both nature and spirit appear evil and unreal, are evil and unreal. When united, as in Shakespeare's final plays, spiritual beings and mankind are both beautiful, things of life. In Dante, the spiritual element in creation is equated directly with the divine: this category, however, including the final miraculous element in creation which is paradoxically conditioned by the spirit-matter marriage it controls. In the Bible, both God and man in the Old Testament have qualities we to-day might call evil. But it is really only the separation between God and man that is ultimately evil: the God-man relation is out of joint. In the New Testament, there is harmony, realized in the Incarnation, the perfect Creation. And conversely whenever and wherever a God-man harmony is realized, an Incarnation is accomplished, the Christ—who must not be too rigidly limited to the historical Jesus—is born again. Such creation is ever something greater and nobler than either 'God' or 'man' in separation, or the two together out of harmony. The Church has significantly recognized Incarnation to be the very heart of reality.

Dante's *Divina Commedia* continually discusses the mystery of creation. Francis chose a 'bride' and made her his for life: the bride was 'Poverty'. So,

> Their concord and glad looks, wonder and love,
> And sweet regard gave birth to holy thoughts.
>
> (*Paradise*, XI, 52-57)

So they gained 'hidden riches'. Notice how clearly the creative life is imaged in terms of human love, marriage, and birth. There is no more nobly erotic poet than Dante, and his vision flowers everywhere according to the laws of organic poetry. The good life is thus creation and all creation holds a magic power:

> Spirit, substantial form, with matter joined,
> Not in confusion mixed, hath in itself
> Specific virtue of that union born,
> Which is not felt except it work, nor proved
> But through effect, as vegetable life
> By the green leaf.
>
> (*Purgatory*, XVIII, 47)

A most valuable passage, applying to all creation. Especially it here enriches my argument. The poetic product has just such a 'specific virtue' born of a union: and it is only felt in its work on our minds, the effect it may have if we so allow it. Its 'virtue' is conditional on our receptivity. And notice the 'vegetable life' and 'green leaf'. Dante's poetry is throughout organic creation and speaks in terms of the created world: all such imagery emphasizes creation. Elsewhere in Dante we have a sharp distinction of 'substance' and 'informing virtue' as the elements of creation (*Paradise,* VII, 130-134). God imprints heavenly virtue on earth, and 'doles out time with his beam' (*Paradise,* X, 25-29). And ever this creation is not only a union of elements, but a new thing. The meeting of lovers thus makes a 'new nature':

> . . . love is that inclining,
> And a new nature knit by pleasure in ye.
> (*Purgatory,* XVIII, 26)

Moreover, natural laws themselves—it may be better to say 'natural laws as we usually think of them'—cannot create. There is always a descent of the divine. Thus in a pregnant passage (*Paradise,* VIII, 126-150) Dante describes how nature, if she were not ruled by Providence, must ever produce men no finer than their parents:

> Were it not
> That Providence celestial overruled,
> Nature, in generation, must the path
> Traced by the generator still pursue,
> Unswervingly.
> (l. 138)

The lower nature cannot necessarily accomplish creative newness. Or we can say that nature properly understood is essentially creative, which is equivalent to calling it miraculous. The central thought will be the same: the miracle of creation and the fact that the final result is the product, not the sum, of its two elements. And this is why the Christian religion, in describing the perfect, that is, the essential man, tells us of his divine birth. The New Testament is a vision of absolute creativeness, a penetrating revelation of essential life: which necessarily includes a divine birth. Birth and creation, if we are not to falsify them, must ever contain a miraculous element: which is a necessary concession to our clouded minds.

Therefore there is really no process of creation. It is, finally, miraculous and immediate. Dante has a dazzling passage on the timeless creation (*Paradise*, XXIX, 13-38). The Creator is imagined as 'beyond time's limit' and 'inhabiting his own eternity', yet unfolding his 'eternal love' into 'new natures like unto himself': in which we see how closely this Creator resembles the poet. Dante continues:

> . . . nor before,
> As if in dull inaction, torpid lay;
> For, not in process of before or aft,
> Upon these waters moved the Spirit of God.

That is, however we must, for our intellectual safety, think sometimes in terms of the elements, yet the ultimate reality is not the factors but the product. 'Creation' has a dimension beyond the flat surfaces of any theory: it is solid. In this sense it is set beyond our intellectual categories, beyond time. In talking of it, we may, sometimes must, refer to those elements, reduce creation to a time process: but we must recognize that this is only a provisional necessity. And if it be objected here that the New Testament itself thinks in terms of incarnation and therefore of time, I answer that all high prophecy necessarily speaks largely in terms of the intellectual fallacies it aims to remove. On every level the breach between the spiritual and material is an evil: a moral evil, an intellectual falsity, a technical weakness. All art, all prophecy, is concerned with healing this gash, this gaping wound. Thus a divine being comes to visit man to reunite him with God: that would not be necessary had there been no severance. And this severance depends partly on our consciousness of it. The New Testament throughout both reminds us of it and points us to a reintegration: it would lift us beyond time, and introduce us to immortality, which is essential life. But to think in terms of this integration whilst using language which does not suggest it may be the greatest of all fallacies, leading direct to a neglect of the mysterious element in creation. A baby is not to be considered the result of a purely 'physical' process since 'purely physical' to our minds holds a very limited content. So Dante describes how the 'babe' comes from the 'animal' (*Purgatory*, XXV, 64):

> Know, soon as in the embryo, to the brain
> Articulation is complete, then turns
> The primal Mover with a smile of joy
> On such great work of nature; and inbreathes
> New spirit replete with virtue, that what here
> Active it finds, to its own substance draws;
> And forms an individual soul, that lives,
> And feels, and bends reflective on itself.
> And that thou less mayst marvel at the word,
> Mark the sun's heat; how that to wine doth change,
> Mixed with the moisture filtered through the vine.
>
> (*Purgatory*, XXV, 70)

Notice again the rich comparison that concludes a theoretical passage: Dante is a prince of poets in his richness of natural suggestion.

Dante, like Shakespeare, recognizes the divine element in creation. Elsewhere he writes how the created product varies according to the degree of 'lustre' imparted by the higher reality; how all natural and human birth is to be thought on as the result of such a process; how artistic creation is of the same kind; and how the perfect example of creation is found in the New Testament. This is the passage—he is writing of the 'triune love':

> Descending hence unto the lowest powers,
> Its energy so sinks, at last it makes
> But brief contingencies; for so I name
> Things generated, which the heavenly orbs
> Moving, with seed or without seed, produce.
> Their wax and that which moulds it, differ much:
> And thence with lustre, more or less, it shows
> The ideal stamp imprest: so that one tree,
> According to his kind, hath better fruit,
> And worse: and, at your birth, ye, mortal men,
> Are in your talents various. Were the wax
> Moulded with nice exactness, and the heaven
> In its disposing influence supreme,
> The brightness of the seal should be complete:
> But nature renders it imperfect ever;
> Resembling thus the artist, in her work,
> Whose faltering hand is faithless to her skill.
> Therefore, if fervent love dispose, and mark
> The lustrous image of the primal virtue,
> There all perfection is vouchsafed: and such
> The clay was made, accomplished with each gift
> That life can teem with; such the burden filled
> The Virgin's bosom . . . (*Paradise,* XIII, 57)

The Incarnation is seen as the perfect Creation: but all human and natural birth, all artistic work, are lesser sorts in the same kind. In another pregnant passage (*Paradise,* II, 105-148), we hear how creation is ever sown from above. From one heaven to the next beneath the divine seed is propagated:

> Thus do these organs of the world proceed,
> As thou beholdest now, from step to step;
> Their influences from above deriving,
> And thence transmitting downwards . . .

The 'sacred orbs', that is the stars and planets, are as 'mallets' in the hand of the great 'workman', they are inspired by 'blessed movers'. And the whole glory of the skies takes the 'image' and 'impress' of the 'deep spirit' which moves their sphere. This impregnation of the stars by the divine is associated directly with the organism of man:

> And as the soul, that dwells within your dust
> Through members different, yet together formed,
> In different powers resolves itself; e'en so
> The intellectual efficacy unfolds
> Its goodness multiplied throughout the stars.

So 'virtue' is said to 'enliven' the various bodies with which it is 'knit'—'as life', says Beatrice, 'in you is knit'. So,

> From its original nature full of joy,
> The virtue mingled through the body shines,
> As joy through pupil of the living eye.

Elsewhere Dante considers the universe as a tree whose life is 'from its top' (*Paradise*, XVIII, 25).

This thought of all creation being vitalized from above rather than below is excessively important. I shall emphasize it again shortly. The 'cause' of creation, if we must have a 'cause', is not in the past but the future; not below, but above. So elsewhere Dante tells us how the root of creation is God, and morality is to be in harmony with this: that is, to be in harmony with the 'origin' of creation. We are not to derive our morality from a 'created thing', but rather follow the laws themselves of creation. The highly moral life is the creative life. It will always be original, in harmony with the great origin of life (*Paradise*, XIV, 82-87). It will be noted that though we variously regard our more 'spiritual' element in different poets the marriage of nature and spirit is always to be considered the condition of 'creation'; whereas their disharmony is death. The expressly 'divine' quality —with all that that word suggests—in Dante's creation is, moreover, to be related to the simple fact that creation is always new, drawing its life from above, not below; pointing us to the future, not the past.

Birth is new, miraculous. And those alchemists who looked for a miraculous discovery in the Middle Ages saw that it must come about in terms of a marriage. Goethe has a fine passage on this alchemical theory and Prof. Latham writes an interesting note:

> In this passage Faust describes processes still familiar to the chemist, in the fanciful jargon of the alchemists. The *Red Lion* and the *Lily* are chemical substances, possibly preparations of gold and silver respectively. To these are attributed different sexes. They are 'wedded together' in a retort, which is the first 'bridal-bower', under the influence of the uniform heat of a 'water-bath'. Then the retort is exposed to the naked flame, and thus the newly-wedded pair are driven over as vapour into the receiver, the second 'bridal-bower', where, if the experiment has been successful, a richly-coloured sublimate is formed. This sublimate, resulting from the union of the two, is regarded as their offspring, and is known as the Young Queen. It is in fact the Philosopher's Stone, which transmutes base metals into gold, and is a panacea for all diseases.
>
> (Goethe's *Faust*, Everyman Edn. p. 166)

This passage is valuable. The emphasis on marriage is most interesting, and the 'Young Queen', who contains the very principle of Life, corresponds to Dante's Beatrice, Shakespeare's idealised heroines, Goethe's Helen. Indeed, one of the most powerful life-symbols in Goethe's poem is Homunculus: and his birth happens partly in terms of alchemy. The middle ages knew a strangely perfect integration of science and poetry. The Renaissance divorce was no doubt necessary: but a new integration must eventually follow.

Creation gives us ever a totally new thing, transcending its elements. This is implied by Dante's thought in many of the passages I have quoted and in the aspirations of medieval alchemy. The word 'process' is therefore provisional only: hence Dante's thought that creation is ultimately to be considered as outside time. In my earlier chapters I have enquired into this process, so that, by regarding the New Testament as a blending of the historical and poetic, seeing it as two lines crossing and diverging, we may be enabled to catch some glimpse as to how it was made. This has been necessary to counteract our sceptical tendencies, which continually think in terms of the temporal succession. The New Testament is a fact and a marvellous fact. But as soon as we start to reason as to its origin, or the origin of certain events, we begin to question its authority: and mainly to this sceptical consciousness have I addressed my examination of the artistic process. It has been a valuable step to understanding. But we can not stop there. Having accepted the book as a marriage of elements, mingling the historical with the imaginative, we must next see it as a new birth, a product transcending its factors. It is in this sense exactly that all art-forms are authentic pieces of life: the creative mystery burns from them. And from such a view I always write my considered interpretations of any poetic result.

It is true that the action of both the New Testament and, say, *Macbeth,* speaks in terms of a body-soul dualism: but that, as I have suggested before, is because all great literature is addressed to our clouded consciousness and therefore speaks in the dualistic mode it would supersede. So, of our two examples the one glorifies the Incarnation, and the other shows the essential evil, and indeed the unreality, of the elements when not harmonized. Both works are mainly concerned in removing this very dualism. That is ever our ideal; and in the action of *Antony and Cleopatra* the dualism is all but resolved. Moreover, though the action within the drama may be often couched in dualistic terms, yet the drama itself, the art-form itself, is already a created whole. Its artistic unity alone resolves all dualisms in its content, and it has therefore advanced beyond all normal categories. It is, finally, to be regarded as an immediate birth, a virgin birth. This is clear from any just consideration. A poet who makes a metaphor may well be unable to say whether the image or thought-content came first. There may, indeed, have been a process: but we only deduce it from the result. In the same way, we should never be so concerned about aesthetic theory were it not that the final creation seems so important. Our 'process', and its elements, are all therefore abstractions from the result: and my earlier chapters have laboured to reintegrate these abstractions in terms of modern thought, without doing too much violence to the poetic fact. They might be unnecessary for anyone who already accepts the New Testament and the Shakespearian play as visionary wholes quite transcending any elements in the process of their creation; which elements are, in any case, mere abstractions from the result. And this result, as we saw in analyzing human experience—and creation is always experience, just as experience is creative—is finally always incommensurable with its factors.

To think too rigidly in terms of the artistic process is, indeed, excessively dangerous. It paralyses interpretation, which depends on a recognition of creative newness not only in theory but in practice. And when I begin, as I shall in the middle chapters of my book, to put this theory into practice, many who have followed my argument hitherto will immediately find difficulties rising in their minds as to the soundness of my method. It has happened, time and again, with my Shakespearian interpretations. People ask whether Shakespeare can be considered consciously to have 'intended' this or that effect which I emphasize; or point out that, by failing to have regard at every point to Shakespeare's source—the story on which he builds—I wantonly impoverish my work. These arguments form no contact whatsoever with my interpretations. It is essential to my method to regard the art-form as new, pointing ahead, transcending all particular sources and intentions. In art such as Shakespeare's, numerous rays of truth, historical narrative, Elizabethan stage technique, the author's personal experience of men and manners, his thought and passion, and the emotions, too, of the real people who once trod the earth and whose story the poet recaptures—all these are as rays to which the poetic act is as a lens, concentrating them in one burning point, transforming a passive light into an active heat, burning into reality, into the future, dynamic and penetrating. The result is different in quality and power from its supposed causes. And such, on a still grander scale, is the New Testament. But if we limit our receptivity by continually remembering that this effect was necessitated by out-worn stage conditions, that by the story the poet is using, and so on, and let these hamper our appreciation of effects which otherwise could be considered rich in profound significance, we are committing the greatest of blunders. We are continually un-making the poet's creation. Such critics will try to place themselves at the poet's elbow, to catch and isolate the thought he is putting into the poem, to unthread his personal philosophy. It cannot, fortunately, be done, and if it could it would tend to destroy, rather than interpret, the work of art. Hence, too, the frequent attempt to imagine Shakespeare 'the man'. If found, he would, as a man, be no more interesting than other men. We would, in any case, do far better to study the personal life and thought of a living poet of significance, such as Mr. T. S. Eliot: and I think he would agree that it would not be easy to isolate the exact philosophy he, personally, puts into his poems.

Indeed, if interpretation were to extract from the art-form only the thought or emotion put into it deliberately and consciously by the poet, that is, those essences that clearly pre-existed or in some other way were independent of the creative act, it would be valueless. Moreover, it would suggest that the poet might have done better to express his thoughts directly rather than entangle them in irrelevancies: and would thus constitute an attack upon poetry itself. We will suppose, for the sake of simplification, that *Antony and Cleopatra* is a creation resulting from two elements, one consciously personal, and the other purely objective. I omit all considerations of the 'unconscious mind' since clearly this brings in categories my critics wish to neglect. We have, then, (i) Shakespeare's conscious philosophy and conscious emotional nature, and (ii) Plutarch's *Antonius* and perhaps the Dark Lady of the Sonnets. These may be allowed to cover the two worlds, the inner and outer. Now, though my two interpretations of *Antony and Cleopatra* in *The Imperial Theme* emphasized respectively the 'spatial' and the 'temporal' aspects, yet both were interpretations not of any such integrated elements as I have just noted but rather of separate aspects of the completed creation: and this completed creation was something quite transcendent to the poet's conscious mind and the source or sources on which he worked. Interpretation thus does not at all aim to extract what was originally integrated. When I interpret Dante, my results are, I hope, different from the scholastic philosophy he put into his poem. Most modern criticism starts from the assumption that the original creation was a mistake. Interpretation does not try, like such criticism, to reverse the creative process, but rather receives the whole creation as a unique thing, pointing to the future. It then does the best it can to interpret, in whatever terms seem most adequate, the magic and mysterious reality. It will recognize, if asked, that there seem undoubtedly to be subjective and objective elements in the work under inspection, but will never let thought of either repress the awakened imagination. Only by having regard to the true nature of poetic creation and by refusing to be fettered by false reasonings will interpretation ever produce any really valuable results. Then, respecting the laws of creation, it will be itself creative.

Now in my previous chapters I have certainly argued in terms of causality, and have admitted two constituent elements in creation. But I have done this in a general and vague way, and purely in the interests of the created whole. Whether looking ahead or back, I start always with the art-form itself. We can, when inspecting our completed creation, see that there has been, in some sort, a marriage of elements. But we only deduce this from contemplating the completed work which transcends these, and therefore we see now how provisional our reasoning must be, and how the parts can never limit the meaning of the whole. This is quite different from the criticism that, comparing Plutarch's *Antonius* with Shakespeare's *Antony and Cleopatra,* notes carefully which words and incidents are added by Shakespeare, and next boldly regards these as more significant than the rest; and, correspondingly, refuses to allow the fullest possible symbolic meaning to an event which comes directly out of Plutarch. For, by becoming constituent to a new whole, every part is dynamically changed. Creation is a multiplication of elements rather than an addition: conversely, you cannot solve the mystery of poetry by a subtraction sum. We may indeed enlist, as I have done, thought of the artistic process positively, wherever it may be of creative service to the created result, or the cause of creation; but never negatively, to impoverish it. For the created whole must always be our starting point and primary concern. If it helps us to enrich our interpretation of Dante, we may have regard to Aquinas, though too much reference is risky: but we must not let Aquinas hamper our intuitions. Any one piece of the Aquinas philosophy must be interpreted primarily always in terms of the whole poem into which it has been incorporated; not in terms of the whole, the *Summa Theologica,* from which it has been abstracted. Thus too much knowledge of Aquinas is quite likely to prove actually dangerous.

As this is a matter of great importance, and one which, in practice, though not in theory, is nearly always neglected, I shall next refer to some helpful passages from other writers. Here is the first:

A mechanical complexity is the sum of its parts. Put them side by side and you get the whole. Now vital or organic is merely a convenient metaphor for a complexity of a different kind, that in which the parts cannot be said to be elements as each one is modified by the other's presence, and each one to a certain extent is the whole.

(T. E. Hulme, *Speculations*, p. 138; quoted by Michael Roberts in *The Criterion*, April, 1932).

Next, I quote from Smuts' *Holism and Evolution:*

That is the essence of a whole. It is always transcendent to its parts, and its character cannot be inferred from the character of its parts. (p. 350).

The following is relevant to works of art:

A poem or a picture, for instance, is praised because it is a 'whole', because it is not a mere artificial construction, but an organic whole, in which all the parts appear in a subtle indefinable way to subserve and contribute to and carry out the main purpose or idea. Artistic creations are, in fact, mainly judged and appraised by the extent to which they realize the character of wholes (pp. 100-101).

Finally, consider this with reference to poetry:

If an external 'cause' is applied to an organism or a living body it will become internalised and transformed, and will be experienced as a stimulus, which in its turn will be followed by a response. The response is not the mere mechanical effect of the cause, and this is due to the complete transformation which the latter has undergone. In the moment which elapses between stimulus and response a miracle is performed; a vast series of organic changes is set going of which comparatively little is known as yet. The inorganic becomes organic, the alien stuff of the environment is recreated into the stuff of the living organism. . . . Anything passing through the organic whole thereby becomes completely changed. *Any action issuing from it has the stamp of the whole upon it. The procedure is transformative, synthetic, recreative, holistic, and the result is 'new' in one degree or another.* (p. 143)

I italicize the concluding sentences, and would emphasize their importance to a proper understanding of poetic interpretation.

And here I may also quote from a great poet, writing of his greatest work, to support my argument. Browning tells how his poem *The Ring and The Book* is the result of his own mind's activity at work on an old tale:

> . . . thence bit by bit I dug
> The lingot truth, that memorable day,
> Assayed and knew my piecemeal gain was gold,—
> Yes; but from something else surpassing that,
> Something of mine which, mixed up with the mass,
> Made it bear hammer and be firm to file.
> Fancy with fact is just one fact the more;
> To wit, that fancy has informed, transpierced,
> Thridded and so thrown fast the facts else free,
> As right through ring and ring runs the djereed
> And binds the loose, one bar without a break.
> I fused my live soul and that inert stuff
> Before attempting smithcraft . . .

'Fancy with fact is just one fact the more'. In this sense, Shakespeare's *Julius Caesar* is as true, indeed truer, than Plutarch. Browning turns over his idea, juggles with it, throws it up and catches it, in his peculiar way. He is ever examining different aspects of things—hence the plot of *The Ring and The Book*. Here he is again at it:

> What's this then, which proves good yet seems untrue?
> This that I mixed with truth, motions of mine
> That quickened, made the inertness malleable
> O' the gold was not mine . . .

This helps us to understand the New Testament and symbolic work generally. The power and value is unquestioned, yet it 'seems untrue'. But it is true in an even more concrete sense. 'Is fiction which makes facts alive, fact, too?' the poet asks. And the implied answer is, 'Yes'. He goes on to say how man may 'project' his surplusage of soul in search of body, but must have something to revivify if he would create, how though breath cannot light a 'virgin candle', it can yet fan a dying flame. Thus he is true to both aspects of creation: the subjective and objective. The gold was not his: but he moulded it. The fancy was his, but it needed something beyond itself on which to work. The final result is as much a fact as those facts that help its making. It is more. It is a creative act.

And here is another pregnant passage from Browning's *Abt Vogler*. The musician is regarding his work as an earth-heaven marriage:

> In sight? Not half! for it seemed, it was certain, to match man's birth,
> Nature in turn conceived, obeying an impulse as I;
> And the emulous heaven yearned down, made effort to reach the earth.
> As the earth had done her best, in my passion, to scale the sky:
> Novel splendours burst forth, grew familiar and dwelt with mine,
> Not a point nor peak but found and fixed its wandering star;
> Meteor-moons, balls of blaze: and they did not pale nor pine,
> For earth had attained to heaven, there was no more near nor far.

Our usual process of creation, a marriage ceremony or incarnation. And Browning also recognizes that there is a miracle within the creative arithmetic:

> But here is the finger of God, a flash of the will that can,
> Existent behind all laws, that made them and, lo! they are!
> And I know not if, save in this, such gift be allowed to man,

> That out of three sounds he frame, not a fourth sound, but a star.
> Consider it well: each tone of our scale in itself is nought:
> It is everywhere in the world—loud, soft, and all is said;
> Give it to me to use! I mix it with two in my thought:
> And there! Ye have heard and seen: consider and bow the head!

So also an historic detail or piece of traditional symbolism in the New Testament, a phrase of Plutarch's in Shakespeare, a piece of scholastic logic in Dante, all may at first seem 'nought' to us to-day. Yet in their context they are rich in significance derived from the new whole they help to build: and a final interpretation regards the symbolic rights of every part, however humble, knowing that each holds a meaning not its own but none the less powerful for that. Each part is splendid by reason of its vassalage to the whole; like liveried servants, or soldiers, or priests of God, whose uniforms endue them with extrinsic rights.

Now it may seem that by regarding art as so impersonally miraculous and refusing to regard it as a personal revelation I impoverish its appeal. Surely there is a sense in which Shakespeare's work is Shakespeare's? There is. *Macbeth* represents an experience of conflict. And the experience was, ultimately, Shakespeare's. But a vivid experience is not a personal philosophy nor even an 'attitude to life.' Moreover, it is conditional on the objective world, it is, indeed, a fusion of Shakespeare's mind with that world. A man cannot create, nor have any experience, without a certain objective reality: for even poetic images, dream-shapes, one's own body, all must be considered objective to the experiencing centre. Melville writes well on this necessity of creation:

> The world is for ever babbling of originality; but there never yet was an original man, in the sense intended by the world; the first man himself—who according to the Rabbins was also the first author—not being an original; the only original author being God. Had Milton's been the lot of Caspar Hauser, Milton would have been vacant as he. For though the naked soul of man doth assuredly contain one latent element of productiveness; yet never was there a child born solely from one parent; the visible world of experience being that procreative thing which impregnates the muses, self-reciprocally efficient hermaphrodites being but a fable.
>
> (*Pierre*, Book XVIII)

We must, however, allow the poet to have the advantage on his side. His soul contains the 'latent element' of productiveness. In Shakespeare, we remember, the 'soul' impregnates the 'brain'. The spiritual or psychical reality is the more decisive factor. In Dante, the 'divine' element, as I have shown, must be taken to cover the final miracle of the spirit-matter union, a miracle incommensurable with its parts. Creation thus comes from above rather than below; its cause is in the future rather than the past, the poet's mind rather than his material. And though Browning fused his 'live soul' and the 'inert stuff' before attempting 'smith-craft', yet he himself is clearly the 'smith'. Prospero is master of both Ariel and Caliban. Therefore, in so far as a miracle can be explained at all, we may say that the final mystery of creative work in literature is to be credited to the poet's 'judgment'. But this is a vague word. I do not mean a reasoning faculty; intuitive rather. I therefore conclude that the poet writes, ultimately, from the imaginative consciousness discussed in my first chapter. In this consciousness, to which the act of composition raises him, he is more than man as usually understood.

He may, after descending from creative work, and returning to his normal consciousness, forget things he knew while in the act of composition. So creation, as the poet writes, itself creates the higher faculty which finally exercises judgment; and all art, born of this change from the one to the other consciousness, acts as a gear-change, raising others from the lower to the higher, from the intellectual to the romantic mode. Poetry is thus the expression of the poet's imaginative or romantic consciousness: and this simple term, 'romantic', is itself to be related to essential life, which life is wronged by our usual categories of 'intention' and 'memory': indeed, it quite transcends the cause and effect sequence. It is simpler than all this: it is the consciousness of a man in love. Thus pure 'experience' and the 'imaginative consciousness' are convergent: and both are to be equated with the greater life and immortality to which we aspire. In this, and only in this, sense, is poetry personal. Therefore the poet's sources or supposed intentions must never be allowed to interrupt or modify our interpretations.

The essence of artistic creation is newness. The fusion is, in a final interpretation, to be considered perfect at every stage and the result always new; or rather every part, which may be purely historical, straight out of a 'source', or personal, is to be seen not in relation to its origin, the whole from which it has been abstracted, but in relation to the new fusion of the whole into which it has been integrated. And only by not asking at every turn whether this or that is Plutarch or Shakespeare can we possibly be receptive to these new relations, and see the new whole in all its finer meanings. The 'not asking' is, indeed, implicit in any creative response. Conversely, to ask is to deny the primary unity of creation. Therefore, in a final interpretation, we must not even draw any too rigid distinctions between what I call 'direct symbolism', symbolic events and speeches, and pure narrative. All is to be received as artistic fact, without question. Hitherto we have been wandering darkly among the mysterious woods and hills of poetry: and that has its own fascination. We have tried to understand the experience of creation. Now I ask that we be prepared to see our territory as a landscape: we have come out of the woods and overlook them from a mountain height. No longer shall we have regard to any process, but the work of poets and the New Testament alike will be seen as things in their own right, to be received each as a perfect whole, if we receive them at all. For all this applies, too, to the New Testament. I have shown how some vast poetic beam is there seen playing on the world of history. It has been useful, in order to relate this mysterious book to our sceptic minds, to regard it as two lines, poetic and factual, crossing and diverging. We cannot stay there, however: we must next be able to see it as a completed and perfect whole, which perfection is potentially existent in each part. Therefore we must, finally, not ask at every turn whether the events are historically true, or pieces of direct symbolism. Such provisional distinctions have been valuable hitherto, and we can always return to such analysis when we wish. But the book finally transcends those categories of poetry and history, imagination and fact, which it fuses together. Here again we must not ask, and this 'not asking' will be the condition of the richest creative understanding.

In my next chapters, I take seriously, as creative visions truer to-day than when they were written, some works of admitted strength: the New Testament, the poetry of Shakespeare, Dante, and Goethe. But I do not search for what was originally intended, by man or divine author, in these works: I show what they can, and therefore must, mean to us to-day. I shall, however, expect many criticisms that would invalidate a profound interpretation of a symbol by referring to that symbol's 'cause'. It is a current blunder to think that, when we find a cause, or supposed cause, for anything, we have limited its significance. The reasoning, in so far as there is any, is puerile. Things do not exist alone, and the only cause of any one event is the whole state of the universe the instant before. Moreover, poetry exists, not in the historical order, but the real world: in terms of that only can it be said to have any cause. It is an event in the life-stream of the real, of which biography and history are abstractions. Its true causes, if it has any, are hidden. A succession of molehills rise one by one: but each is not caused by the preceding one, but by the mole we cannot see. And this mysterious hidden life is essentially creative: its cause is in the future, not the past. Yet we go on refusing to face the creative visions of poetry: and every time, if asked our reasons, we are driven to false arguments in terms of history, sources, intentions, false causes of one kind or another. Do we care, at a railway station, where our train comes from? If it goes to the station to which we would travel, do we refuse to enter it because we have no interest in the town whence it started? Yet poet after poet swings by in his fiery chariot, while we sit down to write his biography, analyse the 'influences' that directed his work, interpret vision in terms of neurosis, find reasons for this and that, until the poetic substance is dead in our hands, mutilated limb by limb, slain by causality.

It is not so bad as that, you will say. But wait till you have read further, and see if arguments do not rise to your mind, as they would to mine did I let them, suggesting that a certain meaning cannot be applied to a symbol with whose derivation it seems incompatible.

False associations must not be allowed to destroy our vision. Too often we think of Dante only in terms of Aquinas, Shakespeare was a working playwright, Milton was a disappointed puritan. As for Lyly—euphuism; Wordsworth had a love affair in his youth; Shelley, Godwin's political theories; Keats, Fanny Brawne and the Quarterly; Browning was a Victorian and D. H. Lawrence fond of his mother. Mr. T. S. Eliot, modernism in technique. And whenever anyone is rash enough to follow my interpretative method, he will at once be stigmatized as a follower of myself, and his work be credited—or rather debited—with all my private failings. But what we will not do is to face the literary product, rich in meanings, potent to heal and save, a life-giving sun. We will not open our minds to that divine fire, nor let their petals be fanned by its summer breeze of truth. We are as buds refusing the hour of their unfolding. I ask that we let poetry work its way with us, relax ourselves to its mastering and creative strength, think in terms of imagery rather than logic, the future rather than the past. For all great work is of the present and the future, not the past. We must recognize its Virgin Birth. If we search mainly for its origins we shall be like one who, looking in a pool, troubles the still mirror by stirring up the sediment beneath, and sees his true reflection turned first to a dancing antic shape with hideously elongated sideways grin, next quickly and mercifully befogged and dissolved in the rising mud. That is what has happened in Shakespearian studies. It is the same with the Bible. But neither Shakespeare nor the Bible are out of date: in both we can see, if we will, the true image of the modern world. Let art be as a still mirror. Or as a drama. How can a man in the wings of a theatre, with machinery around and above, looking from a ridiculous angle on to the stage, hope to receive the subtleties of an expert producer? I ask that we sit rather in that dress-circle of the mind to which all poetry is directed.

PART II

POETIC INTERPRETATIONS

VI. THE POET'S PARADISE

TO the true adept and initiate, nothing about poetry will appear more important than poetry itself. Only by regarding the poetic result as primary can we, finally, see its exact purpose and direction and its meaning for life. But though secondary, we have seen—or guessed—the process of composition to be a creative process, analogous to human birth. We have seen, too, the poetic whole to be organic, its technique and subject matter both revealing similar qualities. I pass henceforward to a view which makes no powerful distinctions between content and technique, and thinks not at all in terms of processes. Yet similar essences to those I have discussed will reappear. Here, too, we shall find in our proper interpretations continual life-themes of which our concepts of creation, marriage of elements, incarnation and birth have been shadows only. We are to see now the rounded whole. That whole cannot be fully interpreted. But our only hope of any valuable interpretation rests on our steadfast determination to see first the thing in itself, and next, to remain true to the more purely imaginative impressions.

All poetry is concerned with creation and life: and, being so concerned, is also bound to speak often of destruction and death. At the extremes, we have death-visions and life-visions; and the most intense poetry is usually found at these extremes. The words 'life' and 'death' are all but ubiquitous at intense moments. The poet naturally responds to the glories of the created universe, its contours, its colours. And he sees, too, its significance: every image is dynamic, a present and picturesque fact pointing to its own potential splendour. The poet is ever seeing through the shapes which present themselves to us all to that whole more concrete and physical, more rounded reality whose significance is ultimate. All poets are as men in love. But they know too that there is death. Throughout our literature we have, at one extreme, impressions of disease, disorder and destruction; sin, cynicism, loathing; darkness and death. Set over against these are physical beauty in nature or man; concord in the community; romantic valour and love; birth and creation; light and life. Vast and easy simplicities, you will say. But all poetry obeys the easy yoke of truth, and is limited by the eternal wonders of the created universe. It urges us thus to know our life, to own it, to live it: and to do this it speaks by symbol and parable; by images of flower and harvest, the trees and beasts of the field and air, the infinities of sea and sky, the profounder infinities of human birth and human love. To possess this glorious life, to find union with it, man hungers inwardly, too often insatiate and starved. Now satanic literature tells everywhere the reverse tale: loneliness, thwarted longing, and death. And to these death visions we must give a wide and understanding sympathy, that we may see how they blend into those other visions of paradisal life on which our hopes are set.

We must, then, focus these vast distinguishing impressions in literature. Details are changeable, essences persist. First I note shortly what I mean by 'death' literature. Old English poetry is burdened with woe; and Chaucer, though happiest in a middle path where neither ecstasy nor despair find place, yet does not shirk the knowledge that tragedy overwaits all human adventure. But with the Renaissance, where so fine a blaze is ignited revealing new vistas in the poetic and the actual world, this very fire serves often to cast a deeper gloom, a more dread abysmal fear, than any in our earlier literature. Webster, who reached a poetic intensity and sombre magic comparable with Shakespeare's, dramatizes not life but death-in-life. His stage is as a torture-chamber, or a graveyard: and the greatest kindness he can do the persons of his imagination is to remove them from the one to the other. Here a cold pain freezes the mind into a nightmare paralysis. In other, and lesser, Elizabethans, we find often the Websterian philosophy variously reflected. The stage of seventeenth century imaginative prose is draped in black. Donne preaches a death-philosophy, seeing the best men most cruelly tortured, and warning all mankind not to forget the dissolution that awaits them; a Christian faith, however, lighting these cavernous glooms with a little candle, fluttering very uncertainly in the vaulted dark. Browne puts up a sterner fight. His solemn cadences are enlisted against the darkness. That darkness, by the slow revolutions of his planetary thought, shows at last its obverse of light and we listen as the arithmetic of language tells out the answer to our equation of death:

> There is nothing strictly immortal but immortality. Whatever hath no beginning, may be confident of no end, which is the peculiar of that necessary essence which cannot destroy itself.

But the immortality he would assert is itself so dim a reality, that he, too, has little more than Donne for our aid. His immortality is largely parasitic on thought of death: no positive life-conviction. This Christianized age in our literature is, paradoxically, a very death-like period, and therefore it is not strange to find its soil bringing forth that amazing book *The Anatomy of Melancholy.*

Wherever we find intensest literature, there is death, or life. The Augustan period is, as a whole, clearly less intense, the imagination here is more relaxed: and its finest works, in Dryden, Pope, or Swift tend towards satire, a mode which reacts from the partiality, the littleness, the faults, of human life, but scarcely plunges into those universal glooms, those dark profundities, which vitalize the most powerful death-literature. But when intensity returns, we have Gray meditating on a Country Graveyard, and then the Romantic Revival, with its fiery strength, its ambitious hope, its frequent obverse of despair. There is no grimmer poet than Tennyson. His early work is thick with the black substances, the nightmare fears, the hell-consciousness that is, as it were, the very spade and rake to dress and manure the gardens of Paradise. For these death-visions, as I shall show, are not final. Yet they are everywhere apparent. In Carlyle, in Melville, in Hardy, to-day in Eliot, the death-consciousness paradoxically creates its wondrous poetic life. And all these poets are disciples of an age-old tradition. Their message was writ down in Ecclesiastes: 'All is vanity and vexation of spirit'.

Death-literature is born from an intense life-desire. It concentrates rather on what is not than what is, and desiring the one it hates the other. Therefore powerful death-visions will often be dramatized in stories whose action presents an ambitious and aspiring protagonist: one who reaches out for the impossible and creates his own destruction. A good example is Marlowe's *Doctor Faustus.* The hero is dissatisfied with literature and science, and theology threatens him with lasting damnation. His world is dark with despair. Where light has failed him he reaches for essential darkness to aid him: hence his adventure into Black Magic and his compact with Mephistophilis. We must observe, however, that the joys he desires are nobly paradisal things: he questions Mephistophilis on the secrets of the universe, or he aspires to the divine vision of Helen. Aspiration is the key to his story. And the same idea vitalizes *Tamburlain:*

> Nature that framed us of four elements
> Warring within our breasts for regiment
> Doth teach us all to have aspiring minds.
> Our souls whose faculties can comprehend
> The wondrous architecture of the world
> And measure every wandering planet's course,
> Still climbing after knowledge infinite,
> And always moving as the restless spheres,
> Will us to wear ourselves and never rest
> Until we reach that ripest fruit of all,
> That only bliss and sole felicity,
> The sweet fruition of an earthly crown.

Tamburlain itself is not a darkly satanic work: but the quotation is valuable. Here an unrestful ambition is set on realizing an earthly paradise, 'an earthly crown': and see how this is imagined as a consequence from man's infinite capacity, his universal mind. So all satanisms in literature or life arise from man's own mind, an imagination not quite tuned to creative life, a too ambitious aspiration towards paradise, a leap into the future regardless of the present.

The Miltonic vision is similar. Milton's Satan is proudly equipped in mind and body. He falls from ambition only, from knowing his own merit and striving to give it place and approbation. Through this sinful desire to too great a pre-eminence he quickly loses grandeur and strength. The loathsome horrors of the death-consciousness are to be related here closely to Satan's companions, Evil and Death. Evil is both his child and harlot. She is significantly born from his head and by her he has a child, Death. Evil and Death thus come into being from Satan's ambitious desire. The symbolism is pregnant. And continually in our poets 'sin' and 'death' are correlative terms. Consciousness of sin and evil, in oneself or elsewhere, is a death-consciousness; the opposite is life, essential life. Often, too, the death-consciousness is inbound with sex. Since it is born from an unruly life-desire, and since there are few greater life-desires than sex, this is natural enough. Thus in Milton, Evil is born from an introverted and unnatural self-concentration in Satan, and Death from a further incestuous union. And the same impressions emerge from a careful understanding of Byron's *Manfred*. Here a change is apparent. Both Marlowe's Faustus and Milton's Satan are clearly to be seen themselves, as persons, evil in some sense: put crudely, we tend to blame them. The Romantic Revival, however, stresses everywhere the divine spirit in human aspiration. Hence in *Manfred* our hero dares the spirits of nature, even, it would appear, God himself, rather than submit his tameless soul to any yoke. He is great as they. He challenges Arimanes on equal terms. He lives agonizedly in memory of past sin and constant striving to his ideal; time is a rack on which he is stretched, tugged in a conflict between past and future. To light and love he aspires. But a loathly fear is in him associated with some hideous evil, some sexual horror: yet too a divine face, like one he wronged, intermittently threads the poem. To that he yearns. Death approaches, and he meets it with scorn. Manfred, guilt-stricken but unrepentant, redeems himself by his faith: faith in his own self and its nameless ideal. So our satanic heroes grow less dark; and in Shelley's *Prometheus* the rebel becomes the saviour of mankind.

On the one side a sense of guilt, a loathly horror: and death. On the other, fleeting glimpse of a purpose, a direction, in this satanic quest. In Melville's *Moby Dick* Ahab enlists his strength against the White Whale, symbol of the evil in an evil universe. And yet the evil may be thought to originate in Ahab. The issue is not clear: in these visions it often is not clear. But the book is weighted with the death-consciousness. And in Emily Bronte's *Wuthering Heights* there is a similar hero. Heathcliff, like Ahab, is set on revenge. These existence has wronged and they must right the balance. And yet, plunging reckless as they do into the dark, they obey a law that knows no death. A mighty purpose propels them, a purpose they themselves do not understand. So Heathcliff tries to explain, just before his death, that he has done no evil, that his hope is now all but in his grasp. 'I tell you I have nearly attained my heaven, and that of others is altogether unvalued and uncoveted by me.' We may think that he wins Catherine in death. No satanic hero is blacker, more evil in his acts, than Heathcliff: and yet none more clearly is impelled by and moves towards love. All evil is the thwarting of a love, as all death is the thwarting of life. Death and love are powerful antagonists in Tennyson's *Maud*. There the death-consciousness is challenged by love, the drama is a death-love contest. Aptly, Tennyson named it a 'miniature *Hamlet*'.

I cannot here demonstrate in detail the presence of these death-themes, nor prove the close relation existent everywhere between 'death' and 'evil'. But to any sensitive reader the justice of my remarks will be patent. It is all, too, in the Bible. There sin brings death and banishes man from Paradise. And his sin may be related to sex in that Adam is tempted by Eve; and next, to man's hunger for knowledge. Knowing evil, he henceforth suffers the death-consciousness, from which all our satanic literature derives. Aspiration is an important idea in the Bible. In the Old Testament man builds his Babel with reckless pride, and the result is disharmony, disunion, misunderstanding. But at Pentecost the Holy Spirit, in the New Testament, restores that lost union of man with man. The symbolism of 'language' and 'tongues' is powerful in these incidents, speech being the very bond of union.

But whether we are faced by pessimistic vision, such as Hardy's, where the persons are blameless, or a sombre work like *Paradise Lost* where a sinful protagonist meets punishment, or a book like *Moby Dick* where the evil is variously to be related to the hero or the universe against which he fights, there is no ultimate difference. We do well to think first of books, not authors' opinions or protagonists, and, whenever we focus a certain death-quality, to relate it to other such elsewhere. Vast masses of our greatest literature unroll the same statement, showing how in some sense man and his universe are out of harmony and how this dislocation takes the form of evil, death, sin. But the sin is not wholly and only man's. It exists rather in the inharmonious relation between man and God, or man and nature, and either may appear to be the evil force. This is clear in *Manfred;* but it is even clearer in the Bible. The God of the Old Testament is sometimes as definitely evil as man. But evil is not really applicable to units at all: it exists only in and through a relation. In the Old Testament it is the God-man relation that is out of joint and therefore evil. Similarly with death: no man can himself, as a man, be dead, but, faced by the loss of what he loved, he experiences a sense of death. Or he may, while alive, for yet other reasons, be seen to live a death-in-life. Death is, ultimately, an inharmonious experience. Satanic literature, in various forms, recreates such experiences.

Therefore, however powerfully we find these death-visions expressed, we must always see the evil as, finally, relative in some sense: either as a disharmonious relation or, which amounts to the same, as a good force misdirected. M. Maritain writes interestingly on these satanic visions:

> The capital importance of the parts played by Baudelaire and Rimbaud lies in the fact that they made modern art pass the frontiers of the spirit. But those are the regions of direst peril, there the weightiest metaphysical problems fall upon poetry, there the battle is waged between the good and the bad angels, and the bad angels are disguised as messengers of light.
>
> *(Art and Scholasticism)*

This is a fine statement: but it is always dangerous to pronounce a moral judgment against poetic creation. M. Maritain forgets or passes by the cardinal faith held by every poet, the faith that all instincts and passions are necessarily good in essence: that every evil is a thwarted love. So it is rather the good angels that disguise themselves as messengers of darkness. Dante can put us right here:

> 'Creator, nor created being, e'er,
> My son', he thus began, 'was without love,
> Or natural, or the free spirit's growth.
> Thou hast not that to learn. The natural still
> Is without error: but the other swerves,
> If on ill object bent, or through excess
> Of vigour, or defect. While e'er it seeks
> The primal blessings, or with measure due
> The inferior, no delight, that flows from it,
> Partakes of ill. But let it warp to evil,
> Or with more ardour than behoves, or less,
> Pursue the good; the thing created then
> Works 'gainst its Maker. Hence thou must infer,
> That love is germin of each virtue in ye,
> And of each act no less, that merits pain . . .'
>
> (*Purgatory*, XVII, 87)

'Thou hast not that to learn'. It is true: the poet knows this, by this alone he writes, expressing dark and bright essences with like joy in his work. All evil is a search, a desire, an unincarnated longing. Our satanic heroes strive for a nameless unincarnated ideal: the abstract craving of Faustus, the unruly self-pride of Satan, Manfred and his elusive dream, Ahab and his introverted hate against that thing which the Whale symbolizes but which it yet is not, Heathcliff and his ghostlike Cathy. In so far as man fails properly to incarnate his life-desires his agony writhes inwardly, casting blackness into his universe. In *Macbeth* and *Julius Caesar* I have shown how evil takes the form of discarnate or naked spirit. So also Shelley writes of himself as tormented through having 'looked on nature's naked loveliness.' We might compare the Earth-spirit in Goethe's *Faust*. The same thought is found in Spenser. So, too, Acteon, seeing Diana naked, is punished swiftly, turned into a beast, devoured by his own hounds, like Evil in *Paradise Lost* whose womb is gnawed by the loathly creatures it has borne. All these visions express the same statement:

there is no hell comparable with sight of a paradise unattainable on earth. The Holy Spirit must thus be directly equated with Satan in so far as it can be supposed to seek, but not find, incarnation. But it is wiser to say that Satan is but the reflection in the material world cast by the mighty brooding Spirit of God that ever awaits more, and still more, incarnate life.

I assert two main streams in our literature: the turgid Phlegethon of Death and the bright Eden-waters of Life. But it is also true that the greater part of our popular literature is set between the poles of intense life and death experience. Here we find a vast territory, satire, the novel of manners, comedy in general. These accept things as they are, criticizing them, laughing at them, copying them, mildly introducing us to ourselves. But death-literature sends Yorick's skull 'to my lady's chamber': it rejects life, because it remembers death. And life-literature does much the same. It rejects false appearances but reveals another, more radiant, life. Human civilization, with its intricacies and irresponsibilities and insincerities, scarcely by itself rouses it to action. Sometimes it may create dreams of magnificence and kingly glory, feasting and rich apparel, in barbaric splendour. But it concentrates mainly on great human simplicities: on romantic love, marriage, and birth; and perhaps immortality. But these are shown in a wide context: they are flowers springing from a natural world, themselves kin to the budding leaf, the fertile soil, the nesting birds. Intense life-literature is ever naturalistic. All poets are nature poets, and all nature poets are poets of life. Now, though these extremes of life and death may seem far apart, they are not really so. Most poets work in both manners, and we often find them passing through a death period to a serene vision of essential life. This life is paradise, the paradise that is created whenever the desiring spirit finds a perfect object for its love. It is the paradise of the love-consciousness, and whatever the paradisal poet presents is ever vitalized by the elixir of romantic sight: so that his lovers, his birds, his trees and flowers are radiant. They flame and burn with a thousand sparkling joys, alight with the holy joy of love and life. This is the paradisal naturalism of the poets.

Sometimes we find a poet given over mainly to satanic literature, such as Webster, or one dedicate mainly to happier intensities, such as Bridges. But most adepts in one style are adepts also in the other, and paradisal and satanic poetry are on the whole to be together distinguished from the more trivial sorts, the novel of manners, the satirists, the wits. Now we are not to worry greatly whether satanic or paradisal visions refer to things of this life or another. The one sort may be rich in Hell impressions, and these may seem to refer to a future existence; or they may present a hell on earth. The other may dream future paradises in earthly imagery, or see earth itself transfigured by paradisal splendour. There is no ultimate distinction. All literature presents experience to us as we read: wherever or however it be expressed, the impression is primary.

Medieval romance literature is rich in erotic perception and human idealisation. The lover sees a divine ideal in his lady. Similarly, the medieval love-lyrist may address a strongly erotic appeal to the Virgin Mary. Medieval literature with its elaborate Christian allegorization and romantic vision comes near to that marriage of poetry and Christianity it is my purpose in this book to celebrate. But in England, anyway, we have no perfected paradisal literature on a comprehensive scale until the Renaissance. Our original Teutonic stream had been much altered by the Romance influence; the Medieval tradition was still further altered by the new learning. As we inspect this amazing revival to-day, we can suggest that its 'cause' was a 'marriage'. The Medieval and Christian tradition meets a strong and masterful lover in a newly arrived Hellenism. But a renaissance is a 'rebirth'; and any birth is different from its causes, not wholly implicit in them. The Renaissance is therefore, like all sudden creations, a miracle and mystery: a sudden blaze of life. In English literature we can detect elements Christian, Medieval, and Greek. The chivalric ideal is blended with Platonic philosophy; medieval alchemy, astrology, and medicine interpenetrates the new science; the universe is variously Ptolemaic or Copernican. Classical deities are as powerfully impregnated with poetic belief as any symbols from Orthodox Christianity. All these are appearances to be observed and noted: but they do not take us far in explanation. All we can say is that we find a strongly heightened life-apprehension, and the poetry is certainly best considered to flower direct from this.

The Elizabethan poet does not decorate his thoughts with classical references: his mythological persons are alive, he possesses them as truly as any Greek, and they blend exquisitely with his English country setting. Lyly is a master in this kind. He is one of our greatest authorities on romantic love, and his theme is ever exquisitely inwoven with Greek mythology. Greene, in *Friar Bacon and Friar Bungay,* can write of the Maid of Fressingfield with a direct sense of physical beauty and a delight in the pastoral setting that is typical and to-day uncapturable. The Elizabethan poet was often in paradise; an earthly paradise. From such paradisal sight Greek Mythology was born: and wherever it recurs, the poet does well to use Greek symbols. The pastoral element is, too, very important. Deriving in one sense from the Greek, through Theocritus and Vergil, it finds in Spenser a perfect poetic medium. The pastoral paradise is a place of simple love, direct sensuous pleasure in physical beauty, a paradise where man enjoys and instinctively expresses the spontaneous life within. The sin consciousness has dropped from him. This is our poets' paradise, pagan if you like; pastoral generally, certainly beautiful and waking a universal response. And such a paradise exists wherever man, contemplating a present fact, finds his spirit wholly blest in that communion, without further desire, or unrest.

A similar age of paradisal poetry flowered at the Romantic revival. Nature again is most important, but only one poet, Keats, retrod the slopes of Arcadian delight with Elizabethan ease. Probably Spenser helped him most, but Greek mythology was a language for which he scarcely needed a tutor. Shelley is ecstatic with paradisal vision, especially in *Epipsychidion* and the *Prometheus*. Wordsworth's nature mysticism is relevant here, but it often lacks the true paradisal ring and erotic perfume. As aesthetic theory, *The Prelude* is a document of unsurpassed importance: as poetry, it varies. His Immortality Ode, however, is as fine a presentation in the kind I am noticing as we have anywhere in so short a poem. From a cluster of the usual impressions—sun, a spring day, music, the shepherd boy and the young lambs, bird-song, trees and grass and flowers, all, as it were dancing in the intense heat of visionary perception, rises the dominant symbol, the Child. Now, whereas Shelley and Keats are often whole-heartedly dedicate to the erotic ideal, Wordsworth is somewhat inhumanly naturalistic, and his very nature is therefore too often presented unromantically. Here, where for once he incarnates his mysticism in vivid paradisal shapes and sense-impressions, there flowers too the human symbol of creation, a human child. Throughout our poetry, in the Elizabethan Cupid, often in Shakespeare, in the Holy Child of Milton's Nativity Ode and Crashaw's lyrics, in Wordsworth, in Shelley, indeed everywhere, the child is a most important life-symbol. Blake is full of 'child' thought, building his poetic paradise. The child is again the very heart and centre of Pompilia's narrative in Browning's *The Ring and the Book;* and so on. Certainly I cannot here do more than scatter a few random remarks: the material is too rich. But wherever we find a vivid and optimistic poetic life, we shall find such impressions as these: a radiant nature, sunlight, often birds and lambs, a happy pastoral setting for the dominant themes of human love and birth. We can say that all these impressions are, as it were, a grammar of symbolism by which the poet transmits that consciousness I call 'romantic', the life-consciousness, the experience known as love. And this ecstatic love, though usually met in sexual terms, may be known variously. A poet, certainly, is, and should be, capable of falling in love with anybody and anything.

The romantic vision sees a spirit-flame blazing in the actual fact, whether the actual fact be man, woman, child, bird, beast, or flower. The fact is alight with spiritual and prophetic significance. Therefore in poetic imagery the impressions of 'light', 'flame' or 'fire' are almost exactly correspondent to the concept 'spirit'. Consequently, those poets who are most spiritual present a blaze of light. Shelley is a good example, Crashaw another. Their work flames, shoots meteors and arrowy sparks across the imagination. Take any typical Shelleyan poem and count all the 'light' or 'fire' impressions: their number will probably prove startling. Such poets aim to startle us. But consider again the love-experience. There is no immediately apprehended flame on the loved one's face: the visual correlative is arbitrary. It is, however, natural, too, as may be seen from the colloquial term 'flame' to denote a lover. Similarly with all mystical experience, there is probably no 'fire' or 'light': but these terms inevitably come in to help description. The poet, shall we say, experiences vividly a fact together with its vital significance. To say what he has to say is not enough, as a rule, to describe the fact alone: he shows it therefore as burning, fiery with the right brilliance of a splendid creation. So God appears to Moses as a burning bush. The extremes of paradisal and death poetry are, usually, to be seen in terms of vivid light and abysmal dark.

But many poets refuse to over-illuminate their poetry. Keats and Shelley form an interesting comparison. Shelley is primarily a visual poet: his world scintillates and flashes with innumerable brilliances; and it is spiritual, ethereal, volatile, swift; mysterious and magical. Keats, however, writes for all our senses—the sight, hearing, touch, taste, smell. His descriptions have therefore a more rounded perfection, his poetical world is more solid. With him nature, too, is far nearer earth than

Shelley's: the ripe plum, the flowers at his feet as he listens to the nightingale, the green-robed senators in the woods, all are close, real, magical often, but always warm with natural life, asking to be touched and smelt rather than rocketing away from us with tails of fire to disappear before we have come to know them. Keats' world is rich in both sombre and happy impressions, but it is never excitable: all is subdued to a single pervading unity. It is paradisal and satanic at once, like *A Midsummer Night's Dream.* His *Ode to the Nightingale* is typical. One stanza is full of horrors, the setting is dark, a wood by moonlight: the final effect is both happy and sad, but with an overmastering beauty and a rich magic surpassing light.

I therefore draw this distinction within our paradisal world. The natural tendency is ever to express the highest poetic glory in excitable light-imagery; but there is a yet more perfect poetry, whose wonder is nearer to the actual yet no less intensely beautiful. Whereas the first tends to visionary ecstasy, the latter embraces reality with all the senses, and is more placidly serene. Keats' poetry is more peaceful and assured as well as more dimensional than Shelley's. Death and life effects blend into one design, all rich in splendour. And it is less spiritual in that the spirit-world is so perfectly incarnate in the poetic act that little light-imagery is needed to balance our habitual blindness. It glows and blushes, but never flames. Some lines from Blake will make this distinction clearer:

> God appears, and God is light,
> To those poor souls who dwell in night;
> But does a human form display
> To those who dwell in realms of day.

There is no more important distinction to be made when regarding the poetic paradise. Where effects are mainly paradisal, the first thing to look for is the amount of fire and light generally. The more of such imagery is being used, the more attention is being given to the spiritual world as apart from the world of creation. In paradisal poetry too much light is certainly dangerous unless you be a Dante; but in satanic visions a fire-nature contrast may, of course, as in Goethe's *Faust,* or Shakespeare's *Macbeth,* be used profoundly to point a spirit-matter contrast or conflict.

In poetry the depths are, paradoxically, ever on the surface. My remarks are thus not drawn from any intellectual inferences as to the poet's mind or the process of his poetic art: they derive primarily from a plain and simple regard to the poetic substance, its surface impressions. Poetry, by its very nature, concretely and exactly embodies what we call, perhaps wrongly, its content. Now, in so far as we are receptive to these impressions we shall find our poetic understanding continually enriched: and, to further that understanding, we must watch first for life and death imagery and see how they intertwine and contrast with each other.

Let me give some concrete examples. Here is a fine satanic passage from Webster:

> I'll tell thee a miracle:
> I am not mad yet, to my cause of sorrow.
> Th' Heaven o'er my head seems made of molten brass,
> The earth of flaming sulphur, yet I am not mad.
>
> *The Duchess of Malfi* (IV, ii, 25)

Earth is here a Hell. Or life may be a living death, as when the hero in Tennyson's *Maud* is brought to the furthest agony:

Dead, long dead,
Long dead!
And my heart is a handful of dust,
And the wheels go over my head,
And my bones are shaken with pain,
For into a shallow grave they are thrust,
Only a yard beneath the street,
And the hoofs of the horses beat, beat,
The hoofs of the horses beat,
Beat into my scalp and my brain . . .

So, too, in Wordsworth's Immortality Ode a negative consciousness is compared to the 'darkness of the grave.'

Tennyson's *The Palace of Art* and *The Two Voices*, with their many impressions of mental agony, serve well to illustrate this death-consciousness endured by poet after poet. In *The Palace of Art* the poet tells how he builds his home of lonely vision, but how instead of bringing him joy it introduces his soul directly to horror and despair. Here is a sample:

But in dark corners of her palace stood
  Uncertain shapes; and unawares
On white-eyed phantasms weeping tears of blood,
  And horrible nightmares,

And hollow shades enclosing hearts of flame,
  And, with dim fretted foreheads all,
On corpses three-months-old at noon she came
  That stood against the wall.

His soul feels a supreme horror, a sense of evil, guilt:

She, mouldering with the dull earth's mouldering sod,
  Inwrapt ten-fold in slothful shame,
Lay there exiled from eternal God,
  Lost to her place and name;

And death and life she hated equally,
  And nothing saw, for her despair,
But dreadful time, dreadful eternity,
  No comfort anywhere.

His soul is 'alone in crime', 'shut up as in a crumbling tomb,' and surrounded by a 'solid wall' of 'blackness'. Tennyson is a prince of death-poets. Though he may work, as in parts of *Maud,* in the paradisal mode, too, the mode that sees Maud as 'queen rose of the rose-bud garden of girls', yet his poetry as a whole never for long forgets the darker realities. The massive dirge of *In Memoriam* is typical, and *The Passing of Arthur* a solemn, but not a radiant, conquest of despair.

Or, instead of a death-consciousness in life, we may have a drama set in infinite spaces with superhuman actors, as in Milton. But exactly the same experience is being transmitted. Here we have it again, in Book II of *Paradise Lost:*

> Thus roving on
> In confus'd march forlorn, th' adventurous Bands
> With shuddering horror pale, and eyes aghast
> View'd first their lamentable lot; and found
> No rest. Through many a dark and drearie Vaile
> They pass'd, and many a Region dolorous,
> O'er many a Frozen, many a Fiery Alpe,
> Rocks, Caves, Lakes, Fens, Bogs, Dens, and shades of death,
> A universe of death, which God by curse
> Created evil, for evil only good,
> Where all life dies, death lives, and nature breeds,
> Perverse, all monstrous, all prodigious things,
> Abominable, unutterable, and worse
> Than Fables yet have feign'd, or fear conceiv'd,
> Gorgons and Hydras and Chimaeras dire.

Here we have the quintessential death-vision. Notice how powerfully the death-concept is emphasized.

But now see the paradisal poet at work. Read Spenser's bridal-song in *Epithalamion.* He tells how there is to be music, the pipe, tabor, timbrels, dances of 'damsels' and 'boys', all praising 'Hymen'. The lady appears as 'Phoebe', her eyes like 'saphyres', her body a cluster of white splendours—forehead of ivory, cheeks like the blush of apples 'rudded' in the sun, lips as cherries, her breast a 'bowle of cream', with 'budded lilies'; her snowy neck a 'marble tower', her body a 'palace fair'. What riot of purified sensuality! The woods ring to the joyousness of it. But through all this shines a diviner suggestion, 'the inward beauty of her living spright'. So the day is 'holy'. The bright evening star appears in the east, a 'fair child of beauty, glorious lamp of love', leading the host of heaven with its 'golden crest'. So the poet prays for the joys awaiting the night. The star twinkles and laughs at all the joy it sees on earth, and the Bride is decked for nuptial pleasures, laid in bed in lilies and violets, with 'silken curtains', 'odoured sheets', 'arras coverlets'. She is like Maia in Tempe, on the flowery grass. All paradisal impressions cluster to honour his marriage-song, this hymn to Life itself. Now on this night all satanic things are banished. Horrors of death and nightmare are barred. No 'lamenting cries nor doleful tears' are to sound, there are to be no 'deluding dreams' nor 'dreadful sights'; housefires, lightnings, evil spirits, witches, the owl and raven—indeed, the whole *Macbeth* world—all are banished this nuptial hour. And the poet prays for increase in his love's womb: first to the moon, Cynthia; next, to Juno, goddess of marriages; and last, to the higher heavens, the realm of blessed saints. Thus is the pinnacle of human life-experience sung by this poet of paradise in terms of light and flowers, all rich extravagance, Hellenistic myth and Christian grace.

So Spenser creates a paradise on earth. Next, I quote shortly from Shelley. Here is an example where immortality rises as a fiery rose from love and life. Shelley's *Epipsychidion* dreams a love-consummation of excessive splendour. This love will be rich as 'the trees of Paradise'. He will enjoy so ideal a union with his 'bride' that love will endue them with powers greater than death:

> . . . more strength has Love than he or they,
> For it can burst his charnel, and make free
> The limbs in chains, the heart in agony,
> The soul in dust and chaos.

They will sail in a bark whose 'nest' is to be a 'far Eden of the purple East', a 'Paradise'. There nature's radiance itself shines with a lover's brilliance:

> Till the isle's beauty, like a naked bride
> Glowing at once with love and loveliness,
> Blushes and trembles at its own excess . . .

All is here immortality, immediate, deathless, utter union and communion, a burning day-spring and inconquerable life. No paradisal poet is more scintillating than Shelley. His visions are all but intangible with too much light; but while they last they are irresistible. In *Prometheus* he is at his best. The vision here is wholly transcendental. Asia, corresponding to Dante's Beatrice, is seen in radiant transfiguration and divine glory. There is music, then a song. Voices in the air are heard, singing:

> Life of Life! thy lips enkindle
> With their love the breath between them,
> And thy smiles before they dwindle
> Make the cold air fire; then screen them
> In those looks, where whoso gazes
> Faints, entangled in their mazes.
>
> Child of Light! thy limbs are burning
> Through the vest which seems to hide them;
> As the radiant lines of morning
> Through the clouds ere they divide them;

And this atmosphere divinest
Shrouds thee wheresoe'er thou shinest.

Again, observe the light imagery.

I offer one example of what is perhaps a more perfect kind of paradisal poetry, wherein something more solid is offered, something also truer to normal experience, something which blends life and death, the positive principle, however, dominating. Here is a stanza from Keats' *Ode to a Grecian Urn:*

Ah, happy, happy boughs, that cannot shed
Their leaves, nor ever bid the spring adieu,
And, happy melodist, unwearied,
For ever piping songs for ever new.
More happy love! More happy, happy love!
For ever warm and still to be enjoyed,
For ever panting and for ever young,
All breathing human passion far above
Which leaves a heart high sorrowful and cloy'd,
A burning forehead and a parching tongue.

Observe how sober the expression of 'boughs', 'leaves', and 'spring'; the exquisite melody of the third and fourth lines; the vividly physical imagery in the last line; the yearning for a love which is peace, an ideal love suggested, not by personal emotion or vision, but a very tangible Grecian Urn; the longing for a perfect love, the knowledge of death, the creation of a warm poetic life. And observe, too, the complete absence of fire or light imagery. In this kind Keats is a master. But I do not suggest that the more brilliant paradise is only found in weak poetry. Fire and light imagery will be absolutely necessary in any lengthy work at all optimistic in suggestion and, if properly controlled, the resultant whole may still correspond to the Keatsian style: *A Midsummer Night's Dream* is such a work. Moreover, Dante's *Paradiso* is one blaze: and the result is such that adverse criticism would look rather silly. So, though only the rarest poetic style can accomplish the Keatsian effect, its warmth, its flowery ease, yet it is perhaps primarily a lyric style and could scarcely make a great play of universal power by itself. Yet wherever we find a great work whose total effect has a similar warmth and richness, and whose final beauty includes the darker essences, we may be reminded of Keats. Whether Keats could ever have written such a full-length work we cannot say. *Hyperion* is scarcely comparable with Dante's *Divina Commedia.* But though we may be forced to regard Dante as a greater poet than Keats, we may, finally, be inclined to say that Shakespeare is a greater than Dante, in that his greatest creations are never so lavishly illuminated. This distinction will be found valuable when we come to the New Testament.

It is, indeed, inevitable that poetry should pursue these paradisal rhythms if it purpose to make some verbal equivalent to the romantic vision. Imagery of flowers and radiant nature, especially the rose, will recur time and again; birds and their nests, especially bird-song, are frequent; harvests, vines, fruits of all kinds accompany themes of human love and birth. And so on. And all this is blessed by the sun and moon and stars. Hellenistic mythology is very often more richly helpful than Christian suggestions. In their life-visions poets tend to paganism: and their satanic heroes often reject religious and Christian aid as utterly irrelevant. Faustus first refuses it, then cries out for it too late, Milton's Satan knows there is no forgiveness for him, Manfred and Heathcliff just brush it aside. Indeed, in our attention to death and life literature we find always an instinctive reliance on paganism to elaborate a life-impression. Crashaw is the only English poet I know of most vivid power and assertive assurance who consistently uses orthodox Christian symbolisms for paradisal effects. Wherever a poet is optimistic, he will invariably speak of light, love, flowers; colour will embroider his page and bright images sparkle out in all his thinking. Contrast to-day the impressions in Mr. Eliot's *Waste Land* and *The Hollow Men*—especially the latter, one of the finest death-visions in our literature—with those in *Ash Wednesday, Animula,* and *Marina,* to observe how death-imagery, darkness and blindness, chaos and disorder, gradually gives place to happier suggestion—the 'veiled sister', 'brown hair over the mouth blown', the 'blue' of larkspur, flowers generally, bird-song, children, and so on.

Whenever the mind is in perfect union with its world, or some part of that world, we have the 'vision splendid', the vision of saint and lover and poet: and this must express itself in natural and human imagery. Crashaw, who addresses a violent eroticism to the Virgin, does much the same as Shelley whose Emilia Viviani in *Epipsychidion* becomes transfigured by love. For we are to forget the process and see only the result: wherein both poets equally blend the divine and human, and in very similar fashion. So, too, Dante is no more eschatological really than Shakespeare. One incarnates an eschatological world in natural imagery, the other presents the actual world with a strong poetic idealisation. If we say that Dante is the more spiritual, that will be mainly because his work blazes with far more fire imagery than Shakespeare's. Indeed, all our well-worn words, Paradise, Eden, Elysian Fields, all our sense of immortality, are interpretations of immediate life-experiences. There is nothing more ultimate than love and life and all poetry, all religion, works in its cause.

Wordsworth, in his preface to *The Excursion*, writes:

> Beauty—a living presence of the earth,
> Surpassing the most fair ideal Forms,
> Which craft of delicate Spirits hath composed
> From earth's materials—waits upon my steps;
> Pitches her tents before me as I move,
> An hourly neighbour. Paradise, and groves
> Elysian, Fortunate Fields—like those of old
> Sought in the Atlantic Main—why should they be
> A history only of departed things,
> Or a mere fiction of what never was?

And in this sense we may see how far all paradises and radiant actualities are one in poetry: poetry may bring paradise to earth or see earth as paradise. Indeed, its very function, at its highest, is to wed man to his own life, which marriage is Paradise. This is how the marriage is performed:

> For the discerning intellect of Man,
> When wedded to this goodly universe
> In love and holy passion, shall find these
> A simple produce of the common day.
> —I, long before the blissful hour arrives,
> Would chant, in lonely peace, the spousal verse
> Of this great consummation: and, by words
> Which speak of nothing more than what we are,
> Would I arouse the sensual from their sleep
> Of Death, and win the vacant and the vain
> To noble raptures; while my voice proclaims
> How exquisitely the individual Mind
> (And the progressive powers perhaps no less
> Of the whole species) to the external World
> Is fitted:—and how exquisitely, too—
> Theme this but little heard of among men—
> The external World is fitted to the Mind;
> And the creation (by no lower name
> Can it be called) which they with blended might
> Accomplish:—this is our high argument.

The thoughts here correspond to those in my early chapters and should be familiar. Wordsworth asserts that true life exists when the mind—which must include emotions—and its object are in love-unison. The opposite to this union will be discord, conflict: and satanic visions present often tempests, as in Shakespeare, contrasting with the music of union. This union is, as Wordsworth says, 'creation'. From such springs poetry, whether paradisal or satanic, itself always creation. Poetry is the vital image, positive or negative, of such experience, carving out natural imagery of flower and leaf, shading them with thought, colouring them with Coleridge's 'predominant passion', till all makes one music, waking us to life as birds salute the dawn with song.

The poetic world suggests that man has developed a faculty that banishes him from Paradise. This endues him with a sense of sin and death and causes unrestful aspiration and desire. Lust and crime reach forth, desiring: and all evil deeds result from unrestful aspiration. But as English literature unfurls, the dark thing is turned slowly to the light, and in the Romantic Revival especially we see the essential splendour of all human aspiration. The desire is good, though action be disorganized. All evil is a kind of lust. Sin is an introverted and pervertedly imaginative thing. And evil is death. Both sin and death arise in our minds from an unruly pushing forward, jostling aside the present to catch an impossible future. Death arises from life-desire, as lust from love-desire: both are good things gone astray. But whenever this desire is seen in terms of present and immediate forms, life-forms, love-forms, a paradise springs from the desert, and streams interlace the parched sands.

The immediate and present is then rich, pointing forward. And whenever a poet's imagery delights us, it will be creating for us such a paradise, the present fact glows with future significance. For death-literature is no mean thing. Its strength is great as its obverse, because it is itself the obverse of life-desire. All satanisms are thus as creative as paradisal visions. But the greatest lyric poetry of all, perhaps, may be said to exist in the Keatsian style, where death and life are blended as variously shaded petals on one rich flower.

This essay is merely an introduction to those immediately following. It makes no attempt to comprehensiveness, nor does it aim to convince the unsympathetic. If it serves to introduce the reader anew to my method of interpretation and to show how it may be applied to the whole field of great poetry, that is its furthest ambition. Next, I present miniature interpretations of Dante's *Divina Commedia,* Goethe's *Faust,* and Shakespeare's plays. My purpose will be to show in what sense they express life-visions, noting especially the great importance of the erotic ideal in all three. After, I offer two essays on the New Testament. It will be necessary to mark carefully wherein the New Testament is different from the poets, and to what extent the poetic and Biblical statements can be called similar.

VII. RENAISSANCE PROPHETS: DANTE, GOETHE, SHAKESPEARE

I

IT IS usual to suppose that Dante's great poem *La Divina Commedia* is permeated so thoroughly with scholasticism and contemporary reference that it cannot be readily understood without considerable learning. But this is not so. A great poem is not so limited. Whatsoever has been integrated into an art-form derives prolonged vitality from that whole which is its new setting: and that whole is not readily antiquated. A careful inspection shows Dante's work, like that of other poets, to be built mainly of imaginative effects: these are primary. The philosophy and historical references find their places in the imaginative scheme, and when seen like this their significance is generally not hard to understand.

The poem is in three parts: *L'Inferno, Il Purgatorio* and *Il Paradiso*. It narrates Dante's progress through Hell, Purgatory and Paradise. But what are we to say of these if we do not ourselves believe in any so rigid an eschatology? In what sense can an admirer be said to accept Dante's attitude and conviction? The answer is simple. We can suggest first that the whole is to be seen as Dante's personal spiritual progress, from an evil to a blessed state: but this alone does scant justice to the firmly objectified system to which he introduces us. In this objective reality he himself believed. Therefore we must blend our facts, and say that the poem expresses Dante's own experience of an objectively conceived evil, or grace. We need not believe what

Dante believes, but we must believe in his belief, thus tuning our minds to his experience. Then we shall see that the people he finds in Hell are there because he sees them as Hell-forces. Persons are not evil: evil needs ever a relation, a reciprocity. Therefore Dante's progress through Hell shows Dante's experience of evil in terms of people he knew or books he has read. We can follow exactly his Hell-experience without at all agreeing to his judgment on pagans. All poetry must be read like this. The constituting elements in a poem or play grow out of date in a year, an hour, a minute. The symbolized experience is dateless. Dante's *Inferno* is such an experience endued with poetic immortality.

I cannot give much space to the *Inferno*. It is the best known and probably the easiest to follow of his three divisions. Its suggestions are obvious. We have grim life-forms: monsters, reptiles, harpies, furies, minotaurs, mastiffs, and so on. There is a forbidding naturalism: jagged crags, rocks, dark abysms and desert sands, mud and slime, rivers of blood, torrents and cataracts, fiery rain, fog, whirlwind, storms, earthquake. Tempests and shipwreck occur as in Shakespeare. We find both agonizing fire and freezing cold. It is a dark starless world lit by hungry tongues of red flame. The trees are horribly human, suffering when their leaves are torn. The human figures are men raving, cursing, weeping, without end or hope. They suffer in varied undignified postures, head downwards with only the legs appearing above ground, fixed in separate fiery compartments like tombs, their heads reversed so that they see backwards only, or condemned incongruously to hold their decapitated heads while speaking. It is hideous, incongruous, ludicrously horrible. They are whipped, flayed, pronged; stung by hornets and scorpions; buried in mud and slime, and down-beaten if they show their faces. Or their limbs are disjointed, scattered. They are naked—this is noted continually—begrimed, mutilated. It is a dark, impossible, nightmarish thing, this Hell: a hideous living distortion, a prolonged death. For it is Dante's expression of the death-experience. True, it is presented in terms of life, live beings. This is inevitable. You cannot write long on nothingness. And, indeed, there is no nothingness and what we call death is ever a living experience, parasitic on life. No absolute death is possible. Death therefore ultimately means horror, incongruity, chaos, despair. This is what Dante paints.

The *Purgatorio* is brighter. Indeed, it gets continually more bright as the progress ascends. In Hell we have fire. There flames of wrath and torture flicker, casting black shadows among its crags, and round its deepening circles. But the Mount of Purgatory is like our human world. Light and dark effects alternate. The sun's position is noted, canto by canto, its appearance discussed. Such light imagery alternates with darkness and mist, and some of the persons here have their eyes stitched up and grope in darkness. In Dante there is constant reference to 'sight', 'eyes', and 'light'. God is a 'high Sun' (VII, 26); Vergil, Dante's 'luminary' (VI, 29); and love a 'flame' (VI, 38). The ascent from Hell to Paradise is one from raging fire to sunlight and thence to a diviner blaze. And in Purgatory we have often a sweet naturalism. Spirits approach nervously like sheep: the simile is beautifully developed (III, 78). Country life generally presents some exquisite imagery. Virtue winnows good from evil like chaff (XVIII, 65), and good fruit is not gathered from an ill plant (XX, 42). Statius tells how the 'sparkles' of the *Aeneid* were the 'seeds' of his own poetic 'flame', how it is 'a bright fountain of celestial fire that feeds unnumbered lamps' (XXI, 94), typically Dantesque phrases blending fire, vegetation, and water imagery. Dante and Vergil, his guide, come to a wonderful tree in a valley whose 'herbs and flowers' surpass in colour the finest gold and silver. The tree has 'goodly fruitage', (XXII, 129) and from it come voices counselling temperance. It is a purgatorial tree, whose unreachable perfumes and fruits are an agony to the sufferers, inflaming them with desire. So the paradisal imagery is upbuilt. Ever there is a heaven and a hell in these sweet suggestions. All paradisal joys are themselves desirable and right: but evil warps the true instinct. Hence the highest desires are imaged in terms of food and drink. Man is to cull pleasing fruit in Paradise (XVII, 85), the river of life, Eunoe, is a 'beverage' (XXXIII, 136). Beatrice allays Dante's 'thirst' (XV, 74), she is a 'viand' (XXXI, 129). All is finely naturalistic and physically described in Dante: and as Paradise is neared, we have a radiant nature, an ecstatic joy, a riot of sense-splendour. They pass the wall of fire, and Dante is in the Terrestrial Paradise.

This paradise is beautifully drawn for us. It is a 'celestial forest', breathing 'delicious odour' (XXVIII, 7). The 'feathered choristers' (XXVIII, 14) warble there: indeed birds are everywhere in Dante's paradisal imagery, beautifully and sweetly imagined in their wheeling or aspiring flight. At the wall of fire Dante's desire is like 'a young stork' that lifts its wing for flight, and then drops it afraid (XXV, 10). This earthly paradise is a paradise of glorious nature, bird-song, soft airs, sweet odours and rippling waters. All is richly imagined. And here Dante finds the lady Matilda, by the 'yellow and vermilion flowers', a human radiance crowning the radiant nature. Her eyes shoot 'splendour' on him, she smiles a welcome. It is a paradise of love-sight, and the trees rustle with a strange music. He is afraid. But she tells him to fear nothing, for this is a place of 'laughter unblamed and ever-new delight' (XXVIII, 98). Dante's Paradise is one where sense-joys are consummated, not rejected.

And then comes Beatrice. The poet elaborates his tale, height by height, to this moment. The stage is set, the Terrestrial Paradise meticulously imagined, other lovely ladies are her harbingers. A 'lustre' shines, there is music in the 'luminous air' (XXIX, 14-21):

> Before us, like a blazing fire, the air
> Under the green boughs glowed. . . .
>
> (XXIX, 32)

There is a procession: first, 'seven trees of gold' which are next seen to be 'seven tapers'. Behind, a tribe in whitest raiment. The poet beholds

> The flames go onward, leaving, as they went,
> The air behind them painted as with trail
> Of liveliest pencils . . .
>
> (XXIX, 73)

Next come 'four and twenty elders', singing. Then there are four animals, 'each crowned with verdurous leaf' (XXIX, 87), each with six wings plumed, the plumage full of eyes. Next, a car triumphal, drawn by the Gryphon, half-bird, half-beast:

The members, far
As he was bird, were golden; white the rest,
With vermeil interveined.

(XXIX, 108)

So, in this car, Beatrice is attended by a procession symbolizing the Old and New Testaments, drawn by the Gryphon, half-bird, half-beast, symbolizing the union of the divine with the animal nature; some say, indeed, the Christ. Nymphs circle in dance, one ruddy like 'clear flame', the next 'emerald', the third snowy white. Then there are seven figures wearing not lilies like the first troop, but roses, till it seemed 'that they were all on fire above their brow' (XXIX, 146). Crowned and garlanded with burning roses. Lilies are scattered, roses and lilies; there is music, and dance. As sunrise from breaking clouds, so from this cloud of fire and song, of many-coloured dance and flowers, appears Beatrice, in white veil, with wreath of olive, mantled in green and robed in living flame. The beauty is too great, and Dante falls in contrition and despair.

Then he drinks in the wonder of her eyes, which reflect the mystic Gryphon. In them, he reads the ultimate mystery, the mystery of the divine interlocking the natural: in Beatrice's eyes, only there. So the *Purgatorio* blooms and flames with a vivid, glorified nature, a nature whose trees and flowers burn with the flame of life, the green flame of trees, the red flame of the rose, the white ray of the lily. It is a paradise both pagan and Christian. The air is perfumed, the cheek fanned by the brush of an unseen wing, the kiss of a Gospel thought. Through sense-forms so sweet we approach the feast, the 'viands' and rich fruit, the nectar of Paradise. And Vergil gives place to Beatrice; poetry to romantic sight. No poet presents, indeed, a more glamorous erotic vision than Dante; none rates higher the arrow-flame of love. Here Beatrice is all but directly equated with the Christ.

In the *Paradiso*, the same qualities persist: a glorious naturalism, a blaze of fire and light, circling dance, Beatrice. These are interthreaded by profound thought and historic figures of grace: Solomon, Thomas Aquinas, St. Peter, Justinian. So we watch the ascent through various spheres, the moon, sun, planets, stars, to the final vision ineffable. But all is miraculously sensuous: never are we left in a vacuum. A pure poet, Dante ever creates with life-forms, sense-forms, and even in his own vast blaze of light his images are never burnt up, melted, dissolved. These are our main imagistic impressions here: food, trees, foliage and flowers; fishes and eagles; fire, eyes, arrows; love and light generally; the rose; circlings of all kinds, dance, music, and song. There is swiftness and especially spinning motion, a whirlflame of concentrated, top-like, static speed. The whole vision expands that swift ecstasy known by short flashes on earth. It prolongs the lightning paradise of a rose's perfume, the swift arrows of lovers' glances. These are expanded to a whirling yet utterly peaceful blaze of sweetness enjoyed and possessed.

I note only certain dominating symbols. Nature, as always in the poets, is important. The warmth of Christ is a force which 'gives birth to flowers and fruits of holiness' (XXII, 47) and St. Peter, the founder of the Church 'set the goodly plant' which, once a stately 'vine', has since become 'unsightly bramble' (XXIV, 109). Dante is himself a 'leaf' of a tree whose root is his ancestor (XV, 84). So the whole paradisal progress is an ascent to the topmost branches of the universal Tree. They are in the fifth sphere, of Mars:

> On this fifth lodgment of the tree, whose life
> Is from its top, whose fruit is ever fair
> And leaf unwithering, blessed spirits abide . . .
>
> (XVIII, 25)

And later they move from 'branch to branch' and approach 'the topmost bough' (XXIV, 114). The whole universe is one vast, paradisal tree: the Tree of Life. This process is continual in the *Paradiso*. The Terrestrial Paradise is left behind in the *Purgatorio* and natural phenomena might seem to be necessarily left behind, too. But without them there can scarcely be any poetry, certainly no vivid Paradise. Henceforward we have, besides metaphors and similes, a gigantic naturalism, flaming from our paradisal blaze. The whole ascent is thus the climbing of a vast Tree.

A grand natural imagery is often thus born from the supernaturalism being presented. It happens with fishes. Fishes are often charged with optimistic suggestion in the poets. They suggest swiftness, darting, glinting flight. Like birds, they often accompany love-thoughts. All this may sound arbitrary. But consider this passage, where the appropriateness of the poetic figure is the measure of the truth in my remarks:

> As in a quiet and clear lake the fish,
> If aught approach them from without, do draw
> Towards it, deeming it their food; so drew
> Full more than thousand splendours towards us,
> And in each one was heard: 'Lo! one arrived
> To multiply our loves!' and as each came,
> The shadow, streaming forth effulgence new,
> Witnessed augmented joy.
>
> (V, 97)

The same process is even more striking with the bird image. As in the *Purgatorio,* we have here many birds in our metaphors. Eagles especially are important in both sections. There are the 'celestial falcons' (*Purgatory,* VIII, 103) that do battle against the serpent of Eden, and the other Eagle, suggesting the Roman Empire, that battles with the holy chariot at the end of the *Purgatorio.* The eagle suggests strength, power, and majesty; especially in its sun-gazing eye and strength of wing. An eagle lifts Dante up the Mount of Purgatory, and its flight is nobly described. In Paradise eagles are again important. Beatrice gazes on the sun 'as never eagle fixed his ken' (I, 46). Constantine is an 'eagle', 'the bird of Jove' with 'sacred plumes' (VI, 1-8). Now the celestial lives are imaged as a flock of birds:

> And as birds, from river banks
> Arisen, now in round, now lengthened troop,
> Array them in their flight, greeting, as seems,
> Their new-found pastures; so, within the lights,
> The saintly creatures flying, sang; and made
> Now D, now I, now L, figured i' the air.
>
> (XVIII, 67)

Thus is 'blazoned' the phrase 'Diligite Justitiam'. The specks of fire then separate like 'sparkles' shaken from a flaming brand, and arrange themselves into one vast Eagle form:

> And when each one
> Had settled in his place; the head and neck
> Then saw I of an eagle, livelily
> Graved in that streaky fire . . .
>
> (XVIII, 98)

So those myriad lives form into one vast organic life:

> Before my sight appeared, with open wings
> The beauteous image. (XIX, 1)

Each is a 'ruby', reflecting the Sun. The beak of the bird speaks, and afterwards, like a 'falcon', it 'rears his head and claps him with his wings' (XIX, 33). Again it waves its wings, 'labouring with such deep counsel' (XIX, 93). Next the Eye of the Eagle, the part that 'sees and bears the sun in mortal eagles' (XX, 29) demands attention. The fires 'glittering in mine eye', it says, are 'chief of all the greatest' (XX, 32). And so on. All this towering poetry is interwoven with speech from those blessed beings. The image dissolves and there is next a golden ladder with 'splendours' descending, like rooks that speed to the fields at dawn, while some 'wheel around their airy lodge' (XXI, 29-35): so seemed 'that glitterance wafted on alternate wing'. Never did the bird imagery, so sacred to the poetic imagination, receive so resplendent expression as here, as the blessed make one towering bird of Paradise, the Eagle of Life.

Or these happy lives form themselves into a wreath or crown. Crowns and wreaths are continually mentioned in the *Purgatorio* and *Paradiso.* So the blessed make a crown with Dante and Beatrice the centre. Three times 'those burning suns' circle them (X, 73), and then another company out-circles them and both circles revolve, blending motion to motion, song to song (XII, 1-5). They are next wreaths of roses:

> about us thus
> Of sempiternal roses, bending, wreathed
> Those garlands twain . . .
>
> (XII, 16)

They sing of the ultimate mystery of the Trinity and the Incarnation. And there are other roses. The rose is powerful in Dante. Love raises assurance 'full-blossomed' in the bosom 'as a rose before the sun' (XXII, 54). Beatrice once asks Dante why he gazes at her and does not turn to the 'beautiful garden blossoming beneath the rays of Christ'. For here, she says, 'is the rose wherein the Word Divine was made incarnate' (XXIII, 71). In form of a rose-circle Dante creates one of his finest visions. He sees light flowing like a river, a wondrous land of flowers, 'rubies chased in gold' (XXX, 67). The central divine light spreads out in a circle and all beings up-risen from earth form themselves into a resplendent rose. 'Into the yellow of the rose' Beatrice leads him (XXX, 122-127). And then again he views it as one whole:

> In fashion as a snow-white rose, lay then
> Before my view the saintly multitude . . .
>
> (XXXI, 1)

Next angels, like a 'troop of bees', cluster to where their 'fragrant labour glows', then rise and stream back again, their faces 'of flame' and wings 'of gold' (XXXI, 7-17). The rose is the Christian Church; the Church is a flower, or again a 'fair bride' (XXXII, 114). The associations are obvious. Love and the rose are correlative to the poetic imagination. So brimful of the very perfume of erotic delight is Dante's Christianity.

This rose-circle and the circling wreaths blend with other circles and circlings. Dante's great poem is built round circles. Hell is divided into circles, and the purgatorial ascent is made in spiral circlings. Throughout the *Purgatorio* there is circle-imagery, the sun's disc, or the moon's, birds 'wheeling', dancers circling, the universal spheres revolving. There are crowns and wreaths, and the smaller circles of lovers' eyes. In the *Paradiso* the image is yet more powerful. The celestial lives are often described as whirling or dancing. They move with 'whirling speed' (XVIII, 38), then come near and return to their 'orbs' again. They sweep in wide circles or revolve in their own spheres. This is typical:

> I had not ended, when, like rapid mill,
> Upon its centre whirled the light.
>
> (XXI, 71)

The 'light'. Often he calls them 'splendours'. One of them and its companions all cluster 'into one' and roll upward 'like an eddying wind' (XXII, 95). They are ever imagined in spinning motion like the revolving spheres they inhabit. Indeed, they and their heavenly spheres are never properly distinct. Continually we are told of the 'revolving spheres', the 'sweet harmony' made by divine voices among the 'wheels' of heaven (VI, 129). The whole paradisal ascent is one from sphere to sphere, to the outer sphere of the divine: yet also the divine is seen as the centre of concentric circles. For the sphere or circle is a symbol of harmony. So Dante's final vision, at the end of his poem, is a mystic circle. It is ever a poem of circles, and here the ultimate ineffable is a 'circling' mystically joined to a human form. In this final vision he understands the mystery, read before in the circles of Beatrice's eyes, the mystery of

> Three persons in the Godhead, and in one
> Person that nature and the human joined.
>
> (XIII, 23)

Even in this paradisal blaze Dante remains the poet of incarnation.

And all this is related to Beatrice. She is the condition in which it is visualized. Though 'fulminating streams of living radiance' play round us and we are 'swathed and veiled in dense impenetrable blaze' (XXX, 50), this blaze is one with her blazing beauty, the radiance of her smile and 'laughing eyes' (X, 58) is ever beside us. All the fire-imagery lends splendour to her, she to it. Herself she blazes with immortal sight, her glory increases as they rise, and light and still more light sparkles in her eyes and in her smile. Once she tells Dante that, did she smile, his 'mortal puissance' would be turned to ashes (XXI, 4-10). The erotic vision is here equated with the divine: in it, in it only, the incarnate Logos is directly apprehended, the dualism of the Gryphon resolved, the ineffable circle of light enclosing the mystic Trinity directly understood.

II

I pass to Goethe's *Faust*. This is very powerfully a poem of incarnation. Dante's poem is a poem of fire. First, the hungry flames of Hell; next, the varying light of Purgatory; third, the light and still blaze of Paradise. But we must see how skilfully the poet incarnates his spirit-world into natural forms such as the Eagle, the Rose. And Goethe's *Faust* more strongly still stresses the idea of incarnation. It is his final statement. The poem is rough and chaotic: it expresses the experience of a life-time, speaking in terms of Renaissance aspiration and the erotic intuition, often looking back to ancient Greece, and considering to what extent poetry may recreate the future of our life. The final ideal is that of creative work, and the whole is crowned by a Christian immortality. Historicity and time are to be considered flexible: the experience only is important.

Here we have a vast nature, chaotic, often seeming discordant, but ever-active and dynamic, a vast seething, torrential and creative energy. Goethe gives us 'creative Nature, limned in vivid imagery' (13). The poet, he tells us, can show the 'one sweet harmony' (14) of the whole built of a myriad discords—'into the whole how all things weave' (13). His poem thus has an organic unity, though its pattern is less neat than Dante's. His imagery, like the creative nature it paints, is never static. 'With growth and with travail the earth is a-thrill' (27). 'Is'—everything is vividly and dynamically immediate. 'The vale is a-bud with the boon of hope' (27) All is motion: 'Doth not the world in all its streams sweep on . . .'? (51) Again :

> How from the window of the chancel there
> Upwards the never-dying lamp doth glimmer!
>
> (126)

It is all a 'changeful weaving' (15). Jewels 'flash with myriad hues prismatic' (191) and watch fires 'shoot red flames athwart the night' (258). To Goethe motion's charm outsplendours static beauty:

> Self-blessed is Beauty—cold and listless,
> 'Tis grace alone that makes resistless.
>
> (271)

'Might, tumult, frenzy' (359) beat in his world, and he loves cataracts 'in thousand twists and turns swift plunging to the vale' (388). Cataracts are indeed especial favourites of his. The Walpurgis Night is a swirling ascent, Faust and Mephistopheles speed by on black horses, in Part II there is continual change, an interthreading dance of elements, conflicting, blending, creating.

The poem roughly corresponds to Dante's Purgatory in outline. It is full of satanic and paradisal elements, but the stage is this earth and the conflict purgatorial. Hence it is characterized by 'mists' and 'mountains'. The moon is 'misty' (138), there are 'misty vapours' and 'cloud wreaths' (219, 220), a 'vapourous cloud' (254). Here is a stage direction: 'Mists spread abroad veiling the background and the foreground too at pleasure' (325). Faust appears from out a cloud (356), then watches it float away. Even if we have morning, it is the 'morning's misty haze' (367). There is much more: it is a poem of mists and clouds. Rocks and mountains are everywhere. Here are some stage directions: 'Woodland and Cave', 'Rocky cove of the Aegean Sea', 'High Mountains', 'Mountain Ravines, Forest, Cliff, Wilderness'. At the end there are 'Holy Anchorites scattered up the mountain-sides'. The Hartz Mountains are the scene of the Walpurgis Night festival. Vast cliffs, forest-clad mountains, grand and rugged nature generally, are impressed on our imagination. Faust would like to hover round 'mountain-caves' like a spirit (12), for the 'rugged pine-clad highland' is ever dear to Goethe (32). 'Upwards and onwards' (32) is his poem's theme, and mountains are its symbols. Seismos boasts of his mountain-making prowess (275-6). The battle toward the end of Part II is waged largely in terms of mountains. 'Great are the mountain's forces' (370). I cannot note more here. But Goethe's nature is ever vast. Active nature is his pride. Plunging torrents, sprouting verdure, hills thrown up from the furnaces boiling at earth's centre, turbulent seas, shifting mists and clouds and glinting sunset skies, all are constituent to our vision of evolutionary and creative magnificence, creation's ever-changing glory.

Now one most important dualism persists in Goethe's nature-thought. Indeed, it is the conflict of the whole poem. Fire and water are throughout opposed. Both are active forces, but whereas water is more gently creative, fire is rather satanic, fierce, unrestful. Fire is an unruly passion. Faust speaks of 'the fire within my bosom raging' (103), Mephistopheles 'fans' in his heart 'devouring fire' (112) for Gretchen, Mephistopheles' own bestial lust is a 'flame' (282). Raging fire is continually suggested. The poem turns on Faust's frenzied desire: and this desire is imaged as a fire. Hence Mephistopheles, the satanic principle, is a thing of fire: aptly, he is dressed in flaming red. Many of Mephistopheles' tricks are associated with fire. In Auerbach's Cellar wine is turned to flame, 'the flames of Hell' (72). In the Witch's Kitchen there is a great cauldron 'over the fire' (75), and from it 'a great flame bursts out and flares up'. The Witch 'splashes' flames towards Faust with a ladle: 'splashes' is typical, since often Goethe sees fire as liquid. What should be liquid is, as here, in the satanic world, fire. Mephistopheles is himself a 'monstrous birth of filth and fire' (122).

There is a Court-Masque in Part II where we watch a curiously interesting rhythm. First, simple and picturesque nature is suggested by pretty rustic figures and persons of Hellenic myth; next, art in general, civilization and greed are dramatized; third, there is a fiery conflagration. A 'well of fire' fascinates the god Pan. 'Froth of pearl' spurts out, it is a thing of 'flame and foam'. There 'golden blood' is seen to 'boil and bubble' (212). Again, a water-fire blending. Pan's inquisitive but risky interest in fire is powerfully symbolical, Pan being the God of Nature. His beard is burnt and the whole entertainment is now a blaze (218-219). It 'crackles' and 'darts', maskers seem to burn, the Emperor himself burns, it is a disastrous termination to the gaiety. It all suggests how luxury and greed sully nature's happiness and desecrate art, how simple nature is deformed by man. Nature, art, a greedy civilization: it is a descending sequence. Goethe writes the moral:

> O Youth, O Youth, wilt never thou
> In the pure measure of joy contain thee?
> O Majesty, wilt never thou
> All-powerful, yet let Prudence rein thee?
>
> (219)

The fire of lust is quenched by 'misty vapours' and 'cloud wreaths': water conquers fire, 'softly steaming, smoothly welling', and magic asserts itself over 'spirit-malice' (220). Notice how fire is 'spirit' and malicious; but how water acts 'softly', 'smoothly'.

Now this is a universal opposition in Goethe's *Faust*. Continually it is suggested. Consider the arguments in Part II, about the relative importance of fire and water in creation of mountains. Mountains, we remember, are symbols of highest excellence in Goethe. They are heroes of the natural world, suggesting, too, the heroic actions of men. Anaxagoras supports fire, Thales water. The pigmies and cranes fight it out. Pigmies and mine-folk continually are associated with fire, metals and mountains. The mountain mine-folk work with metals, and the gnomes in the masque are directly associated with gold. Fire, pigmies, metals, gold and greed, are all associated. Now Mephistopheles and Faust argue too: clearly Mephistopheles will support fire, saying how the mountains are creations of hell-fire, but Faust will not have it so. He will not complicate his intuition of natural beauty and heroic excellence by such subterranean questionings (358), however his companion urge the importance of the abysmal flames, and Moloch's hammer. The heroic battle at the close of Part II is won for the Emperor by mountain waters and mountain fire. The mine-folk are called in by Mephistopheles for the occasion. The battle, was, indeed, won by cascades first, and Faust is mainly interested in these: whereas Mephistopheles is shown as more interested in the fire-works. Faust certainly uses the victory for his own advantage, and boasts of the mountain's fiery forces. But this is what he often does: he profits by Mephistopheles' fire, usually regretting it after. The mine-folk and their smithies and metal workings are often noted: they often suggest hard metal as against organic nature. And also, too, they symbolize widely that which is behind creation, the Shakespearian 'nothing', unincarnated eternity. Whatever passes above in the world is shown them by their 'spirit-power' in the 'eternal silence' (370). The same is told us of the 'mothers' to whom Faust goes for Helen, fleeing from the 'existent' into the 'unfettered realm of form' (231). This is a spiritual, fiery quest: the key he takes is lit 'with flames' (230), and we are told in detail that it is more dreadful than any voyage over the ocean's billows. The satanic principle in both Shakespeare and Goethe is seen alternately as fire or a dark nothingness, Goethe's 'nethermost abyss' where are 'forms of all things that be' in 'the Eternal mind' (231). This is the land of the 'Mothers'. And all this fire and these adjacent suggestions correspond to 'unincarnated spirit'; whereas water suggests incarnation, organic nature. After the masque, Mephistopheles observes that the Emperor has survived fire and next offers a happy conquest of the sea: continually we find the two together associated or contrasted.

But the fire is not always directly satanic. Whereever there is a violent force in man or nature, we may have fire suggestion. Faust's love for Gretchen was a fire. After the disaster he sees how he sought to kindle 'the torch of life' and was penned in 'a sea of fire' (182). From this image, he passes to the 'cataract': and the transition marks an important change of direction. He will turn his back on the fiery sun and

> The cataract, that through the gorge doth thunder,
> I'll watch with growing rapture.
>
> (182)

Here the fire-water opposition is vivid. And 'the torch of life' is a significant phrase. Wherever we have essential power of life nakedly apprehended, there may be fire. The Earth-spirit early in the poem appears in fire. 'A ruddy flame flashes. The spirit appears in the flame' (14). It is a 'Creature of Flame', and strikes fear in the beholder. It is the naked beauty of Nature dangerous to man, the naked loveliness that Shelley writes of. So throughout this early part of the poem fire-imagery is powerful. Moreover, Homunculus, who is an unincarnated spirit ever searching to be born, is likewise fiery. He 'flashes' (252). Again, 'the glass hums and flashes mightily' (259). The creation of Homunculus is an adventure into the life-origin itself. Homunculus is a spirit of aspiration and fire: so is Euphorion. Euphorion's fiery love causes the maiden he would win to turn to flame: she 'bursts into flame and flares aloft' (348). He shakes the liquid fire from him: fire of his own passion.

Ever Goethe is working at the fiery life-principle, its aspiration and desire, its longing and inevitable failure. The whole poem is a song of fire and life-aspiration. And wherever love or any desire is too hasty, it is unrestful, and usually associated with fire. Not that Goethe desires peace. A static paradise is no paradise to him, and his well-loved cataracts may themselves be equated with turbulent passion: 'I am the cataract', says Faust, imaging how his desire seems fated to crash ruinously down on Gretchen's life (115). Goethe's Faust desires life, creative life. The whole poem dramatizes a struggle to turn the life-fire into organic and creative action: hence the use of fire and water to fight the Emperor's battle. 'Creation' is a word continual in the poem. Water, it is clearly stated, is creative: fire, unless wisely directed, destructive. His use of these is exactly explained by a Shakespearian passage:

> Methinks King Richard and myself should meet
> With no less terror than the elements
> Of fire and water, when their thundering shock
> At meeting tears the cloudy cheeks of heaven.
> Be he the fire, I'll be the yielding water:
> The rage be his, whilst on the earth I rain
> My waters; on the earth, and not on him.
>
> (*Richard II*, III, iii, 54)

Yet the life-fire forces Faust too often to destruction: his love-fire ruins Gretchen, his ambition-fire sets Philemon's cottage in luridly described flames. Poetry indeed may be a substitute, a proper outlet for the life-fire, and hence the spirit of poetry in the Masque dispenses 'flamelets' to those he favours, splashing them with fire (209, 210). But the last word is with purely creative action: water rather than fire. So Faust at the close turns his attention to mastery of the ocean, to draining a marsh. True, he is opposing water here; but water and fire are alike passionate forces, to be controlled. Water is docile at the last: fire, at the last, is yet, in Goethe, a Hell, as Mephistopheles describes it at his final discomfiture (409). Thus our poem opposes the wisely creative life with the instinctive and fiery passions: nature's lovely surface with the subterranean forges and smithies that throw them into place: nature's outward form and her blazing inner life, 'water' and 'fire'. Water is given the poet's explicit favour, but yet fire makes the poem. In the masque, where the gnomes and the nymphs again suggest the fire-water opposition, the gnomes claim that their 'purpose' is 'at bottom kind' and friendly to men. So Mephistopheles, the scarlet-robed fire-principle, is essential to the plan of Heaven: and indeed he is employed by the Deity to awaken man to action. The only doctrine that fits our paradoxes is that of incarnation. Hence Goethe's final word of the creative life, incarnating in creative action the life-fire which, not properly incarnated, brings destruction and evil.

Next I outline the story: or, rather, its main events. Faust is old and weary of study. For life only he longs. Abstract thinking has served him ill. He is on the point of suicide, hoping death may bring him what he craves. But Easter hymns recall him to life. Then by black magic he summons Mephistopheles. It is important to see that Mephistopheles, though fiery bright and a cheery soul, is our negative force. He is a 'spirit of denial', 'the spirit that denies'. All created life he would recall to the 'void'. Sin, destruction, evil, are therefore his element (40). He opposes 'light' and the 'bodies' it illuminates, preferring darkness and chaos (40). 'Light' is thus to be associated with 'bodies' and creation; fire with chaos and destruction: for fire incarnate in bodies is light. Still, however, creation wins continually from Mephistopheles, life multiplies itself in earth, air and water. 'Flame' only remains his own (41). He is a 'Son of Chaos' fighting against 'Creative Might' (41). Faust scorns him, yet accepts his aid, confident, however, that nothing the devil gives will satisfy him. So he embarks on his course, which is first an immersion into physical life-pleasures. He ruins Gretchen speedily. Yet, once he meets her, his better nature fights his lust: she raises his noblest thoughts, he is in touch with divine things. All this is strongly emphasized. His love is a religion:

> Call it then what thou wilt!
> Call it Bliss! Heart! Love! God!

He has 'no name for it', name is only 'sound and reek', 'a mist round the glow of heaven' (118). His love-ecstasy is absurd to Mephistopheles, who only recognizes lust. But both are entwined in Faust, and Gretchen's tragedy ensues. Faust's life-desire thus slays life's richest flower, his first life-adventure causes a death.

Nature's assured power redeems him from despair, and he is next at the Emperor's Court. There is the Court Masque, followed by the vision of Helen, and the union of Helen and Faust. Part I has shown us the limitations of unfettered instinctive desire: it leads to death, not life. Here we have art as a substitute. The whole of this section, including the firmly realized 'Helena', is as a dream-world, belonging to the world of poetry. The instincts too rashly projected into life in Part I are here seen as projected, incarnated, into vision, into art. It starts with an entertainment for the Emperor. This Masque shows a lovely modern pastoralism, which gives place next to nature-figures of Greek myth, love of nature developing naturally into Hellenism; leads up to the appearance of Poetry, the Boy-Charioteer; and ends in the conflagration. Afterwards there is the vision of Helen, typifying the Greek ideal of Beauty. To present this vision to the

Emperor, Faust has to descend to the Mothers, creatures of eternity, the discarnate origins of life and creation. Notice how closely all this is related to Renaissance poetry, and how the poet, Faust, presents to the Court an art that needs first a dreadful and lonely voyage. All this section of the poem is true to the Renaissance love of Hellenism. Aptly, it is shown first as entertainment, and next its wider issues developed. This is true to the history of literature, in England, anyway. The Elizabethans were likewise entertainers. In all these activities Faust is helped by Mephistopheles.

The vision he wins does not satisfy Faust. He needs must gain something more permanent, must find a Helen that does not vanish, and goes to Wagner, his old pupil, who is at work on a medieval experiment, seeking the principle of Life. Wagner succeeds, and creates Homunculus. Homunculus is, as it were, the furthest creation of Medieval Science, and he serves to lead Faust to Helen. But we are told that he does not properly 'exist', he is a fiery spirit awaiting incarnation. He, too, desires the Hellenic quest on his own and, after much searching, and after deciding to 'exist' through water rather than fire, finds his ideal, Galatea. Galatea comes drawn in a car, with wondrous procession, just like Beatrice, save that this is a sea-ceremony. A hymn is sung, honouring especially the water 'whence all things are created'; the radiant vision draws near; Homunculus spills out his life-flame in ecstasy, anointing Galatea with his own brilliance; and another hymn is sung, this time to Eros; Eros who marries Homunculus' fire to Galatea, Queen of the Waves.

> To Eros the empire, whence all things first blossomed!
> (305)

All the elements are next praised in turn. Fire and water are at peace, in marriage union. It is an amazing and wonderfully powerful climax.

Meanwhile Faust meets Helen. Medievalism blends with the Hellenic ideal, and gives birth to Euphorion. The whole Helena, celebrating the marriage of an erotic paganism with medieval Christianity which it is my main purpose to forward in this book, demands exact attention, but here it is enough to note again the stress on Hellenism and the erotic ideal. And there is creation. Homunculus is succeeded by another and greater child, Euphorion. Euphorion is the child of the Renaissance, as Homunculus of the Middle Ages: he is thus associated directly with Byron. But Euphorion in unfettered aspiration dashes out his life: it is typical of Goethe that he dies while too rashly scrambling up mountain cliffs. And Faust and Helen part. The poet sees the Renaissance intuition and the later Romantic aspiration alike coming to an end, scarcely less permanent than the life-experiments of medieval alchemy. Something Euphorion lacks, some restraint, some profounder purpose. But all the best in these sections is radiantly paradisal with Hellenism, a glorified nature, a wondrous erotic vision. Helen, while she is present, is absolute Queen, and even Lynceus, who seems to represent the medieval Church, admits he has failed to see her because her light blinded him.

Two other sections only can be recorded. First, how toward the close Faust devotes himself to creative, altruistic, work: and in that finds peace at last. Second, how at death he rises up the mountainous ranges to meet again Gretchen, for only by such romantic blessedness can man rise to Paradise. It was the same in Dante. The conclusion is exquisite. Paganism gives way to Christianity, but the Christianity, as in Dante, recognizes the sovereign rights of the Eros:

> Here the ineffable
> Wrought is with love.
> The Eternal-Womanly
> Draws us above.
>
> (422)

The greater Renaissance poets are all alike. Christian, they yet approach Christianity directly through the erotic intuition.

Goethe's mighty poem is rich in paradisal passages. Indeed, the word 'paradise' itself is frequent. Sometimes we have ordinary nature-description, radiantly expressed; sometimes, a transcendental vision in natural terms. Early in Part I Faust regretfully describes the glories of the natural world that he cannot fully possess in his own life. Later voices sing to him of a rich paradisal existence in terms of natural glory and human joy. As Faust wakes in Part II he sees a glorious prospect: 'A very Paradise about me lightens!' (181). That is typical. Again, there is the paradisal Hellenism and especially the sea-paradise in the Classical Walpurgis Night. Descriptions of water-paradises are frequent in the poem, and the river Peneus important at one point as a stage setting. Or again, a radiant Arcadia is described towards the close of the Helena, with all the usual pastoral effects. It is to be a 'fruitful land', with whispering sedges and 'fairest bloom'. Since Goethe writes it, there are giant rocky mountains and gushing springs. It is a world of life:

> Pan shields them there, and Life-nymphs there in legions
> In the moist cool of bushy clefts dwell free,

> And striving yearningly to higher regions
> Rears itself, branchwise, crowded tree on tree.
>
> (339)

Here all men are healthy, content, immortal. Again,

> The blooming child to fatherhood unfoldeth
> By favour of this limpid day;
> We stand amazed, and still the question holdeth
> If men, if haply Gods are they?
>
> (339)

It is a vision of man become divine in union with essential life. Such radiant paganism is set against a dark medievalism. Homunculus, intoxicated with vision of an Hellenistic water-paradise, thus addresses Mephistopheles:

> The North thy heritage is.
> Thy birth was in the misty ages,
> The waste of priesthood and of chivalry . . .
>
> (254)

He is only at home 'in the murky', says Homunculus. Yet Goethe's poem is interthreaded by Christian thought, too. There are Faust's childhood recollections, springing to mind as the Easter music breaks into his darkened life. The whole of Part I is impregnated strongly with Christian feeling, especially when angelic voices, at the end, assert Gretchen's redemption. Most of Part II is pagan and Hellenic. But it ends with a Dantesque ascension. Indeed, the whole story melts into the divine at either end. There is the prologue in Heaven, and Faust's final rising to Gretchen in Paradise, while Mephistopheles is tormented by a hailing shower of roses.

So Goethe, in his own mighty fashion, blends the pagan and erotic intuition with the Christian. Primarily, he writes of nature and man's place in nature; of creation and creation's miraculous strength. Civilization is often associated here with greed of gold and too lavish entertainment. The Emperor throughout is a weakling and spendthrift, carried away by superficial pleasures, and the glory of his court is to be contrasted with the fresh splendours of nature, or the simple sweetness of human life when in harmony with the laws of creation. There is constant suggestion of simple and erotic human happiness; of country music, song and dance, blending with the song and dance of nature. Goethe's poem tingles throughout with eroticism and the thrill of life and birth. He does not favour a flashing and sophisticated civilization, richly robed and crowned with temporal glory. But it is nevertheless true that he everywhere makes peculiarly powerful poetic use of clothes. Mephistopheles is in red, Faust in medieval dress when he is united with Helen, Euphorion's mantle and lyre are left after his spirit flames upward, and so on. Still, most of our most powerful optimistic effects are those of natural simplicity and beauty rather than civilized grandeur. Life, nature, creation and the Eros are his main themes. He sees life as both turbulent and creative. It is one vast paean in praise of life. Love, beauty, birth continually bubble up, irrepressible: a mighty life pulses in this mighty song, a multitudinous and mountainous life-force. Two main principles emerge from Goethe's symbolism: the fire-principle and the water-principle, the latter being understood to blend with both air and earth in opposition to Mephistophele's flames. The one is fierce, violent, hasty; the other, sometimes turbulent, yet on the whole more gentle, soothing, creative. Both are necessary. Mephistopheles is himself part of God's organic scheme, fire seethes at the mighty heart of the mountain. So the conclusion is this only: that the fire of life be incarnated in creative and organic action.

III

Next, I shall very shortly notice the work of Shakespeare, throwing it into relation with Dante and Goethe, and, since I have elsewhere written Shakespearian interpretations at great length, confining myself to broad generalities only.

Consider Dante and Goethe in point of 'incarnation'. Roughly, we may say that, throughout the poets, flames are likely to be satanic, light is usually paradisal, and fire is indeterminate. In so far as fire is incarnated, used, directed, or generally helpful, it is good; it may equally be dangerous. Now, Dante's Paradise is one blaze of fire: but this fire is continually incarnated into natural life-forms. He sees essential life as light forming into transcendent bodies. In Goethe there is less light: he deals rather direct in bodies. Here, as in Dante, flames suggest hell-forces. But fire generally in Goethe is also to be seen as dangerous, although it is closely related often to life, and the ultimate good is therefore a fire housed in the actual. The two statements, especially if we remember that to Goethe Mephistopheles and his flames are part of the divine purpose, are not wholly dissimilar. But whereas Goethe's poem implies that incarnation is the ultimate solution, and Dante allots a third of his poem to a very absolute Hell, we may, provisionally, call Goethe the more Christian poet at heart, in that there is with him no absolute negation, and finally all evil is to be seen as discarnate essences which are themselves, in their places, excellent enough. And, indeed, Dante clearly states this too, as I have shown. And yet again, if we allow Dante's Hell to correspond not to the New Testament Gehenna—which is only a very minor strand in the pattern there—but rather to the death-forces of any kind therein—disease, sin, fear—we shall be forced to regard Goethe as just a little too optimistic: and in this sense Dante is the more truly Christian, in that he faces the darkest facts. Consider a third aspect. Dante's system is harmonious: all, from Hell to Heaven, is a system of circles, and the resultant whole is as one circular or spheral harmony. But Goethe's world is chaotic. True, he himself, in the Prologue in the Theatre, says that the poet's business is to discover an organic harmony in the mighty discords of nature, and this he certainly does. Yet Dante's harmony is more than organic, it is intellectual, symbolical, pictorial, what you will. His poem is perfectly harmonious in every way, and from every view.

In all these matters Shakespeare is found to steer, as it were, a middle course: for example, whereas Dante stresses the divine and Goethe the natural, Shakespeare as certainly stresses the human. Consider, too, Shakespeare's light-imagery. The heavenly bodies are used in his poetry as in Dante's Purgatory: they may be cloud-eclipsed, or radiant. Love is associated with the sun or moon in unveiled splendour, evil with Acheronian fog and cloud. With fire there are variations. In *Romeo and Juliet* the love-theme is imagined as a spurt of flame in the dark, a lightning, an ignited explosion: it is a life-force dangerous but sweet. It illuminates a not very lovely world with angelic splendour: but quickly it is burnt out. In *A Midsummer Night's Dream* a dark but moonlit world is, as in *Romeo,* an apt setting for the glimmering uncertainty of such love: and this is contrasted with the dawn and daylight majesty of Theseus, a Christlike figure who incarnates spirit in a steady, unwavering, beauty of life.

In *Julius Caesar* fire-imagery is vivid. It makes the action romantic and colourful, yet is certainly also to be related directly to essential disorder. The fires of revolution blend with the supernatural fires and the whole is a vision of disorder, discarnate essences volcanically upheaving to overturn Olympus, or Caesar. *Macbeth* shows a pattern similar to *Julius Caesar* where the evil is darker. Darkness here is lit by glimmering light, and enriched by the red of blood. As in *Julius Caesar,* there are supernatural phenomena. Evil is again seen to exist in terms of discarnate forces: either spirit untuned to nature or nature unco-ordinated and undirected by spirit.

In *Antony and Cleopatra,* we have our paradise. Here there is less fire than in *Julius Caesar,* however. Sun and moon and stars are unveiled; nights are 'gaudy' with torches, and so on. But there is less pure fire-imagery than might be expected. Cleopatra, at her dying, is 'fire and air', and indeed love in Shakespeare is 'a spirit all compact of fire'. Love is fiery, as in Goethe, dangerous or divine according to circumstance. The fire is, however, in *Antony and Cleopatra* mostly housed in natural phenomena and dramatic event, in human life and love. There is enough fire-imagery to direct our understanding: not enough to dissolve our human sympathy in a pure transcendentalism. And in the final plays, such as *The Winter's Tale* and *The Tempest,* the process is still clearer. The Shakespearian paradise is explicated in natural image, human delineation and plot-rhythm: in symbols of all kinds; in music; but never in a Dantesque blaze. Ariel, the spirit, may be fiery, but *The Tempest* as a whole is not. Neither does Shakespeare, as Goethe, give slight emphasis to the darker, nightmarish, things. *Macbeth* is a Hell comparable with the *Inferno*. True, Goethe touches such darkness when writing of the Mothers, or when Mephistopheles introduces himself as the champion of destruction: but fire, not darkness, makes his main tragedies, his evil is a lurid, picturesque thing, and his Devil a permanent asset for fancy-dress balls. But one would scarcely go to a dance as Banquo's ghost with 'twenty trenched gashes' oozing blood. As a whole, I find Shakespeare to be a poet like Jesus and Keats: a poet of incarnate life. Goethe is close, but lacks the universality of Shakespeare and the New Testament in limiting himself to the happier potentialities and passing by the black forces of nightmare horror. Dante's Hell is grim enough to satisfy the most exacting. He is a poet of extremes, whether of gloomy or optimistic impressions. Thus his paradisal blaze is close to that of Crashaw and Shelley and makes contact with St. Paul's Epistles; though it must be remembered that he writes not only visually, like Shelley so often does, but for all the senses, and amazingly incarnates his fire-blaze into natural forms. Jesus and Shakespeare appear, indeed, to be opposed slightly in this matter to St. Paul and Dante. Blake's lines are apposite:

> God appears and God is light
> To those poor souls who dwell in night;
> But does a human form display
> To those who dwell in realms of day.

Dante is a poet of both hideous evil and life so blazing that it becomes pure light; Goethe the poet of nature and fire; Shakespeare, the poet of humanity. Like Goethe, Shakespeare writes primarily in terms of nature and man, and is thus a poet of incarnation; and like Dante, he steadily faces both the radiance of victorious love and the ultimate horrors of evil, seeing evil, however, as Goethe sees the lesser satanisms of his imagination, rather in terms of forces not properly incarnate than as ultimate realities: which philosophy of evil is made explicit by Dante, too, in a philosophical passage I have quoted already.

I have shown that Dante aims at a perfect harmony, expressing it, however, as often as possible in natural terms, whereas Goethe, subduing his imagination to a seemingly chaotic world, is primarily true to nature, and only secondarily recognizes, in the Prologue in the Theatre, that a poet must resolve natural discords into a unity. Goethe's poem is organically naturalistic in form and content. We may say that Dante attains a perfect and circular harmony, at a certain sacrifice of truth to the chaotic nature of experience: whereas Goethe attains a certain truth to nature with a sacrifice of intellectual harmony. Here, too, Shakespeare holds the balances exactly. For his whole universe is as a massive world revolving on the tempest-music opposition. This I have shown in my book *The Shakespearian Tempest.* Tempests suggest conflict and discord, personal or political; music is the language of harmony, union, love. Dante's massive poem has a single, perfected harmony built of circles and circlings of all kinds, concentric spheres, and so on. Goethe's fire-water opposition is his final unity, and fire and water may each often be equated with Shakespeare's tempests: they are both expressly dynamic and active elements. Therefore the tempest-music opposition in Shakespeare is more final than either Dante's or Goethe's scheme, since it contains both. Indeed, it is the main purpose of Shakespeare to present the conflict of conflict and union, to make a harmony of harmony and discord, to blend nature and divinity in man. Now tempests and the fierce beasts which are usually associated with them suggest brute nature; music, the divine. Between these two the Shakespearian drama is enacted: and they, nature and the divine, correspond roughly to the works of Goethe and Dante. Shakespeare's music is often the 'music of the spheres', recalling Dante, in whose Paradise there is also much music, and his tempests clearly remind us of the chaotic nature-world of *Faust*. In *Faust,* music occurs sometimes at paradisal moments, but it has nothing of the emphasis given to it by Shakespeare. Indeed, we see that the Shakespearian tempest-music opposition is really a Goethe-Dante opposition: and through Shakespeare we finally reach a Goethe-Dante harmony. There is, therefore, no more ultimate symbolism than these tempests and music, unless it be the Christian Trinity itself. Of that, I shall write later.

I need not show in detail how powerfully the Shakespearian vision is ever incarnated into life symbols. His nature poetry may be grand as Goethe's, paradisal as Dante's. This I have shown elsewhere often enough. The oak, pine and fir-tree are important symbols throughout. Tempests are ubiquitous. Shakespeare, human though his drama may be, is ever sublimely naturalistic too. Sylvan glades and woodland life accompany love in *A Midsummer Night's Dream* and *As You Like It;* or we may have a garden and rich flowers as in *Twelfth Night;* or Perdita and her flowers at the sheep-shearing festival in *The Winter's Tale;* or the rustic masque—just like Goethe's—in *The Tempest.* Shakespeare, like Goethe in the Classical Walpurgis Night, may give us a water-paradise, as in the description of Cleopatra on Cydnus in *Antony and*

Cleopatra. Both fishes and birds, powerful in *Antony and Cleopatra,* occur in other lyric, idyllic contexts, corresponding to the fishes and birds in Dante's Paradise. This we find, too, in *Romeo and Juliet,* in a passage describing Paris' beauty:

> The fish lives in the sea, and 'tis much pride
> For fair without the fair within to hide. (I, iii, 89)

And Juliet compares Romeo to a 'bird' (II, ii, 178). Nature is variously paradisal or ominous—as in Dante's Hell—throughout Shakespeare, and the sun, moon, and stars take large part in his human and cosmic drama. To Shakespeare, at the top of his vision, the human is the cosmic, the cosmos itself becomes human. Cleopatra's dream-Antony is the universe, her universe an Antony; Prospero is, certainly, man, and yet Prospero is as surely God. Shakespeare is the mighty poet of incarnate life.

And because Shakespeare puts faith in man and man's civilization, he vitalizes his poetry with continual life-effects of feasting, raiment, gold. Feasting as in *Timon, Macbeth,* and *Antony and Cleopatra,* is often vivid and important: in *The Tempest,* a banquet is a dominating symbol. But food may suggest equally life and greed. As in Goethe, where the luxury of the court is so powerfully satirized in point of feasting, so the Court of Denmark in *Hamlet* may be soiled by inordinate and unrestrained festivity. Rich clothes are likewise often important: either as a legitimate part of the glory of human life, or things which are a vanity, a superficial attribute to glory but not themselves intrinsically afire with significance. In the early romances Shakespeare satirizes extravagant fashions; Macbeth, who seizes a glory he cannot own, is absurdly possessed of a title that sits on him as a giant's robe 'upon a dwarfish thief'. Dress is important in *Macbeth.* But Cleopatra dies in her 'best attires' and, at her dying, says

> Give me my robe, put on my crown; I have
> Immortal longings in me:
> (*Antony and Cleopatra,* V, ii, 283)

Crowns, likewise, are continually impregnated with poetic power; and Shakespeare has clearly far more sympathy with temporal royalty than either Goethe or Dante, who respectively tend to reject it in the name of the natural and the divine. Pericles, finding Marina, says likewise, at a pinnacle of Shakespearian vision:

> Give me my robes. I am wild in my beholding.
> O heavens bless my girl.
> (*Pericles,* V, i, 224)

There is Hamlet's 'inky cloak' and Prospero's 'mantle': and so on. Conversely, nakedness is equally important: the nakedness of Edgar in *Lear,* Lear's own intention to be naked as he, and, most powerful of all, the naked Timon glaring his unending hate beside the surging waves of death. Goethe, like Shakespeare, is, as I have shown, also rich in raiment, in spite of his naturalism. Dante shows his sufferers in Hell as naked, but his Paradisal lives are either clothed radiantly or seem to blaze with a fiery nakedness waiting for the 'new-vested flesh' (*Purgatory,* XXX, 15) and 'garments' (*Paradise,* XXV, 129) of the new body they are to receive.

And there is much gold in Shakespeare. Gold may, like clothes, be repudiated as worthless, even as poison: or it may be used to point the richer gold of essential life. 'There is thy gold', says Romeo to the Apothecary,

> worse poison to men's souls,
> Doing more murders in this loathsome world,
> Than these poor compounds that thou mayst not sell.
> I sell thee poison; thou hast sold me none.

But it is yet a life-force, too. He continues:

> Farewell: buy food, and get thyself in flesh.
> (*Romeo and Juliet,* V, i, 80)

The whole incident forecasts *The Merchant of Venice* and *Timon* where gold symbolism is, in both, of primary importance. Gold, or any rich merchandise, is continually used to suggest the riches of love. This is typical:

> Albeit I will confess thy father's wealth
> Was the first motive that I woo'd thee, Anne:
> Yet, wooing thee, I found thee of more value
> Than stamps in gold or sums in sealed bags;
> And 'tis the very riches of thyself
> That now I aim at.
> (*The Merry Wives of Windsor,* III, iv, 12)

The loved one is continually a jewel, a 'rich pearl'. So, too, Dante's Paradise has 'rubies', 'emeralds', and 'pearls', and the divine grace is as 'hidden riches' (*Paradise,* XI, 75). But gold itself and avarice may lead to evil and help to create hell. Goethe is closely Shakespearian: the flash of wealth or merchandise illuminates his drama, but its golden fire turns to a blaze of greed, an incitement to decadence and evil. Throughout our greater poets, such effects have two directions: they may serve, or may oppose, essential life. Like Dante and Goethe, Shakespeare's poetry is rich in varied sense-suggestion and draws its significances alike from natural, human, or divine realities.

The plays from *Hamlet* to *Henry VIII* are, at their most powerful, death-visions and immortality myths. *Hamlet* and *Macbeth* both emphasize death. *Hamlet* is full of loathly horror, disease-imagery, death. The play starts with a ghost, there is a graveyard scene. In *Macbeth* death is an active, rampaging force, loosed murderously on earth. *Antony and Cleopatra* as surely emphasizes a life which conquers death. The play is full of feasting, sense-splendour, a paradisal sea, birds and fishes. In the final plays such as *Pericles* and *The Winter's Tale* this intuition is explicated in a recurrent plot-rhythm. The protagonist is separated from his wife by sin or misadventure, and also loses his daughter. Both he thinks dead. The loss is associated with tempest, the restoration with music. Shakespeare's final plays are impregnated with religious vision and transcendentalism generally. This, with the plot of loss and reunion and their powerful nature and child-symbolism, makes them, more powerfully than most happy ending romances, direct visions of immortality: this I discuss in my essay, *Myth and Miracle.* And here also we find elements Dantesque and Goethean. There are two primary human life-symbols in poetry: the lover and the child. Dante, whose Paradise expands primarily the romantic love-intuition, and who is little concerned with the temporal process, as a process, sees the divine in terms of Beatrice. Goethe, to whom the creative process, as a process, is more important, is concerned with both the lover and the child: hence the many important birth-themes, Gretchen's child, Homunculus, Euphorion. Goethe's world is one of up-thrusting, blossoming life, a creative world. If we now turn to *Pericles* and *The Winter's Tale,* we see that the miraculous restoration of Thaisa or Hermione corresponds to Beatrice's restoration to Dante, or Gretchen's final restoration to Faust; whereas the return of the lost child, Marina or Perdita, will suggest the victorious power of creative love within the temporal process. These plays are plays, then, of love and creation. Dante and Goethe both in different ways stress the importance of creative living: and Shakespeare's final plays, too, are direct myths of creation.

Shakespeare's world is multitudinously varied. Christian eschatology entwines with a pagan naturalism and both with themes of empire and world-glory. The histories show us the pangs of national evolution, the calls of discipline and order; the romantic comedies blend humour with a paradisal eroticism; the tragedies analyse death-forces, the final plays celebrate life's conquest over death. From all this, the most powerful impressions emerging, apart from tempests and music, are those of human love, human birth, human life: and their opposites, evil and death. Shakespeare, like Dante and Goethe, approaches the divine through the erotic ideal: his Juliet, Portia, Desdemona, and Cleopatra are recurrent incarnations of this ideal. In *Antony and Cleopatra,* a pure and seemingly pagan eroticism gives us the finest paradisal vision and immortality intuition in English literature: I discuss it fully in *The Imperial Theme.* Continuing, we have Thaisa, Hermione, Imogen, Queen Katharine. Often the poet irradiates this love by religious and Christian metaphor: a short examination of *Romeo and Juliet* or *Othello* will illustrate this. The loved one is divine, an angel, a 'paradise' of 'sweet flesh', and so on; conversely, jealousy and unfaithfulness bring in damnation, hell, the devil, and such like terms. Continually also, the love-theme is entwined with religious events and persons, especially Friars. So, finally, I note this rhythm. Shakespeare serves mainly the erotic ideal throughout his work, often giving it religious suggestion. Toward the close, *The Tempest,* a universal statement, sums up the whole of the Shakespearian universe. The purely erotic intuition appears as

Prospero's wide and universal love, the child is again important in Miranda, and the marriage of Miranda and Ferdinand brings thoughts of a happier race new-born, a bridal-joy in the new generation which was lacking to the old. The contemplative peace and philosophic forgiveness of suffering age blends nobly with the new and young marriage-joy it has itself created. And, last, we have *Henry VIII*. Here, for the first time, Shakespeare saturates his action with a radiant Christian orthodoxy. The progress from *Hamlet* to *The Tempest* is definitely subjective in comparison with *Henry VIII*. In *Henry VIII*, the poet speaks not through pagan deities, as in the other final plays, but through a Christian symbolism. He returns to a national rather than a philosophical and personal theme, and becomes a national and political prophet, like Dante, Isaiah, and Vergil. Again, as in Isaiah and Vergil, we have a child: this time, the child Elizabeth. Like Goethe's *Faust*, Shakespeare's work develops through the erotic ideal to a Christian symbolism.

Next, I offer two short essays on the New Testament. My purpose will be to show how St. Paul's Epistles and the Gospels may be interpreted as I interpret poetry; how they employ the usual poetic life effects, including the erotic symbol, here recurring as marriage; but how they point further to a wider union, a deeper and more enduring music such as Shakespeare touches in *The Tempest*. My aim is to reveal those richer poetic essences too often neglected, a neglect which from time to time leads to dangerous statements as to the death-philosophy of Christianity. There are dark-effects, death-impressions, certainly: but that is because the New Testament, like all the poets, is fighting for life against death. If ever a book had a message of life, it is this. Our life-poets, from Dante to D. H. Lawrence, are all, consciously or unconsciously, working over again its primal statement. And yet we are tempted by a perverted Christian teaching and numerous false associations to talk and think of its death-philosophy: we might as well talk of the death-philosophy of a richly-laden fruit-tree.

VIII. MANKIND IN GLORY: AN ESSAY ON ST. PAUL

I

THE Christian Revelation is expressed through the book known as 'The New Testament'. But a proper interpretation has sometimes been precluded by an instinctive tendency to regard the life of Jesus in abstracted isolation. And not only this: commentary nowadays continually attempts to abstract those elements especially which help to make Jesus realistic. Now, while we try at every point to relate the New Testament to prosaic thought, we shall never focus its vision: since it is pointing us all the time to something very much more exciting than that. We must therefore see the whole book as an expression, an incarnation, of some resplendent force, a creative energy, tapping new power, new life, for men. This life is bodied continually into vivid life-imagery. To this close mesh of pictorial language and pictorial event we must give the closest attention. Certainly Jesus will be easily the most important single person in our drama: but his true importance will not be apparent in all its splendour till we see not only the poetic quality in his own life and words, but also its reflections in the actions, letters, and prophecies of his successors.

But there is an important difference to be observed. I have already drawn a distinction between poets who use vivid fire or light imagery and those whose words have a more natural bloom, a less scintillating excitement. The two types are well represented by Shelley and Keats. We can even say that Dante's blaze of light tends to falsify reality, departing from the great principle of incarnation. And yet, the poet's creation interprets as it creates: and if fire or light be useful, the means may be justified by the result. So, though Shakespeare, the mighty poet of incarnate life, is in this way truer to the Christian revelation than Dante, he risks misunderstanding. Indeed, until recently, his visionary statement has been quite unread. Both modes, therefore, serve a purpose: and both are found in the New Testament. We have the Keatsian imagery of Jesus' words in the Synoptic Gospels; but where the writer describes some visionary fact, even in the Gospels, there may be a blaze of light such as Jesus never himself uses in his parables. Again, St. John, an highly interpretative writer, intellectualizes earlier imagery in the other Gospels, heightening it, translating it; and St. Paul both interprets by close reasoning and occasionally uses fine images of glory. Glory is not, however, a word to be directly applied to Jesus' own imagery. He is more Keatsian, more quiet, more natural, more homely. And in this he is the greater, not the less, as poet: but the more interpretative books are equally necessary to our full understanding. Therefore I start here by regarding St. Paul's approach to the Christian fact, his explanation, his message. From that I pass, in my next chapter, to St. John. These will serve as an approach to the Synoptic Gospels.

The Acts of the Apostles describe some marvellous events. There are miracles and visions reflecting similar wonders in the Gospels. But clearly there is, too, much powerful realism. A new power has entered the world, and here it is in its first birth. Death-forces are opposed by the day-spring of the

Christian life. Early in the book we have described the coming of the Divine Life at Pentecost:

> They saw tongues like flames distributing themselves, one resting on the head of each, and they were all filled with the holy Spirit—they began to speak in foreign tongues, as the Spirit enabled them to express themselves.
>
> (Acts, II, 3)

All differences are thus melted in this fire. It is an intoxicating elixir. The bystanders think that 'they are brimfull of new wine'. Though Peter denies it, it is metaphorically true: they are filled with the rich wine of essential life.

The miracles done by St. Peter are striking: he wields the power of Jesus himself, dispelling death-forces. And there is Stephen's dramatic martyrdom. Stephen is 'full of grace and power' (Acts VI, 8), and performs 'wonders and miracles'. But he is considered dangerous by the priests:

> Then all who were seated in the Sanhedrin fixed their eyes on him, and saw that his face shone like the face of an angel.
>
> (Acts, VI, 15)

He tries to recall the authorities to true life. They are 'uncircumcised in heart and ear' and always, he says, resist the holy Spirit. Naturally, he infuriates them. Then:

> He, full of the holy Spirit, gazed up at heaven and saw the glory of God and Jesus standing at God's right hand.
>
> (Acts, VII, 55)

They take him out, and stone him. But observe the great strength and visionary assurance this 'spirit' gives: we must remember that 'spirit', a word somewhat debased today, means here not something ghostly but rather the breath of life. Even death is no failure: from Stephen's death is raised up Paul's prophetic life, as from Jesus' death this whole life-inspiration has arisen. Every death is but another seed sown, enriching the harvest of life. While Paul breathes yet threats against the disciples, he is visited by a vision:

> As he neared Damascus in the course of his journey, suddenly a light from heaven flashed round him . . .
> (Acts, IX, 3)

The light is 'dazzling', to use his own word elsewhere. So he is converted to life and starts his great mission: and the Divine choice was well-placed.

Henceforth we see St. Paul in various tribulations, imprisoned, tormented, shipwrecked: yet active ever with a mighty strength, possessing a purpose and direction which turns all impediment to a spurring hope, all failure to inspiration. He is the ambassador of life, serving his master, the great 'pioneer of life' (Acts III, 15). In argument with authorities, in disciplining the new church, in policy of any kind, he is supreme. At any difficulty he is like Dr. Johnson in an argument: he just overturns it. As soon as he is converted, his theological training makes him a truly terrible antagonist. Here is a delightful touch:

> Saul became more and more vigorous. He put the Jewish residents in Damascus to confusion by his proof that Jesus was the Christ . . .
> (Acts, IX, 22)

They plot to make away with him: but he is equal to things like this and escapes in a basket. When he tries to join the disciples they are 'afraid of him'. He must indeed have been a very formidable personality. He is no weakling, and the strength he wields is something of disconcerting power. Nor is he always humble except to his divine master. He can be haughty and overbearing, and yet again loving and gentle. There is one delightful incident when he is imprisoned in Macedonia. But he bears a charmed life which nothing can disconcert: if he is imprisoned, there is next an earthquake and we find him doing his best to re-assure and comfort the distressed jailer. So the jailer and his whole family are promptly converted to Christianity, and the praetor sends orders that the prisoners be released. But Paul stands on his dignity and refuses to go. Here is his reply:

> 'They flogged us in public and without a trial, flogged Roman citizens! They put us in prison, and now they are going to get rid of us secretly! No indeed! Let them come here themselves and take us out!'
>
> (Acts, XVI, 37)

The praetors go to 'appease' them and 'beg' them to leave. Paul and Silas take their time, visiting their friends first, and go away at their leisure: and presumably the authorities breathe a sigh of relief.

All these incidents are characteristic. It is as though Paul is in some sense grown-up, trying to make children behave themselves. There is danger, of course, just as Gulliver may be sometimes in danger among the Lilliputians. But it is an unfair contest. St. Paul is equally at home in practical affairs or theoretical reasoning. Witness his remarks to the Greeks. He comes on an altar inscribed 'To an unknown god'. This calls forth his declaration that God is not 'unknown'; that he is no abstract entity to be set in shrines and carved by human art. Rather he is the great God of Life itself:

> The God who made the world and all things in it, he, as Lord of heaven and earth, does not dwell in shrines that are made by human hands; he is not served by human hands as if he needed anything, for it is he who gives life and breath and all things to all men. All nations he has created from a common origin, to dwell all over the earth, fixing their allotted periods and the boundaries of their abodes, meaning them to seek for God on the chance of finding him in their groping for him. Though indeed he is close to each one of us, for it is in him that we live and move and exist—as some of your own poets have said.
>
> (Acts, XVII, 24)

He is 'breath', 'life': the life we live. Paul urges the Greeks to awake, to know their own essential life. His creed is sublimely humanistic. Notice, too, Paul's apt reference to Greek literature: his education gives him a practical advantage the original disciples never possessed.

Whenever he is in difficulties with the Roman authorities, he always makes use of his Roman citizenship:

> Then those who were to have examined him left him at once alone; even the commander was alarmed to find that Paul was a Roman citizen and that he had bound him.
>
> (Acts, XXII, 29)

He makes equal use of his Rabbinical learning, and splits his Jewish accusers into two parties by claiming to be a Pharisee, suffering for his Pharisaical beliefs. Whilst in Roman custody, he gets wind of a plot and persuades the Roman commander to have him safely removed. Later Tertullus accuses him before the governor Felix:

> The fact is, we have found this man is a perfect pest; he stirs up sedition among the Jews all over the world and he is a ringleader of the Nazarene sect . . .
>
> (Acts, XXIV, 5)

Paul defends himself and Felix anxiously puts off his decision. Meanwhile, he talks to Paul, who loses no opportunity of evangelizing and quickly frightens the poor man:

> He sent for Paul and heard what he had to say about faith in Christ Jesus; but when he argued about morality, self-mastery, and the future judgment, Felix grew uneasy.
>
> (XXIV, 24)

All this is typical. Finally Paul appeals to Caesar. Nothing can stop him. He is always turning the tables on his adversaries. On the way to Rome he warns the captain that their ship will be wrecked; and when the voyage grows dangerous it is he who comforts, advises, and indeed commands the whole situation. It is always the same. He acts as though those round him were silly children, but, when they grow troublesome, he is a master at using whatever weapons come to hand. When he does get to Rome, he has comfortable lodgings and a soldier to 'guard' him—or serve him?—and settles down to more evangelism:

> For two full years he remained in his private lodging, welcoming anyone who came to visit him; he preached the Reign of God and taught about the Lord Jesus Christ quite openly and unmolested.
>
> (Acts, XXVIII, 30)

So he wins again.

St. Paul's life in the service of Christianity is perhaps the most amazing on record anywhere: and certainly its fruits have been equally amazing. He was, indeed, a necessary link in the Christian growth. In every way, he was necessary. The original simple and apocalyptic vision, or fact, or whatever we may call it, had to be related to current affairs, the thought of the day. Moreover, the

Christian community had to be organized. Before Paul's arrival on the scene, the chances in its favour were not impressive. Martyrdom alone—such as Stephen's—is not enough: a practical force was needed, and Paul aptly chosen. He was peculiarly fitted for the task: a Roman citizen, yet versed in Jewish theology; a born organizer, and a powerful poet; a man of great driving force—witness his enthusiastic persecution of Christians—yet capable of infinite patience; arrogant and gentle by turns; one of the greatest visionaries the world has seen, yet with a most careful regard, as his letters show, to comparatively prosaic detail. By circumstance and nature he was uniquely equipped for his gigantic work: that of incarnating the Christian poetry in decisive and militant action.

In the Epistles he shows himself a most practical and, indeed, almost terrifyingly efficient organizer, as well as a powerful and intrepid thinker with a gift for glorious phrases. The first Epistle to the Corinthians well illustrates his efficiency. He has heard certain unfavourable reports about them, but he begins gently, persuasively, urging them to leave their private quarrels. He hears that they have divided themselves into followers of Paul and Apollos, and thus shown that they do not understand the first principles of Christianity. He gives them much general counsel, trying to help them in their difficulties, telling them to interpret what is spiritual in spiritual language: what the cynic foolishly rejects must be read with a spiritual eye if it is to be understood. True, he has not told them all this before: he had to address them as 'worldlings', 'babes in Christ', to feed them with 'milk', not 'solid food'. And they still, he says, are not ready for 'solid food' (1 Cor. III, 12). Observe the word 'solid'. He urges them to Christian commonsense. This is how he rounds off his exhortation:

> So you must not boast about men. For all belongs to you; Paul, Apollos, Cephas, the world, life, death, the present and the future—all belongs to you; and you belong to Christ, and Christ to God.
>
> (1 Cor. III, 21)

Notice his paternal gentleness; and also the terse comprehensiveness with which he sweeps away the impediments of foolishness. Indeed, he aims to tell the blunt truth always, to preach the Gospel 'with no fine rhetoric, lest the cross of Christ should lose its power.' (1 Cor. I, 17). 'Power': Paul is ever full of 'power'. So he tells his pupils, with loving gentleness, that he does not at all wish to make them feel ashamed, merely he instructs them as well-loved children. He is sending Timotheus to help them and explain things. He would be gentle. But let them not think his gentleness is weakness. If they do—well, this is what he says:

> Certain individuals have got puffed up, have they, as if I were not coming myself? I will come to you before long, if the Lord wills, and then I will find out from these puffed up creatures not what their talk, but what their power amounts to. For God's reign does not show itself in talk but in power. Which is it to be? Am I to come to you with a rod of discipline or with love and a spirit of gentleness?
>
> (1 Cor. IV, 18)

There they have it. The personality that persecuted Christians without remorse has changed its direction without losing one whit of its 'power'. Paul radiates power, in action or writing alike.

II

His thinking is likewise powerful. Not that he sets great store by thinking. His philosophical passages must all be read in their very practical contexts. The main thing is Christ: intellectual reasoning he uses only to explain away difficulties. He elbows his way through the intellectual world with something of Dr. Johnson's Olympian manner:

> I demolish theories and any rampart thrown up to resist the knowledge of God, I take every project prisoner to make it obey Christ . . .
>
> (2 Cor. X, 5)

What he tries to make clear is this: that the old order of good and evil is superseded, and a new order, something quite new, has come to birth. The 'Law' is gone. On this he is clear and vigorous. The law implants 'the consciousness of sin' (Rom. III, 20), and produces the 'wrath' of God (Rom. IV, 15). But under the new order of faith we are 'done with the Law' (Rom. VII; 6):

> Such a faith implies the presence of . . . a God who makes the dead live and calls into being what does not exist.
>
> (Rom. IV, 17)

In other words, he announces the royalty of creative life: and this, properly understood, always involves the annihilation of death. A life-consciousness is to supersede sin-consciousness: that is, the death-consciousness. Sin and death are interdependent. 'Sin's wage is death, but God's gift is life eternal' (Rom. VI, 23). Again,

> Thus, then, sin came into the world by one man, and death came in by sin; and so death spread to all men, inasmuch as all men sinned.
>
> (Rom. V, 12)

But now we are all to 'live and move in the new sphere of Life' (Rom. VI, 4). 'Life' is the key-word of the New Testament. And yet the Law is not equivalent to sin. Paul talks of 'the law of sin and death' (Rom. VIII, 2), but that is because the Law produces the sin-consciousness. Yet that consciousness is good, in that it is dynamic, provided we do not stay in it. Here our thinking gets paradoxical. Sin, apart from the law which brings the sin-consciousness, is 'lifeless' (Rom. VII, 8). The Law thus urges toward goodness, which is life, yet by implanting sin in the mind, it brings death:

> I lived at one time without law myself, but when the command came home to me, sin sprang to life and I died; the command that meant life proved death for me.
>
> (Rom. VII, 9)

Sin 'uses' the Law to slay: but the Law itself is not sin. Yet neither is 'this death' final. For the other 'law of the spirit brings the life which is in Christ Jesus, and that law has set me free from the law of sin and death' (Rom. VIII, 2). Therefore He who raised Christ will make our 'mortal bodies live by his indwelling spirit' (Rom. VIII, 11). Everywhere Paul opposes 'life' to 'death' in these passages. He asserts a new 'glorious freedom' loosing man from his 'thraldom to decay' (Rom. VIII, 21), so that Jesus may become the 'first born of a great brotherhood' (Rom. VIII, 29). A resplendent life-intuition blazes in his mind and in it all old rules of behaviour are paled to insignificance. All his reasoning, paradoxical and hurried, thrown out with little care as to form, is secondary to the one primary fact:

> For I am certain neither death nor life, neither angels nor principalities, neither the present nor the future, no powers of the Height or of the Depth, nor anything else in all creation will be able to part us from God's love in Christ Jesus our Lord.
>
> (Rom. VIII, 38)

Even angels are nothing to him. Nothing in fact is anything to him but the one immediate and blazing positive life-experience. All his thinking is now filled by an elixir which infuses him with an immediate and wondrous life.

He writes much of the 'Law' saying how it is now superseded. The Law is negative. It has no positive creative power. It involves sin in that it is wholly dependent on the concept of sin, therefore parasitic on evil. We may say that the two are reciprocally interdependent, each causing the other: and this relation is a reflection of a wider reciprocity. Sin and its correlative the Law both reflect the the disorganized relation between man and God. While there is sin, the Law is necessary. But it is now possible to attain a state where 'sin' and 'the Law' drop away, meaningless and unwanted. The Epistle to the Hebrews tells us that Christ will come to save, not 'to deal with sin' (Heb. IX, 28). The Law is abstract, 'a mere shadow of the bliss that is to be' and it does not at all represent 'the reality of that bliss' (Heb. X, 1): only the poetic phrase can do that, and hence Paul's symbols of glory. The Law, then, being repressive and negative, cannot itself make for life, it has no creative power:

> Had there been any law which had the power of producing life, righteousness would really have been due to law . . .
>
> (Gal. III, 21)

Paul asserts now the splendour of the Christ newborn in man: all who are baptized into Christ take on his 'character' (Gal. III, 27), all are now sons and heirs of God (Gal. IV, 7), all now must therefore let the peace of Christ be 'supreme' within their 'hearts' (Col. III, 15). Man has ceased to be at enmity with life. Therefore Paul strongly opposes all old rules and catalogues which cannot in their narrow compass contain the new resplendent birth.

There is a powerful passage in I Tim. I, 1-11. Here Paul attacks those who study old 'myths and interminable genealogies' which are abstract, dead things bearing on 'speculations' only instead of the 'divine order'. Rather he emphasizes the 'love' of a 'pure heart'. All 'empty argument' he repudiates. Those who engage in it aspire to be 'doctors of the Law', but 'they have no idea either of the meaning of the words they use or of the themes on which they harp'. St. Paul has to fight a pseudo-intellectualism, such as prevails to-day. He knows well enough that 'the Law is admirable, provided that one makes lawful use of it'. But he emphasizes that law exists not for honest people but for the lawless. It is negative, not positive. And those who reach a positive reality in any field invariably throw off the laws on which they have been brought up; and invariably have to fight those to whom the law itself is a satisfying ideal. Paul offers a new wine that cannot be contained in the old bottles. The commands of Moses were an 'administration of death', and the 'glory' of the Old Testament 'fades in Christ' (2 Cor. III, 7, 14). Necessarily, it was not easy to find words to express this new reality. His thought tumbles out, vigorous and powerful, smashing old arguments, concise and splendid in conviction, but not always easy or coherent to a superficial judgment. All must be understood, however, by seeing every argument, every image, he uses, as a surface expression of the one positive experience. Thus his God is not to be associated with sin and the Law; rather He is Birth, Life, and Immortality.

Now St. Paul does not point us to an abstract 'speculation': rather to a very concrete life-reality. Abstract speculations nauseate him. He can use them himself—no one better—but that is because he is talking to children. What he wants is for man to see the solid reality that is his. But is this reality physical or spiritual? What is the relation, we may ask, of Paul to D. H. Lawrence? Our answer depends partly on the meaning we attach to 'spiritual'. Certainly, as Paul uses it, we must not regard it as anything ghostlike. By derivation it suggests the 'breath' of life: and breath is finally inconceivable without a body. Yet Paul clearly says that his 'flesh' fights against the 'spirit': that is, therefore, against its own life. For 'spirit' as used by Paul is not an abstract entity: it usually denotes a simple life-harmony. In so far as either the flesh or intellectual abstractions oppose such a harmony, there is evil. But his use of the word 'spirit' is vague. Therefore the antagonist to Christian life may just as well be spiritual:

> For we have to struggle, not with blood and flesh but with the angelic Rulers, the angelic Authorities, the potentates of the dark present, the spirit forces of evil in the heavenly sphere.
>
> (Eph. VI, 12)

This might well be spoken by Byron's Manfred: our understanding must be elastic.

But the elements to be harmonized must never be confined to the individual: rather Paul envisages a larger harmony transcending any one person. And even supposing we admit that his use of the word 'spirit' seems to emphasize the less physical element in life at the expense of others when referring to individual men, yet, when referring to the community, he is most insistent in his assertion that it is a 'body'. We might suggest that he emphasizes the element in either that is most likely to be neglected: thought of the community of Christ is thus to him highly physical. Thus he urges us to think more about the 'spirit', the central life-principle, in ourselves, and the metaphorical 'body' of the community. But in reality both body and spirit are both equally in both. For the body is not, to St. Paul, a material thing only: like spirit, it suggests a life-principle, an organic harmony. 'Body' is generally—not always—to be contrasted with 'flesh', and may, like 'spirit', be related directly to 'life'. So he draws us to a solid and interlocked marriage-harmony embracing flesh with mind and man with man, in Christ, which is Life.

He sometimes writes that his own 'flesh' is rebellious, fighting against the harmony in which alone the true personality exists:

> That being so, it is not I who do the deed but sin that dwells within me. For in me (that is, in my flesh) no good dwells, I know; the wish is there, but not the power of doing what is right.
>
> (Rom. VII, 17)

This he emphasizes and repeats. Notice how 'I' is the true personality, 'me' the false one: and how, to remedy the paradox, he equates the false with 'flesh'. There is no rigid assertion that flesh is evil: merely that the flesh alone has no 'good' or 'power' to do right. Which is self-evident, since 'flesh' is a strictly limited term. Christians are not 'in the flesh' at all, but 'in the Spirit', since the 'spirit of God' dwells in them (Rom. VIII, 9): observe that each is in the other. The flesh does not exist for them, as such: but he does not belittle the body. Far from it. Flesh, part of the organism, in abstraction cannot be good. But the organic harmony, which he calls either body or spirit, is not limited to the physical: it is a vital organism, an expression of sacred life. Physical vice is to him abhorrent for the very reason that the body is itself divine:

> Shun immorality! Any other sin that a man commits is outside the body, but the immoral man sins against his body. Do you not know your body is the temple of the holy Spirit within you—the spirit you have received from God? You are not your own, you were bought for a price; then glorify God with your body.
> (1 Cor. VI, 18)

'Glorify God with your body': for that body is the 'temple' of Life itself. St. Paul is the very apostle of the body. He deprecates physical vice not because the body is unimportant but because it is so excessively important: far more so than the 'Law', the 'speculations', the elaborate calendars and ceremonies, the 'genealogies', and intellectualities that raise his wrath. To join yourself with a harlot is to be 'one with her in body' (1 Cor. VI, 16): therefore it is no small act, but one of consequence.

He varies his remarks on the wider issue of marriage, considering it best, in the rush and whirl of this new revelation, that Christians avoid it if they can. This, he says, has suited himself: but he makes it very clear that there is no 'sin' in marriage (1 Cor. VII, 28). He is full of a life that leaves him no time for marriages: it is merely a matter of expediency. Yet marriage is important: both husband and wife must give each other their 'conjugal dues' (1 Cor. VII, 3). Again, 'Do not withhold sexual intercourse from one another' (1 Cor. VII, 5). He is sternly opposed to any loosing of the marriage knot, for marriage is a divine thing. And yet again the unmarried are busy 'about the Lord's affairs', whereas the married Christian has also 'to satisfy his wife' and is thus 'torn in two directions' (1 Cor. VII, 32-34). St. Paul wants his people to subordinate all to the immediate practical issue, and therefore counsels celibacy: D. H. Lawrence once did the same. Such men have in them a violent, explosive force, intolerent of rivalries. This is Paul's advice:

> At the same time if any man considers he is not behaving properly to the maid who is his spiritual bride, if his passions are strong and if it must be so, then let him do what he wants—let them be married; it is no sin for him. But the man of firm purpose who has made up his mind, who instead of being forced against his will has determined to himself to keep his maid a spiritual bride—that man will be doing the right thing. Thus both are right alike in marrying and in refraining from marriage, but he who does not marry will be found to have done better.
>
> (1 Cor. VII, 36)

'Spiritual' is here contrasted with a specific physical act: which does not mean that it is to be contrasted with physical life in general. He is tentative, will not commit himself finally on the point of marriage. A widow may remarry if she likes. 'However', he characteristically adds, 'she is happier if she remains as she is', concluding—very modestly for him—'that is my opinion' (1 Cor. VII, 40). He is not dogmatic on this point. And he assumes all the time that he is writing to people who, like himself, are wholly dedicate to the new revelation. But not only is this revelation not necessarily opposed to marriage: it is itself a sort of marriage, certainly a thing very much of the body, and something offering essential life. In a fine passage (Eph. V, 21-33) he compares marriage to the relation between Christ and the Church. The husband is the head of the wife as Christ is the head of the Church. Christ is the divine Bridegroom. Husbands, he says, must love their wives, for so Christ loves the Church, and would have her stand before him 'in all her glory, with never a spot or wrinkle or any such flaw, but consecrated and unblemished'. Husbands must love their wives 'as their own bodies', a man's wife is 'himself', and no man hates his own flesh, but rather 'nourishes and cherishes it'. The body—and here the flesh too—is thus excessively important. And so all of us are 'members' of Christ's 'body': that is, the body of Life in all its grandeur. To Paul, the old saying that 'a man shall leave his father and mother and cleave to his wife and that they shall be one flesh' is here 'a profound symbol' as regards Christ and the Church. Marriage-thought is powerful in his mind and integral to his teaching.

Everywhere St. Paul uses strong physical imagery. He offers no abstract spirituality: something more solid and concrete. The new community is everywhere the 'body' of Christ. The old order is the 'shadow', the new the 'substance' (Col. II, 17). Here is an excellent contrast of abstract intellectualities with Christian realism:

> Let no one lay down rules for you as he pleases, with regard to fasting and the cult of angels, presuming on his visions and inflated by his sensuous notions, instead of keeping in touch with that Head under whom the entire Body, supplied with joints and sinews and thus compacted, grows with growth divine.
>
> (Col. II, 18)

Notice the physical imagery. Like the vast Eagle and Rose in Dante's *Paradiso* it suggests the organic nature of that greater superpersonal Life to which man aspires. It is easy to see how man may have to sacrifice his own bodily desires to serve this greater body of the community. Nevertheless, people 'get the name of wisdom' with their devotions, fasting, 'rigorous discipline of the body' but 'they are of no value, they simply pamper the flesh.' (Col. II, 23). Notice how in these passages intellectualism is the concomitant of the 'sensuous': whereas Paul counsels a harmony where both mind and flesh are unified in what he calls either the 'spirit' or the 'body' of Christ. But he is all the time sternly opposing philosophies that rigidly abstract either flesh or mind from the one unity. He banishes the 'elemental spirits' of the world, and dislikes 'dreams' and 'visions'. Here is another fine passage:

> For He, Christ, is the head, and under him, as the entire Body is welded together and compacted by every joint with which it is supplied, the due activity of each part enables the Body to grow and build itself up in love. (Eph. IV, 15)

Notice the concrete imagery, the ideas of 'growth' and 'love'. And all this 'body' imagery is not to be dissociated from Paul's worship of the individual's body:

> The body is not meant for immorality but for the Lord, and the Lord is for the body; and the God who raised the Lord will also raise us by his power. Do you not know your bodies are members of Christ? Am I to take Christ's members and devote them to a harlot? (1 Cor. VI, 13)

The New Testament is everywhere the very poetry of incarnation, superseding the negative 'elemental spirits' against which St. Paul elsewhere inveighs. We must on no account be led astray by the various uses of 'spiritual': often we must put 'life' for 'spirit'. The confusion here exactly reflects the experience of incarnation which is the message of

Christianity: for body and spirit, man and God, are no longer properly distinct. All this concrete 'body' imagery is used to present a vivid life-intuition. I have shown, too, how he uses marriage thoughts to express the relation of Christ to the Church. Life-essences, life-processes, are everywhere suggested:

> I betrothed you as a chaste maiden to present you to your one husband Christ . . .
>
> (2 Cor. XI, 2)

Those who would find evil in God's plenty are themselves evil. Time and again Paul attacks the false intellectualisms of teachers who see evil of their own making, men

> . . . who prohibit marriage and insist on abstinence from foods which God created for believing men, who understand the Truth, to partake of with thanksgiving. Anything God has created is good, and nothing is to be tabooed—provided it is eaten with thanksgiving, for then it is consecrated by the prayer said over it.
>
> (1 Tim. IV, 3)

The New Testament presents the New Creation: or, rather, the old, seen by eyes opened in a new sanity, by men possessing a new life. So he writes that 'there is a new creation whenever a man comes to be in Christ; what is old is gone, the new has come'. (2 Cor. V, 17).

To such, there is no death. St. Paul unswervingly asserts immortality. But this immortality is no ghostly thing. Clearly, it will be difficult to express: sometimes it seems 'spiritual', in the modern sense; sometimes 'bodily'. But whatever it be that he means, it is solid, weighty, super-physical perhaps, but in no sense an abstraction. See how he writes of the immortal life on earth:

> But we all mirror the glory of the Lord with face unveiled, and so we are being transformed into the same likeness as himself, passing from one glory to another . . . (2 Cor. III, 18)

'The slight trouble of the passing hour' will result in a 'solid glory past all comparison' (2 Cor. IV, 17). Sometimes he is highly poetical and figurative, imagining how the Lord will desend from heaven, and the dead and living alike will rise (1 Thes. 16, 17). This he seems to expect during his own lifetime: but his words express a truth—the truth that a union of heaven and earth—or what men usually mean by those terms—was being accomplished day by day as Christianity upthrust itself into life. Whatever it be, he knows it is 'solid'.

In his grand passage on immortality in 1 Corinthians XV, he carefully elaborates his conviction, giving it coherent form. Christ's resurrection is a fact. Christ put down Death, and was 'reaped' by the divine Harvester. Yet some will ask 'how do the dead rise? And what kind of body have they when they come?' This is his answer:

> What you sow never comes to life unless it dies. And what you sow is not the body that is to be; it is a mere grain of wheat, for example, or some other seed. God gives it a body as he pleases, gives each kind of seed a body of its own.

The 'flesh' of animals varies according to the type. So, also,

> There are heavenly bodies and also earthly bodies, but the splendour of the heavenly is one thing and the splendour of the earthly is another. There is a splendour of the sun and a splendour of the moon and a splendour of the stars—for one star differs from another in splendour. So with the resurrection of the dead:
>
> what is sown is mortal,
>   what rises is immortal;
> sown inglorious,
>   it rises in glory;
> sown in weakness,

> it rises in power;
> sown an animate body,
> it rises a spiritual body.

And so on to his magnificent conclusion:

> Here is a secret truth for you: not all of us are to die, but all of us are to be changed—changed in a moment, in the twinkling of an eye, at the last trumpet-call. The trumpet will sound, the dead will rise imperishable, and we shall be changed. For this perishing body must be invested with the imperishable, and this mortal body invested with immortality; and when this mortal body has been invested with immortality, then the saying of Scripture will be realized,
>
> Death is swallowed up in victory.
> O Death, where is your victory?
> O Death, where is your sting?

Typically, after this glorious rhapsody, he starts, 'With regard to the collection for the saints . . .' Never was there a more practical visionary. But notice his concrete imagery: his metaphors from sowing, the animal world, the sun, moon and stars; how there are first two kinds of 'body'; and then again how the immortal body is as an addition or vesture to the mortal, including it, not rejecting it. All are variable expressions of his one central conviction, that Jesus Christ 'has put down death and brought life and immortality to light by the Gospel' (2 Tim. I, 10).

Death is never to him an unbodied nakedly spectral existence: the immortal life is not ghostly. This is very clear from a less colourous, more contemplative passage:

> I know that if this earthly tent of mine is taken down, I get a home from God, made by no human hands, eternal in the heavens. It makes me sigh, indeed, this yearning to be under the cover of my heavenly habitation, since I am sure that once so covered I shall not be 'naked' at the hour of death. I do sigh within this

> tent of mine with heavy anxiety—not that I want to be stripped, no, but to be under the cover of the other, to have my mortal element absorbed by life.
>
> (2 Cor. V, 1)

He craves not less, but more, life. But all our exact questionings are vain. Body or spirit, both are abstract concepts. It is therefore unwise to reason too insistently, and Paul bases his words always on fact, on immediate experience. This is how he writes of his original vision:

> I know a man in Christ who fourteen years ago was caught up to the third heaven. In the body or out of the body? That I do not know: God knows. I simply know that in the body or out of the body (God knows which) this man was caught up to paradise and heard sacred secrets which no human lips can repeat.
>
> (2 Cor. XII, 2)

To St. Paul the body is, anyway, a thing afire with spiritual power: he sees it with the erotic consciousness of a lover. It burns, flames, splendid with divine life. Clearly, immortality will be to him a very bodily thing, since the body itself is divine. No man loves a ghost. So, though 'the entire creation sighs and throbs with pain' we have a promise and await 'the redemption of the body that means our full sonship' (Rom. VIII, 22). We, too, shall then 'live and move in the new sphere of Life' (Rom. VI, 4). We have been 'brought from death to life' (Rom. VI, 13). Nor is all this strange. The God of the New Testament is the wondrous God of Birth and Creation, one 'who makes the dead live and calls into being what does not exist' (Rom. V, 17) : and these two attributes are finally the same.

We must beware of trying to understand St. Paul's message on either life on earth or future immortality without giving primary attention to his symbols. They, indeed, alone constitute his positive message. He is a visionary; his imagery is exact, his thought often chaotic and paradoxical. So we must note his continual assertion that Christ has brought a death-vanquishing 'life' to men, his marriage-symbolism, his body-symbol, and, where he uses it, his nature suggestion. And though he sometimes asserts that marriage may be inexpedient, this is only because the life and immortality he preaches is itself a splendid marriage. The two marriages are so similar that they may become rivals. And the similarity is most apparent when we find him using the one as a 'symbol', to use his own word, for the other. This is natural enough. He preaches, after all, a life which is love, a love which is immortality. He calls man to universal marriage, to universal love, in Christ: 'above all you must be loving, for love is the link of the perfect life' (Col. III, 14).

St. Paul writes, then, in vivid life-imagery, in terms of the 'body', 'marriage', the risen Christ. With these he is nobly eloquent. His symbolic style is all-important: and yet he is not aiming primarily at poetic power. He has a resplendent gift of phrase, but he does not set out to write poetry. His aim is ever to convince and convert, and next, to organize the new life-forces whose future is in his charge. His theoretical arguments spring not at all from love of theory but from a burning desire to explain what to him is a patent fact. He is forced to fight theory with theory. Sometimes he is accused of falsely intellectualizing Christianity, and taking us away from the purity of Jesus' teaching. Nothing could be more unjust. He writes hurriedly, anxiously, forced to oppose his pupils' pseudo-intellectualism by vital thought, passionate reasoning. But he is always practical, transfixing the heart of his subject, and hurrying on to another point without loss of time. There is nothing of the pedant in him. He writes from an imaginative, not an intellectual centre, and hates the arbitrary rules a theoretical and abstract religion or ethic imposes. All is subservient to his one burning faith in the living Christ. This shines resplendent.

III

It is true, however, that his writing, at its most powerful, tends towards the excessively visionary in its suggestion: that is, its violent assurance makes slight concession to sobriety. He is comparatively poor in the gentler naturalisms we find in the Gospels. Eternal life is, as we have seen, a 'harvest', to which mortal existence is a 'seed'. Again, his missionary work is a 'planting', and God the power that makes the seed grow (1 Cor. III, 6). There is a lovely passage comparing the Christian community to a wild olive tree (Romans XI, 16-24). But these are widely scattered. The contrast between Paul and James is valuable. Read the Epistle of James and observe his clustering nature-images. It is five pages long, and contains imagery of the 'surge of the sea', the 'flower of the grass' and 'scorching wind', 'first-fruits' and 'rank growth', bridles and horses, ships and their rudders, a forest lighted by a spark, 'beast and bird', 'creeping animals and creatures marine', fresh and 'brackish' water, the fig-tree, the vine, mist, harvest, the farmer, the autumn and spring rains. This is what we find again in the Gospels. But it is not Paul's characterizing medium. Rather his most characteristic effects are brilliant and visionary. The divine message is as a rich perfume:

> Wherever I go, thank God, he makes my life a constant pageant of triumph in Christ, diffusing the perfume of his knowledge everywhere by me.
>
> (2 Cor. II, 14)

'Pageant', 'triumph', 'perfume': a glorified language for the glorious revelation, the 'vital fragrance', as he elsewhere calls it, 'that makes for life'. His vision is ever radiant.

He is vividly humanistic. Ever his images are of 'marriage', the 'body', the glorified Christ. He sees primarily not nature but man, and man transfigured, stepping free from death, radiant, of divine stature. It is the exact statement of Shelley's *Prometheus*. The finest passages in the Epistles burn with a white-gold brilliance of light and glory, housed ever in solid imagery, but 'dazzling' like his own vision, reiterating his favourite words 'life', 'body', 'Christ', driving in the one blinding intuition with phrase after hammering phrase. His grandest statements, if gathered into an anthology, would, it is true, lack variety, subtlety, colour: he is no master of light and shade. But, as he says himself, he preaches the Gospel 'with no fine rhetoric, lest the cross of Christ should lose its power' (1 Cor. I, 18). And yet, again, the power of that Cross carves out its own resplendent rhetoric. The Gospel so blazes in his own heart that it makes of his eloquence a golden trumpet, the while his faith splashes the page with liquid flame. 'Power' and 'glory' are favourite words with him, and the power and glory he sees are splendorously bright. It is the same with the author of the Epistle to the Hebrews, whether Paul or another. There Christ is imaged as 'reflecting God's bright glory and stamped with God's own character' (Heb. I, 3). All Christians, says St. Paul, must 'shine like stars in a dark world' (Phil. II, 15). But this glory-imagery is never loosed from concrete symbolism:

> For God who said, 'Light shall shine out of darkness', has shone within my heart to illuminate men with the knowledge of God's glory in the face of Christ.
> (2 Cor. IV, 6)

'The face of Christ': he is ever solidly humanistic. Now he sees darkly, but soon he will see Christ 'face to face'. He proudly carries on in all his phraseology that noble heritage of 'incarnation' which from the start differentiates Christianity from other religions. In Hebrews the incarnate Christ is thus superior to the angels (Heb. I, 1-14), incarnation being the very condition of purest life. St. Paul's vision may thus be limited to the one blazing fact of his Christ and this he may reiterate in 'body' and 'glory' symbolism till we are a little tired, but the Christ-experience, however brilliant it may be, is yet vividly realized at every turn, the image solid and compact from line to line. He thus powerfully contrasts his own poetic language with that of those who talk mystically 'of divine secrets in the spirit' (1 Cor. XIV, 1-19). He has no secrets. His vision is radiantly humanistic: he sees man invested with immortal strength. Here is his call to battle:

> Hold your ground, tighten the belt of truth about your loins, wear integrity as your coat of mail, and have your feet shod with the stability of the gospel of peace; above all, take faith as your shield, to enable you to quench all the fire-tipped darts flung by the evil one, put on salvation as your helmet, and take the Spirit as your sword . . . (Eph. VI, 14-17)

The words ring with metallic clangour and glint like shining steel. But his militant rhetoric is gazetted lieutenant to imperial love alone:

> I may speak with the tongues of men and of angels, but if I have no love, I am a noisy gong or a clanging cymbal . . .
>
> (1 Cor. XIII, 1)

From love his utterance gains its power.

Even his opponents admit that his letters are 'weighty and telling' (2 Cor. X, 10). Weighty indeed: at his best, his words are rounded and heavy, like ingots of gold. In splendid phrase he images the one absolute and eternal principle of Life:

> . . . that blessed and only Sovereign, King of kings and Lord of lords, who alone has immortality, who dwells in light that none can approach, whom no man has ever seen or can see.
>
> (1 Tim. VI, 15)

With such glory his pages abound. Had he so chosen, he could have been a yet mightier poet than he was. Instead, he incarnated his poetic might primarily in organizing the Body of Christ, in planting the immortal tree. Some of the grandest poetry the world has known is struck off, as it were by chance, to explain a difficulty, illuminate a doubt. Effortless, he writes only of what he knows, of what he has seen. Though his letters often shadow in splendid speech a grandeur and a glory beyond words, his primary aim is ever to teach, not to write. Therein is his heart and purpose. For his pupils are to be his living poetry, 'written not with ink but with the spirit of the living God', that is, inspired with the breath of the God of Life; not on 'tablets of stone', but graven on the more enduring tablets 'of the human heart' (2 Cor. III, 3). He works for one end only. He would have all men see and enter the radiance and the glory that awaits their birth in Christ: he would have them wake to their new-found heritage of Life.

IX. THE PIONEER OF LIFE: AN ESSAY ON THE GOSPELS

We do it wrong, being so majestical,
To offer it the show of violence;
For it is, as the air, invulnerable,
And our vain blows malicious mockery.

I

THE fourth Gospel, the Gospel of St. John, is an interpretation of the others. It will therefore be a convenient point for our start. St. Paul's life and letters show us Christianity attaining a practical foothold. But, though very practical, St. Paul himself is visionary and mystic in his approach to the Christ. 'Christ' indeed is hardly a person to him: rather a condition. From his relation to Jesus is born anew the Christ; and wherever this relation, this marriage-union is consummated, the Christ is risen in man. Hence St. Paul may write of Jesus as purely human. But St. John is more theological. That is, he tries to dramatize the mystic relation in objective terms, personifying the divine protagonists. He is as much interested in the relation of Christ to God as St. Paul in that of Jesus the Christ to himself. Jesus, to St. John, is the 'Logos of Life', a phrase he uses in his Epistle. Likewise his Gospel starts:

> The Logos existed in the very beginning,
> the Logos was with God,
> the Logos was divine.

And

> . . . this life was the Light for men:
> amid the darkness the Light shone,
> but the darkness did not master it.
>
> (John I, 1-5)

Throughout he is strongly theological. He tells the story of Jesus with certain variations of his own. I cannot here discuss them all. But I would emphasize the curious way in which he makes his hero, so to speak, self-explanatory. His Jesus is always interpreting himself. This is, however, a legitimate artistic process: Shakespeare's heroes likewise may be regarded as 'interpreting' themselves. Clearly, St. John's Gospel is a necessary link in our understanding.

Jesus here interprets his own imagery: 'I am the real vine' he says, 'and my father is the vine-dresser' (John XV, 1). Notice the word 'real'. The vine-image has less rights on its own: to St. John, it is 'merely a metaphor'. When Jesus meets a Samaritan woman drawing water, he asks for a drink, and says:

> If you knew what is the free gift of God and who is asking you for a drink, you would have asked him instead, and he would have given you 'living' water.
>
> (John IV, 10)

This he expands and explains:

> Anyone who drinks this water will be thirsty again, but anyone who drinks the water I shall give him will never thirst any more; the water I shall give him will turn into a spring of water welling up to eternal life.
>
> (John IV, 13)

Continually Jesus translates his metaphors in terms of 'eternal life'. The disciples ask him to eat and he says that he has food of which they 'know nothing' (John IV, 32). His food, he says, is the will of God. Then:

> Look round, I tell you, see, the fields are white for harvesting! The reaper is already getting his wages and harvesting for eternal life . . .
>
> (John IV, 35)

He counsels men to 'work for no perishing food, but

for that lasting food which means eternal life' (John VI, 27). God gives the heavenly 'bread' and 'life', Jesus himself is the 'bread of life', dispelling hunger and thirst, and so on. Again,

> I am the living bread which has come down from heaven; if anyone eats of this bread, he will live for ever . . .
>
> (John VI, 51)

Notice how the interpretative thought often seems to spoil the poetic impact. Jesus' words in the Synoptics give far more attention to the rights of pure poetry: and so their content is, finally, the richer. The idea and method of interpretation is continually observed by St. John. Jesus here often compares himself to food, telling people they must 'eat the flesh of the Son of Man and drink his blood' if they are to have life. And all these passages must be taken for what they are: the author is dramatizing his own reaction to Jesus' poetic speech. It is all theological and abstract far beyond Jesus' words in the Synoptics. So we see how the life-symbols of the 'vine', 'harvest', 'water', and 'bread', are all here explicitly related to 'eternal life'.

It is the same with 'sight' and 'light'. When Jesus heals a blind man, he here draws a moral from the act:

> Then said Jesus, 'It is for judgment that I have come into this world, to make the sightless see, to make the seeing blind.' On hearing this the Pharisees who were beside him asked, 'And are we blind?' Jesus replied, 'If you were blind, you would not be guilty; but, as it is, you claim to have sight—and so your sin remains.'
>
> (John IX, 39)

Observe how the physical sight symbolizes another 'sight' for which there is no exact name. There is also much light-imagery, similarly interpreted. I have already quoted the opening passage where the Logos of God is directly equated with 'light'. Now Jesus calls John the Baptist 'a burning and a shining lamp' (John V, 35), and says of himself:

> I am the light of the world: he who follows me will not walk in darkness, he will enjoy the light of life.
> (John VIII, 12)

This Gospel has powerful light effects, often explicitly translated:

> Then Jesus said to them, 'The Light will shine among you for a little longer yet; walk while you have the Light, that the darkness may not overtake you. He who walks in the dark does not know where he is going. While you have the Light believe in the Light, that you may be sons of the Light.'
> (John XII, 35)

And soon after, he interprets:

> I have come as light into the world, that no one who believes in me may remain in the dark.
> (John XII, 46)

Light is vivid here.

Elsewhere, often, Jesus interprets his own actions or metaphors. At great length he explains his sonship to God, using realistic terms about 'coming down from heaven'. He is the good shepherd who is 'to give up his life for his sheep'. He acts and speaks with full consciousness of his mission and its implications at every turn. The result is an abstract and theological document. It is interpretative, rather than narrative; intellectual rather than pictorial. And, remembering the importance attached here to light, we may again aptly quote Blake's pregnant lines:

> God appears and God is light
> To those poor souls who dwell in night;
> But does a human form display
> To those who dwell in realms of day.

It seems that St. John writes from a consciousness

nearer the intellectual darkness than St. Paul. St. Paul, glorious and shining as his figurative language is, is ever richly humanistic too. He presents a passionate experience of the mystic Christ; John, a meditative and theological interpretation of Jesus the Son of God. Each sees a slightly different facet of the central reality. I have, however, emphasized only one peculiar quality in the Gospel: that does not do it justice. Moreover, this interpretative quality is not at all a weakness: it is invaluable. Our own interpretations of the Synoptics must always owe it a debt: indeed, it directly points our course. For John is receptive especially to Jesus' imagery and actions, seeing them as a profound symbolism of life. To this he calls our attention. And following him, we shall necessarily inspect carefully the various suggestions and poetic colourings throughout the other Gospels.

II

I shall use the Synoptics together, making my own single pattern from them all; occasionally, however, drawing again from the fourth Gospel. The Synoptics tell the same story, with variations. Those variations cannot here receive discussion. Rather, I shall, so to speak, assume that all three together build an ideal Gospel in our minds; and I attempt to indicate what the outlines of such an ideal Gospel will be. My attempt will not be exhaustive, but merely a rough outline.

The life of Jesus is told by narratives thickly inlaid with powerful imaginative impressions. The life itself is, as I have already observed, often both convincingly factual and artistically significant. It pursues an unswerving and unique tragic rhythm, showing an individual's clash with his environment.

Generally, the tragic hero in literature fails through a fault, although he himself is often conceived on a grander scale than his community. Here, however, the protagonist is in every way a more perfect being than his world, the usual tragic relation being to this extent reversed. Jesus' life distils the very quintessence of human reality: his story presents an absolute, finished, and complete life in perfect harmony with a sublime ethic; that is, with the innermost principle of life itself. For that very reason, it has a purpose and direction which leads it inevitably to clash with its environment: it is a life-force in a death-world.

There is, too, a sublime imagination mysteriously interlocked with our narratives. There are numerous events which possess an immediate richness and significance in their own right: dynamic pictures printed lastingly on the mind's eye. They possess the curious quality of seeming to exist profoundly and poetically independently of their verbal expression: the fact itself is poetical. Such are the Journey of the Magi, led by the Star of Bethlehem; the appearance of the Angel to the Shepherds, announcing the wondrous Birth; the Baby in the country manger; the Massacre of the Innocents, with all its suggestion of evil and tyrannic death opposing birth and creation, yet failing to destroy the powerful Child who is to slay evil in the name of life. We see the boy Jesus disputing with theologians, a picture which reminds us that his mission is not to destroy but fulfill the traditional religion. John the Baptist is poetically important. Like so many incidents here, we feel a universal meaning. It is the way things happen: all great movements casts their shadows before them, they have their precursors, their 'voice crying in the wilderness'. We may feel the same with the Massacre of the Innocents: the chances against any new and splendid birth seem multitudinous, the old world will slay it if it can, yet that birth inevitably occurs, that birth is mysteriously guarded, and the new life springs strong-limbed in death's despite. Jesus' lonely fasting and temptation in the desert is likewise universal: any great endeavour is conditional on a similar solitariness, a similar rejection of the splendours of the world, a similar refusal to leave the pinnacle whose height is a giddy fear, a lonely and loveless exaltation. The miracles in turn are poetically important, rich in meanings. Jesus walks on the waves, stills the raging winds and seas. His life is interthreaded with sublime experience, as when the Voice of God claims him as a Son at his Baptism, or when he is transfigured on Mount Tabor and that Voice again pronounces an assurance and acknowledgment. We have the dramatic entry of Jesus into Jerusalem, his path strewn with foliage. The Last Supper is a deathless memory, the prayer in Gethsemane contains all that a tragic poet need learn, all disloyalty is summed in the thirty pieces of silver received by Judas, the Crucifixion encloses and transcends the furthest agony that mortal life may endure. After the Crucifixion there is an earthquake, the sun is blackened, the Temple's veil torn asunder. Symbolism is pregnant everywhere. The number three is recurrent. We have the Eastern kings who bring three offerings to the Divine Child, the three Temptations, the three disciples who witness the Transfiguration, and their suggestion that three tabernacles be built for Jesus, Moses, and Elijah. There are the three crowings of the cock, and the three crucifixions. Often the women who interthread Jesus' story are three. Three are named as attending the Crucifixion: the same three, according to St. Luke, find Jesus' grave deserted. Likewise, mountains are important: Jesus is crucified on a hill, tempted on an 'exceedingly high mountain', and we have the Sermon on the Mount, the Transfiguration on Mount Tabor, the Hill of Olives. And the wondrous life is perfectly framed in a divine birth and a physical resurrection.

All these symbolic pictures are, however, not, as a whole, radiant and flashing. Most are very quietly narrated. The colourings are subdued. They vary: some are dark with a dark beauty, others light with a beauteous light. But, happy or unhappy in suggestion, they are all magical. Solid, they melt into an aura, a gently shining magic frames them. They are beautiful with a lustrous beauty, tragic with a rich agony, breathing ineffable speech. They are wondrously symbolic and wondrously real at once; like Keats' poetry, the more magic for its seeming reality. We have here no flashing and fiery vision, no apocalyptic splendour; but the Star of Bethlehem shines in the frosty night, a magic light, star-beam in the dark.

These Gospels present a pattern wherein a life-beauty interthreads a dark background. Usually, our life-symbolisms will be found directly related to Jesus himself, most often indeed actually used by him. Next, I observe a general sprinkling of this imagery, imagery suggesting gentleness and peace and life rather than turbulence and death, which interpenetrates our story. The nature-references are mostly pleasant. Birds to the human imagination are essentially lovable creatures. Thus they are apt for divine offering, and so we have the sacrifice performed by Jesus when Symeon, inspired by the Holy Spirit, sought to meet him. This is the sacrifice: 'a pair of turtle-doves or two young pigeons' (Luke II, 24). The Holy Spirit descends like a dove upon Jesus (Luke III, 21). Doves are sold in the Temple (Mark XI, 15). A similar suggestion of gentleness is transmitted by pastoral and shepherd symbolism: the flock is a unity, guarded, guided, fed by the shepherd. So the Angel announces Jesus' birth to shepherds; and, indeed, the idea of sheep is powerful throughout, given a particular emphasis by St. John toward the close of his Gospel. There is a strong element of fishing-life: the disciples are fishermen, Jesus performs miracles with fishes when he feeds the multitude, and he wondrously fills the nets that are empty. Fishes—perhaps partly from Gospel associations—are strangely impregnated with positive beauty in many poets. And still lakes have often a paradisal significance in poetry: with which we may compare the realism of the Gospels, as Jesus and his disciples walk by the shores of Galilee. Moreover, fruitful nature generally is a dominant colouring. We hear of Jesus and his disciples 'crossing the cornfields' and how the disciples 'pulled some ears of corn and ate them, rubbing them in their hands' (Luke VI, 1). There is the fig-tree withered by Jesus' curse (Matthew XXI, 18-22). The 'Mount of Olives' or the 'Olive Orchard' is frequently mentioned. There is the sycamore tree on which Zacchaeus climbs to see Jesus (Luke XIX, 4), and the palms strewn before Jesus on his final entry into Jerusalem. According to St. John, Jesus was buried 'in an orchard' (John XX, 41). Food is often mentioned. In the desert, Jesus suffers hunger and is tempted to turn stones to bread; he performs miracles with food often, he is a prophet who comes 'eating and drinking', there is the festival of the Passover and Jesus' supper with his followers. John the Baptist lives on 'locusts and wild honey'. Drink may be used in relation to suffering. Jesus prays in Gethsemane that the cup may pass from him, he is offered 'wine mixed with bitters' before the Crucifixion (Matthew XXVII, 34), and later is given a sponge 'soaked in vinegar' (Matthew XXVII, 48).

And beyond animal-life, nature-suggestion, and human feasting, we have events which point more directly to civilization or human grandeur. There is the flash of coins, the thirty silver pieces received by Judas, the coin with Caesar's impression, the money-changers in the Temple, the woman who comes to anoint Jesus with rich perfume from an alabaster box. And garments, too, are vivid. Jesus is robed with a scarlet mantle and crowned in mockery by the Roman soldiers, the soldiers draw lots for his raiment. Suffering and nakedness are often found together in poetry; so here nakedness is associated directly with madness, clothes with sanity (Luke VIII, 35). Jesus is crucified in naked suffering; but next his body is wrapped in 'clean linen' (Matthew XXVII, 59), and at his resurrection his raiment is 'white as snow' (Matthew XXVIII, 3). There is the man who flies 'naked' at the arrest of Jesus (Mark XIV, 52); and the radiantly clothed angel at Jesus' tomb (Matthew XXVIII). These are a few scattered examples. The Gospels are poetical in word and incident. The events are solid, rounded, and shine with a strange lustre. Being poetic creations, they are full of life-effects. Moreover, they are organic, and so we find the events and outward facts often reflect the central reality. The Gospels are thus rich in life-suggestions, quite apart from Jesus' words. But in his own words they are more than suggestions: they are the very poetry of his teaching. To this I now direct attention.

III

Jesus' words are rich in reference to natural life. His parables are to be read as poetry. We should not be too hasty to draw morals from them: rather we must always first tune our minds to union with their poetic quality. Only so can we receive his statement.

This is his teaching:

> Are not five sparrows sold for two farthings? Yet not one of them is forgotten by God.
>
> But the very hairs on your head are all numbered; fear not, you are worth far more than sparrows.
>
> (Luke XII, 6)

Or again:

> Look at the crows! They neither sow nor reap, no storehouse nor granary have they, and yet God feeds them.
>
> How much more are you worth than birds?
>
> (Luke XII, 24)

So he draws man to contemplate the carefree existence of bird-life. Himself he knows only too well, however, the cruel severance of man from the sweet peace existing in the instinctive world:

> The foxes have their holes, the wild birds have their nests, but the Son of man has nowhere to lay his head.
>
> (Luke X, 58)

Birds are often love-images, they are gentle, peaceful creatures. So, filled by a universal love, Jesus cries to the city he loves, cries to the cities of the world:

> O Jerusalem, Jerusalem! slaying the prophets and stoning those who have been sent to you! How often I would fain have gathered your children as a fowl gathers her brood under her wings!
>
> (Matthew XXIV, 37)

The Realm of Heaven is as a grain of mustard seed growing and expanding till 'the wild birds come and roost in its branches' (Matthew XIII, 31). Jesus, too, talks of shepherds and sheep. His thoughts are tinged with natural and pastoral imagery. Birds suggest nature's sweetness, happy flight, and nesting love. Flocks direct us rather to see a harmonious relation, in union and concord, between the animal and human kingdom. The scattering of a flock is therefore an image of severe unrest:

> You will all be disconcerted, for it is written: I will strike at the shepherd and the sheep will be scattered.
>
> (Mark XIV, 27)

But here more evidently we receive the full beauty of the image in all its delicacy:

> Fear not, you little flock, for your Father is delighted to give you the Realm.
>
> (Luke XII, 32)

So the joy of heaven over a sinner's repentance is similar to that of a man who loses a sheep, and leaves his whole flock to search for the lost one. Finding it, 'he puts it on his shoulders with joy', and when he gets home he calls his friends together, and 'Rejoice with me', he says to them, 'for I have found the sheep I lost' (Luke XV, 6).

This last is a typical parable. All that such pastoral imagery can do for us, it does. We must not first think too closely in terms of 'God' and 'man'. Rather, first think about the shepherd and his sheep, his care and labour, his skill to know each of his flock, one from the other; and the union and dependence which a flock denotes. Thinking like this we are to read the parable, and then, our minds rich with proper associations, turn to the more abstract application. For Jesus' language is poetry.

The poetry comes first, this he ever elaborates. The application he leaves vague, couched often in the most usual terms: 'heaven', 'God', so on. He is a poet, not a theologian. Often he leaves his story uninterpreted. What is new in his teaching can be seen from this parable. He does not say merely that a repentant sinner is gladly forgiven by God. Had he done so, he would not have been the greatest force the world has known. Rather his statement is this: the universal love that beats at the heart of life is a shepherd-love, and man, to that wisdom, is as a sheep in a vast flock, skilless in his master's providence, easily and foolishly lost; but yet, if deepest care can do it, sought and found at the last. Poetry is not parasitic on Jesus' teaching: rather there is a teaching that flowers from his poetry. He works largely by emotional associations. The Christian flock is naturally, then, to be compared with sheep or lambs: the disciples are to go out as 'lambs among wolves' (Luke X, 3). And Jesus pities the people, harassed and dejected, seeing them as 'sheep without a shepherd' (Matthew IX, 36).

Jesus continually speaks in terms of vegetable life, nature's creative growth and rich luxuriance. Whether he mentions harvests and vines, which are related to food, or other trees, there is no primary difference. To creative and fruitful growth he calls us. Even when he describes a selfish man, there is a harvest-richness in his tale: 'A rich man's estate bore heavy crops', so many that he had no room for the corn. But he builds a great granary and determines to 'eat, drink, and be merry', forgetting that death can cut short his joy (Luke XII, 16-20). Such a man thinks crops are only to be possessed: instead, he might rather have learnt from them, and made his own life richly creative as the waving corn.

For men are as a wondrous grass, earth-born, sun-ripened. God clothes the grass 'which blooms to-day in the field, and is thrown to-morrow into the furnace': how much more will he regard the needs of man (Luke XII, 28-32). Indeed, man is nobler than the grass, his life is rather a corn to be ripened, to store eternal granaries. So the Lord of Creation is a farmer seeming, to the wrong-headed servant, to reap where he never sowed, gathering where he never winnowed (Matthew XXV, 24). The law of creation presents always miraculous increase. Thus the appointed end is like a threshing, a winnowing of wheat from straw:

> His winnowing-fan is in his hand to purge his threshing-floor, to gather the wheat into his granary and burn the straw with fire unquenchable.
>
> (Luke III, 17)

The word of divine grace is like seeds thrown on different soils by a sower, some of it maturing, some dying as soon as sown (Luke VIII, 5-8). But where the ground is good, the seed will bring forth richness an hundredfold. Again,

> It is with the Realm of God as when a man has sown seed on the earth; he sleeps at night and rises by day, and the seed sprouts and shoots up, he knows not how.
>
> (Mark IV, 26)

Observe how simply yet how masterfully the mystery of creative life is put before us. And all these images are not random illustrations: they are themselves more important than their application. Or, rather, they and their application are one. For laborious intellectual applications and interpretations, necessary often though they be, yet falsify the reality Jesus is expressing. He says that the true good is like organic life. Man must not be directed by laws only, by systems of ethic: these alone are powerless. Rather his deeds and thoughts must be themselves creative, so that he act and think from the creative centre only, the life-centre, the centre from which he lives, his words and deeds out-flowering from the great life which his very existence expresses:

> If you had faith the size of a grain of mustard-seed, you would say to this mulberry tree, 'Be uprooted and planted in the sea' and it would obey you.
>
> (Luke XVII, 6)

Man must let his life create itself in thought and deed, as the life in the seed upthrusts and burgeons into bloom. So the life that Jesus plants among men is to grow, creative, 'like a grain of mustard-seed', grow till it be a tree, 'so large that birds can roost in its branches' (Matthew XIII, 31-32). Indeed, when the Realm of Heaven is grown to its full height, in that far summer angelic visitors may well find their pleasure in its sheltering leaves. Yet observe how much even that comparison wrongs its context. For Jesus speaks not with any Pauline splendour in these passages, but with poetry more sacred.

Man is as a tree, and is known by his fruits:

> Either make the tree good and its fruit good, or make the tree rotten and its fruit rotten; for the tree is known by its fruit.
>
> (Matthew XII, 33)

The image is exactly the same at Matthew VII, 16-20. There we are told that men do not gather grapes from thorns or figs from thistles. Again,

> The axe is lying ready at the root of the trees: any tree that is not producing good fruit will be cut down and thrown into the fire.
>
> (Luke III, 9)

So a man who owns a fig-tree in his vineyard comes to gather fruit, but, finding none, he tells the vine-dresser to have it cut down. But the man replies,

> Leave it for this year, sir, till I dig round about it and put in manure. Then it may bear fruit next year. If not, you can have it cut down.
>
> (Luke XIII, 8)

This is a lovely parable: the fig-tree itself is so sympathetically drawn, so amazingly realized in so few words, its fate so strangely weighted with meaning. The fig-tree becomes human in this miniature drama. The parable is left uninterpreted. And we, too, wrong its beauty if we do not see it first without any interpretative associations: letting them next gather round it, or rather flower out from it, till the total meaning is born in our minds.

Now the vine or fig-tree may be human, or man may be as the vineyard labourer:

> For the Realm of Heaven is like a householder who went out early in the morning to hire labourers for his vineyard . . .
>
> (Matthew XX, 1)

Notice how curiously the comparison is made. It is often so. The 'householder' here is 'God'. So either the 'realm' is itself God, or the comparison applies rather to the whole story than the 'householder' alone. Both alternatives are ultimately the same; but the second is our best approach. Often in these parables the 'realm' is like, not a person, but a drama. So also many a story-rhythm in other poets must also be allowed to serve the same purpose. Jesus preaches not a poetic gospel, but rather the gospel of poetry. The story-rhythm, the story-picture, presents a quality, union with which is our entrance to the realm. Jesus tells us the blessed realm is something of love, of growth, of rich luxuriance, yet something again in which we must take our part, as labourers tending the vine of life, or again, ourselves as vines unfurling to the sun, if we would bear fruit. The world is thus one vast vineyard, whose master has two sons, one of whom promised to work in it and did not, while the other, first refusing, afterwards obeyed (Matthew XXI, 28-31). Again, the master sends messenger after messenger to his vineyard, and last his own son:

> There was a householder who planted a vineyard, put a fence round it, dug a wine-vat inside it, and built a watch tower: then he leased it to vinedressers and went abroad . . . (Matthew XXI, 33)

The world one wide vineyard, our task its care, to watch and nurture its growth and 'collect its fruit'. All life is as a vine or fig-tree, a tree of life. All that is creative, is of that tree, all that hampers growth is doomed to death, itself is death:

> Let the fig-tree teach you a parable. As soon as its branches turn soft and put out leaves, you know summer is at hand; so, whenever you see all this happen, you may be sure He is at hand, at the very door.
> (Matthew XXIV, 32)

The world of poetry is such a tree. Its fruits have not, indeed, appeared. But to-day its branches are softening and putting out their leaves, and the summer comes. So Jesus directs us to creative understanding, creative life, in language itself creative, a rich bloom springing from fertile ground and seeding itself where it may. Yet he is never, in these passages, rhetorical, never resonant, never decorative:

> Look how the lilies neither spin nor weave; and yet, I tell you, even Solomon in all his grandeur was never robed like one of them. (Luke XII, 27)

His very words live the gospel that they preach.

Though so often addressing his hearers in naturalistic terms, his life-gospel does not exclude images from human civilization. Indeed, he refers often to two closely connected symbols very frequent in the poets: riches, and raiment. Shortly I shall now notice these. Jesus repudiates excessive desire for wealth. Money as a means to life is important: but it is not an end in itself. He tells how a poor widow who offers a few farthings at the temple shows more virtue than the wealthy who contribute larger sums (Mark XII, 41-44). Money is thus relative: not absolute. Another facet of this idea occurs in the parable where a master engages labourers for his vineyard, and pays them each a shilling irrespective of the work they have done (Matthew XX, 1-16). The story has wide implications: but, like so much else, it strongly opposes the desire for exact tangible reward according to merit. We cannot rate love, or anything else worth having, in figures. Yet, in a story of less realistic suggestion, two debtors, owing different amounts, are forgiven equally: and he who owes the most is the most grateful (Luke VII, 41-42). Forgiveness of debts is a favourite thought. We have a parable showing how a rich man forgives a debtor three million pounds, and how that debtor next fails to forgive a brother-servant owing him twenty (Matthew XVIII, 21-35). Avarice and lack of charity are evil: hence Dives is to be blamed for letting Lazarus suffer, and the rich man who stores his garners, forgetting death, is a fool. But the Good Samaritan (Luke X, 30-35) pays two shillings to help a complete stranger. Another parable tells how a master gives his servants various amounts of gold, and praises and rewards those who increase the wealth in their charge. The moral is:

> For to everyone who has shall more be given and richly given; but from him who has nothing, even what he has shall be taken.
>
> (Matthew XXV, 29)

This is best understood in terms of growth. He urges us ever to make contact with essential life. To one who has in him the principle of growth and creation developed, true wealth comes unasked: without that principle, impoverishment must ensue. For there is nothing static in nature: hence again Jesus' dislike of rigid monetary laws. These parables, often superficially contradictory, all suggest nevertheless that money is a means sometimes to life, but that the only true wealth is life itself, not mechanically but organically controlled. Debts, accounts, exact amounts—all these take us nowhere. The rain of nature falls on the just and unjust alike (Matthew V, 45). At the extreme, we even have the Factor who, about to be dismissed, makes friends for himself by falsifying the accounts of his master's clients (Luke XVI, 1-9). And the more universal meaning is this: money is to be used, even though it, and all use of it, seem evil, in order to make friends for us in 'the eternal abodes'. In this parable it is suggested that the deeper life-realities come first, that all else is to be used in their service. The fact that Jesus so often uses 'money' illustrations itself, apart from all else, gives money some poetic justification. It is as a temporary expedient, so firmly established that it cannot be neglected, but never to be allowed autonomy. Let all be flexible, swaying to the needs of the hour and the breath of love.

The young man who would be perfect, yet fails when told to sell his possessions and give to the poor, is typical: riches may bar man from eternal life.

'Rich folk', indeed, are often in danger (Luke VI, 24). They miss the real wealth, of which gold and silver are colourless shadows only. They forfeit the 'riches of God' (Luke XII, 21), the 'true riches' (Luke XVI, 11). Again,

> The Realm of Heaven is like treasure hidden in a field; the man who finds it hides it and in his delight goes and sells all he possesses and buys that field. Again, the Realm of Heaven is like a trader in search of fine pearls; when he finds a single pearl of high price, he is off to sell all he possesses and buy it.
>
> (Matthew XIV, 44-46)

All these images suggest the same thing. Money is desirable as a means to life: for life is what all desire. But too often the means are confused with the end. Let money then be but the currency of little affairs, while the true search is for essential life. Therefore we are told not to store up treasures on earth, for such are transient: moth and rust corrode, thieves break in and steal. Rather should we store our treasure in eternal coffers (Matthew VI, 19). For 'rich' is the 'reward in heaven' blossoming from the true life on earth (Luke VI, 23, 35). Caesar's coin may be paid to Caesar: the Realm demands a more stable and yet more dynamic currency. Everywhere the thought suggests that riches may be, in metaphor or actual affairs, fluctuating expressions of the more solid and blossoming gold of life; but in themselves, riches are insecure in value, sometimes dangerous. So, when money is, as it were, spilt out, however recklessly, by a pure devotion, the waste is blameless. Jesus will not reprove the woman who comes 'with an alabaster flask of pure nard perfume' to anoint him, even though it might have been sold for 'three hundred shillings' and given to the poor (Mark XIV,

3-9). And every one of these parables, besides what moral it may contain, helps to build here a certain rich beauty interthreading our naturalistic symbols. The Gospels are full of riches: of riches and of richness.

It is much the same with raiment. Clothes, like money, are strong-rooted in man's civilization. Like money, jewels, and riches generally, they are often very importantly used by the poets. Dives in his worldly luxury is seen in 'purple and fine linen' (Luke XVI, 19). The scribes 'like to walk about in long robes' (Mark XII, 38). But men ought not to trouble so much about what they put on, for 'the body is something more than clothes' (Luke XII, 23), and Solomon in his robes of glory cannot match the pure vesture of the lily (Luke XII, 27). Yet, too, the Prodigal is given his father's 'best robe' (Luke XVI, 22). A 'wedding-robe' is most important in one parable (Matthew XXII, 12). Clothes may thus be symbols of life. Clearly, at an extreme, they are so, like money, to the poor: so 'let every one that has two shirts give to him who has none' (Luke III, 11). Again,

> I was a stranger and you entertained me, I was unclothed and you clothed me.
>
> (Matthew XXV, 35)

Jesus uses the metaphor of a new patch and an old coat, to illustrate his life-gospel (Matthew IX, 16). Here, then, also we have two directions. As a means to life, our life-symbol is good: but yet it may cease to be a symbol of life, and then it becomes dangerous.

But perhaps Jesus' richest poetry is that which blends the human and the natural. I pass then to the simplicities of human food and human marriage. We remember how St. John imagines Jesus as saying that he is a 'living bread' or 'living water', that he is come to satisfy a universal 'hunger'. This may direct us to passages in the other Gospels where food is mentioned, but left without explicit interpretation. Such an interpretation, however, is all but implicit in Jesus' remarks to the Syrophoenician woman, that 'it is not fair to take the children's bread and throw it to the dogs' (Mark VII, 27), or his image about putting 'fresh wine into old wine-skins' (Mark II, 22). The Reign of God is 'like dough which a woman took and buried in three pecks of flour, till all of it was leavened' (Luke XIII, 21). Observe the homely realism of Jesus' illustration: here again, it is suggested that true growth is never catastrophic, but rather gradual, flowering from the source of life. Mankind is as 'the salt of the earth', which must not become 'insipid' (Matthew V, 13) or 'tasteless' (Mark IX, 50). A stone is contrasted with a loaf, a serpent with a fish, an egg with a scorpion, in a passage pointing God's care for man (Luke XI, 11-13). Food is often mentioned in Jesus' speech with varied symbolic or realistic content. He tells us we are to feed one another for his sake:

> Whoever gives you a cup of water because you belong to Christ, I tell you truly, he shall not miss his reward.
>
> (Mark IX, 41)

Again,

> For I was hungry and you fed me, I was thirsty and you gave me drink.
>
> (Matthew XXVI, 35)

Food is important, more important than ecclesiastical rules: we are reminded how David eat the loaves of the Presence when he was hungry (Mark II, 26). And when the prodigal son falls on evil times, he eats 'husks' or 'pods' with 'swine': but, returning to his true home his life is made rich with music, dance, and banqueting, the fatted calf being killed to celebrate his return (Luke XVI). So Jesus, the life-bringer, is one who comes 'eating and drinking' (Luke VII, 34), and who feeds the hungry by miracles. To these suggestions the more rigid interpretations of St. John may be applied, provided they enrich, but are not allowed ever to impoverish, our sense of pure poetry. To St. John the interpretation is all-important: to Jesus it is seldom more than part of his whole poetic statement.

Jesus expands the feasting idea often. Once when he is taking a meal he talks about feasts to his host and other guests (Luke XIV, 1-24). He describes how a proud man may disgrace himself by sitting too high. Next, he enjoins his friends when they give a feast not to invite only the rich but rather the poor also. A fine remark comes from one of those present: 'Blessed is he who feasts in the Realm of God.' And then Jesus goes on to make a parable, telling how a man invites his friends to a feast, but they make excuses in turn. Then the poor are invited instead, the rich excluded. There is thought here of wide issues, the banquet is the heavenly kingdom. And this whole conversation, starting from a real feast, shows how close intermeshed, in Jesus' mind, is the image with the thought: either may blossom from the other. The two are never really distinct. The true life expresses itself by feeding the poor; but such a life is also itself a blessed feast.

Jesus, indeed, very often talks about banquets. And it is usually a marriage-banquet. Marriages are continually in his mind and we may say that all our life-symbols culminate in this: marriage festivity being, as it were, the finest flower of the human and natural worlds. To these all our other suggestions of nature's fertility and human life, animals and trees and harvests, raiment and riches and feasting, all are subsidiary; this presents a finer excellence than all the rest. In the conversation I have just described one of the banquets was a marriage-banquet. 'When anyone invites you to a marriage-banquet', he said, 'never lie down in the best place, in case a more distinguished guest than yourself has been invited . . .' (Luke XIV, 8). Again, we have a more elaborate parable on the marriage-banquet in Matthew:

> Then Jesus again addressed them in parables. 'The Realm of Heaven', he said, 'may be compared to a king who gave a marriage-banquet in honour of his son. He sent his servants to summon the invited guests to the feast, but they would not come. Once more he sent some other servants, saying, 'Tell the invited guests, here is my supper all prepared, my oxen and fat cattle are killed, everything is ready, come to the marriage-banquet.'

Eventually,

> Then he said to his servants, 'The marriage-banquet is all ready, but the invited guests did not deserve it. So go to the byeways and invite anyone you meet to the marriage-banquet'. And those servants went out on the roads and gathered all they met, bad and good alike. Thus the marriage-banquet was supplied with guests.

This is the conclusion:

> Now when the king came in to view his guests, he saw a man there who was not dressed in a wedding-robe. So he said to him, 'My man, how did you get in here without a wedding-robe?' The man was speechless . . .
>
> (Matthew XXII, 1-14)

Here the festal hope is beautifully bodied into this marriage-symbol. Again, the Realm of Heaven is compared to ten maidens 'who took their lamps and went out to meet the bridegroom and the bride'. Five, however, took no spare oil. While waiting, they go to sleep. Then 'at midnight the cry arose, "Here is the bridegroom! Come out to meet him!"' As they trim their lamps the foolish maidens find they need more oil. They go to buy more:

> Now while they were away buying oil, the bridegroom arrived; those maidens who were ready accompanied him to the marriage-banquet, and the door was shut. Afterwards the rest of the maidens came and said, 'Oh sir, oh sir, open the door for us!' but he replied, 'I tell you frankly, I do not know you.'
>
> (Matthew XXV, 10-13)

Observe how unnecessary, in one sense, the tale is. The conclusion seems hardly to fit it and might have been expressed very simply alone. But the conclusion is only part of what the parable says. Look at the rest, regarding the whole pattern: the ten maidens, the lamps and the oil, glimmering lights in the dark, the weary waiting set against the coming joy, the anxious watching for 'bride' and 'bridegroom', the arrival and the marriage-banquet. It is all rich, rich in suggestion. Jesus' parables are first poetry, second, teaching. And Jesus often shows he would rather his hearers received the poetry without the teaching than the teaching without the poetry. Marriages are powerful in Jesus' mind:

> Keep your loins girt and your lamps lit, and be like men who are expecting their lord and master on his return from a marriage-banquet, so as to open the door for him at once when he returns and knocks . . .
>
> (Luke XII, 35)

Through such bridal-images we receive his statement. In St. John's Gospel his first miracle is performed, aptly, at a marriage-banquet:

> Two days later a wedding took place at Cana in Galilee; the mother of Jesus was present and Jesus and his disciples had also been invited to the wedding.
>
> (John II, 1)

He is the poet of marriage and all marriage joy.

And yet it is sometimes thought that Jesus repudiates actual marriage. This is wrong.

> Have you never read that He who created them male and female from the beginning said,
>
> Hence a man shall leave his father and mother, and cleave to his wife, and the pair shall be one flesh?
>
> So they are no longer two, but one flesh. What God has joined, then, man must not separate.
>
> (Matthew XIX, 4)

True, some men may be eunuchs for the sake of the Realm of Heaven. 'Let anyone practise it,' he says, 'for whom it is practicable' (Matthew XIX, 12). The one marriage may be neglected for the other; but both are good. In the perfect state all the joy and union that marriage can bring is included:

> You go wrong because you understand neither the scriptures nor the power of God. At the resurrection people neither marry nor are married, they are like the angels of God in heaven.
>
> (Matthew XXII, 29)

Marriage has, indeed, a negative aspect: it is repressive, a law controlling unruly desires. In the Realm, where desires are not unruly, there can be no marriage, as such. All life-suggestions have thus positive and negative aspects. All point to life, yet the partial may at any time be rejected to make the way clear for the absolute: it is better to get into life with the loss of an eye or a limb, than that the whole life, body and soul, be destroyed (Matthew V, 24-30). But nothing is more powerful in Jesus' poetry than the marriage-symbol. His consciousness is never limited to men only. Paul is at heart a bachelor, and can be irritated by women who usurp too much power. But Jesus is rather a lover by nature, loving all things creative, including human love.

Women and children are important in his story. To women he is gentle. He satisfies the Syrophoenician woman who begs him to cast a demon out of her daughter (Mark VII, 26). A delightful domestic incident occurs at Luke XI, 38-42, where Jesus visits a woman called Martha, whose sister talks to him without doing her share of the work and so incurs Martha's reproach. Then Jesus gently excuses her. There is his wide sympathy with the convicted adulteress (John, VIII, 3-11). Similar suggestion of impurity is present in the woman who anoints him with rich perfume (Luke VII, 36-44). Mary Magdala, out of whom he has cast 'devils', is likewise a friend of Jesus. The Crucifixion is attended by 'the women who had accompanied him from Galilee' (Luke XXIII, 49). They are Mary of Magdala, Mary the mother of James, and Salome, and they bring spices to anoint his body after his death (Mark XVI, 1). All three Gospels refer to these as 'following him' from Galilee, or 'waiting on him'. He was clearly loved by them. They seem to honour him for his very independence of them, recognizing that, though he himself has renounced marriage happiness, yet he in some masterly way is renouncing life-instincts in the name of life. So women love him in his loneliness, paying tribute to his manhood. His own mother overwatches his story.

Children also are loved by him. Indeed, they are given high prominence in his teaching. To all poets they are the freshest flowers of life, on whom sparkles dew from the fields of paradise: 'Their angels in heaven always look on the face of my Father in heaven' (Matthew XVIII, 10). Again,

> Let the children alone, do not stop them from coming to me: the Realm of Heaven belongs to such as these.
> (Matthew XIX, 14)

Therefore those who wrong children incur his most bitter condemnation. To get into the Realm, one must become as a little child (Matthew XVIII, 2). Indeeed, all that is natural and all that is human is loved by him, provided that it serve life. His words are life-words, creative words. Himself he is proud to call the 'son of man'. Often, too, as in the parables I have quoted, he seems to think of himself as a bridegroom:

> Can friends at a wedding fast while the bridegroom is beside them? As long as they have the bridegroom beside them they cannot fast. A time will come when the bridegroom is taken from them; then they will fast, on that day.
> (Mark II, 19—20)

The Son of Man and Bridegroom of the World.

As we contemplate this the Pioneer of Life we begin to see him as pure light in a dark world. The tendency is dangerous, unless controlled and directed. We must never see the light of this life as a pallid abstraction, a cold white ray. Light here is interfused with the physical, dependent on the body: not in itself a separate essence. Moreover, Jesus' words on light are subdued, homely, realistic. There is no blaze in his phrases:

> No one lights a lamp to put it in a cellar or under a bowl, but on a stand, so that those who come in can see the light. Your eye is the lamp of the body: when your eye is sound, then the whole of your body has

> light, but if your eye is diseased, then your body is darkened (Look! perhaps your very light is dark).
>
> So if your whole body has light, without any corner of it in darkness, it will be lit up entirely, as when a lamp lights you with its rays.
>
> (Luke XI, 33)

Notice how quietly realistic is this light-imagery, and how far from intellectual subtleties. Yet to interpret its full meaning a book would have to be written. Indeed, this book I am writing is such an attempt. And there have been, and will be, many more, for of the making of such books there can be no end. To Jesus sight illuminates the 'whole body', not the mind only. And this whole body he would have lit by a purified sight. It is something simple he asks: but it is yet mysterious. Simple and mysterious as light itself. It is something, too, that Blake and D. H. Lawrence were trying to explain. Jesus tells, too, a parable where a lost coin is sought with a light (Luke XV, 8). A woman loses ten shillings, and lights a lamp and searches till she finds it. These two parables are simple, their imagery rounded, realistic: the lamp, cellar, bowl in the one, in the other a 'bed', the lost coin, and the woman 'scouring the house' for it. Remember, too, the parable of the ten maidens, their lamps and oil: and contrast this sort of poetry with the flaring brilliances of lesser visionaries. All this is very different from St. John and St. Paul. And the difference is that described by Blake: Jesus dwells ever 'in realms of day', not only his mind, but his body, full of light. To such reality is the only vision and 'nothing is hidden that shall not be disclosed, nothing concealed that shall not be known and revealed' (Luke VIII, 17). Light, to him, is adjectival, never a thing in itself.

All light is itself but a part of life. The whole life is primary, and any part whatsoever may be sacrificed in that cause:

> If your hand or foot is a hindrance to you, cut it off and throw it away; better be maimed or crippled and get into Life, than keep both feet or hands and be thrown into the everlasting fire.
>
> If your eye is a hindrance to you, tear it out and throw it away; better get into Life with one eye than keep your two eyes and be thrown into the fire of Gehenna.
>
> (Matthew XVIII, 8—9)

'Get into life'. There is no thought of 'souls' in our modern abstract sense. Jesus' mind does not work in terms of a body-soul dualism at all. His concrete intuition will be best illustrated by our saying that he would sanction the statement that it is better to get into life with no 'soul' than to save your soul and be thrown into the fire of Gehenna. Indeed, life itself may be sacrificed for life's sake: 'whoever wants to save his life will lose it, and whoever loses his life for my sake, he will save it' (Luke IX, 24). Of the whole life Jesus speaks. Concentration on any aspect, on wealth or on fine clothes, or on bodily pleasures—these may hinder life. So, too, may religious observance, intellectualisation, self-satisfaction. The Scribes and Pharisees are blind guides, 'filtering away the gnat and swallowing the camel', cleaning the outside of the cup and leaving the inside foul. Their piety secretes a death: they are as whitewashed tombs full of dead men's bones (Matthew XXIII, 24). The blind lead the blind, the dead prescribe to death. But 'the body is something more than clothes' (Luke XII, 23). And life is something more than the body—or the mind, or the soul. Just as the first creature to develope sight could only have explained that miracle in terms of smell, warmth, sound; so Jesus would explain his life-message in terms of other, and lesser, life-suggestions. All poets do this. Thus all our life imagery builds up a greater life to which no one part must take precedence; and that life as far surpasses what we call life as the body surpasses its clothing. 'Do that', Jesus says to the lawyer who seeks his help, 'and you will live' (Luke X, 28). Towards life—not of the body, spirit, or mind, but of all and more—the Gospels call us. Thus Jesus himself is necessarily often shown as independent of all but the true life: unmarried, fasting, without worldly wealth, his body nakedly crucified. His own life he finally throws down as the last challenge to death. There is then no death: 'He is not the God of dead people but of living. You are far wrong' (Mark XII, 27).

IV

I have emphasized that Jesus' poetry is richly imaginative yet rarely flashes or scintillates. It moves with an assured mastery, a quiet grace. It is homely, realistic, and magical. Here I point especially to its life-quality. But Jesus moves in a dark world, and if we, too, are to be true to his own realism we do wrong to see him only and always as a white splendour, an immaculate lord of peace. He drives from the Temple those who wrong its sacred stones. When blindness maddens him, he threatens eternal flames, the burnings of Gehenna; a generation of 'vipers' he condemns to weeping and gnashing of teeth; bitter woe he prophecies to all who love their own death, death to the dead, life to those who live. It is better to be drowned in the depths than wrong the child of life. A dark anger burns from him. He images the apocalyptic end where one shall be taken and another left. Then,

> The sun will be darkened, and the moon will not yield her light, the stars will drop from heaven, and the orbs of the heavens will be shaken.
>
> (Mark XIII, 24 and 25)

The Son of Man will appear 'like lightning that flashes from one side of the sky to the other' (Luke XVII, 24) : and the image is one of terror as well as beauty. An image of judgment. All these are reflections cast by the death-world on the pioneer of life, shadows thrown by the dark rocks and frowning fortress he invades. But his own natural words are life-words, in him there is no death, nor threat of death, save it comes from without; from cruelty, from hypocrisy, from wilful blindness.

We should see Jesus, as it were, silhouetted against a world of formalized religion, hypocrisy, envy, evil; and suffering. It is, very often, a world of death. Spiritual death, bodily death. To this he would bring life. His only gospel is life, and life put into words is poetry; and his only ethic is poetry, for poetry put into action is life. So his words tell of the shepherd and his sheep, the harvest and the vine; of food and of clothes, and of marriage. Life-words on his lips, himself a life-force, he feeds those who are hungry, saves those who are lost. He goes about in a world of disease and death. All sorts of diseases he cures: leprosy, haemorrhage, palsy, paralysis, dropsy. Each withered limb he heals in turn, each sense in turn he restores, healing the blind, the deaf, the dumb. Diseases of the body, diseases of the senses. Spiritual torment he relieves, releasing those mastered by devil-possession, dark abysmal neurosis, the *Macbeth* evil, the *Macbeth* guilt. He cures madness, restoring the tameless maniac of the 'tombs' (Mark V, 1-14). Sin he removes with a word and a look, sin and its correlative, death. Twice the dead themselves rise at his command. All partial death, all more absolute death, he cures, himself a thing of life: he shows, indeed, that there is no death. But, though all this he can do, though every disease and every mental evil he can cure for those who ask, though every physical sense he can restore, there may yet be lacking the one essential health, the final sense that sees without sight and hears where no word is spoken, the faith that moves mountains, the heart beating in unison with life. To him all are sick to death. This universal sickness, too, he would heal: by example, by miracle, by poem after poem, by reference to all life-forces and all senses in turn, by love and bitter anger, by his own life and bitter death, this one thing he would make clear to all men, a thing to him so simple, yet more hard to breathe into us than to feed five thousand with a few loaves and fishes, or make the dead rise from their sleep. And yet this thing alone is life: the others, in comparison, but shadows, parodies, ghostly unrealities.

So he speaks in parables, that men may not deceive themselves into a mockery of understanding. To those who have eyes and see not, he leaves his poetry without interpretation. Better that they have the poetry without the teaching than think they have the teaching before they see how it flowers from the poetry. But to his own disciples, whose understanding is tuned to his message, he will add the interpretation (Luke VIII, 15). No symbol, indeed, can ever be understood till the hearer is ready for understanding. So Jesus would avoid an intellectual exploitation of his message. He leaves his own theology and ethic vague and often paradoxical; for he does not think in intellectual categories at all. To him, the body itself 'sees'. All his ideas are physically embodied. He talks about natural life, food, marriage; feasting, wine, rich perfumes are woven in his story; he cures by touching, or by being touched: the very 'tassel' of his 'robe' is magical to heal. He would not have men think so much as 'see', 'hear', and speak. He would have them enter their inherited eternity of fullest life, he comes 'that they may have life and have it to the full' (John X, 10). He ever speaks in poetry for he is calling us to creative life, he tells us to blend our life with the life of harvest and tree and human marriage, to make metaphors and poetic symbols, that is, true creations, of our thoughts and acts. We must live at the heart of creation, be one with the principle of creation, and thus possess our immortality, our life. In creation alone is there life. The Gospels are thus rich with tangible, physical, sensuous and super-sensuous life, pitted against disease in mind and body, evil, and death. That the New Testament should ever have been itself considered a message of death, of intangible spirituality, of pallid, lifeless, and ghostly counsel, is one of the grand enigmas in this mysterious world: more truly miraculous than anything in the Gospels themselves. With God, indeed, all things are possible.

Jesus' life throughout is complementary to his words. By picture-language and by dramatic example his work is done. In word and act he is the pioneer of life. And this essential life of life is throughout both firmly realized and magically mysterious. Most of our symbols and symbolic events here are solid and realistic, yet also framed by a poetic aura, haloed with imagination. So Jesus, as a person, is human and real to us; we grow to know his naturalistic and humanistic poetry, his sympathy and endurance, his flashing wrath and prophetic ardour. But his personality, human though it be, is also symbolic: it, too, radiates a mysterious and mystic power. Moreover, his life as a story in time is likewise framed by light, melting into the divine at either end. His birth is divine, he rises from the dead: his life-story thus blends with the infinite, dissolved in light. At certain moments in his life he is vividly superhuman: when the heavens open at his baptism, at his transfiguration. But, silhouetted against these, we see the powerful darkness of Golgotha, that stark suffering unrelieved, the black cross, the fifth act of death unlit by any limelight from the heavenly sphere, a silence broken by no assuring voice of God. All various colourings here, the vividly incandescent, the utterly dark, and the many rich tints that mingle between these extremes; suggesting categories natural, human, and divine, elements realistic and miraculous—all must be re-created in our sight if we are to possess the whole in its wonder.

It is Shakespearian, in its life-imagery, in its symbolism, its tragic symbols especially. There are the sea-tempests that terrify the disciples (Mark IV, 35-41, Matthew XIV, 22-33), but Jesus walks on the troubled waters, and even 'the winds and waves' obey his voice. The apocalyptic end prophesied by Jesus, when the sun and moon shall be darkened and the graves give up their dead has reverberations throughout Shakespeare; and there is the doom-darkness at the Crucifixion, as the great earth quakes in its guilt, and the *Macbeth* terror is wakened at its own crime. And there are happier symbols: the radiant and transfigured Christ, his divine birth, the resplendent resurrection. The Shakespearian universe is compacted in these pages.

But perhaps the Gospels are nearest of all to *A Midsummer Night's Dream*, a work whose fairy loveliness too often blinds us to its deeper and darker meanings. This play I have analysed in my book *The Shakespearian Tempest*. *A Midsummer Night's Dream* resembles Keats' poetry, in that the horrors and fears which torment mankind are themselves part of something magically sweet, sweeter than any more fanciful and golden paradise. This play is apt here: for in it too we have pastoral life, in farm, crop, or natural growth, in bird and beast, exquisitely and minutely apprehended. But it is a world too where the graves gape wide and the dead stalk along the churchyard ways. There are nightmare fears, prowling beasts seeking whom they may devour, dissensions and mistakes and blindness, darkness and distress. It is all mysterious. A moonlit and paradisal tragedy makes the middle scenes. And then Theseus rises on this world with the dawn, a Christ-Sun, his fire dispelling pagan fears. The whole is crowned by marriage and bridal-music. It is rich, and warm with life. Keats' *Ode to the Nightingale* likewise blends the pale horror of decaying youth with starry fays and moonlight melodies, and the flower-woodland, till death is itself 'rich', and all one deep intoxicating draught of song.

Like such poetry, the Gospels are pastoral, homely, and magical. They too breathe warmth and truth, their words and incidents are flowers budding as we read. They are loaded with both fact and significance: all is symbolically potent and fragrant. They are rich in sense suggestion at every point: their incidents and poetry rounded and complete. They have been thought effeminate. They are so; or, rather, feminine. Feminine in their love and endurance through the ages, their creative passivity, their pregnancy and power for life. They distill the richest essences of literature, all is fertile, creative, packed with quickening poetry. All themes of poetry are here. Hebrew theologians mix with Roman military authorities, and the oriental potentate, Herod, is set beside the royalty of the Christ. Not only is this book poetic: it holds all possible poetry potential in its pages. The Gospels may lack outward blaze and tittilating scintillation, but they are deeper dyed with essential and perduring truth. It is softly, darkly toned, this Gospel art-form, like an Isfahan carpet, smooth and velvet to the touch, whose close-knit silken thread and darkly interwoven colours outlast a hundred more assertive and flamboyantly decorative textures. It is richly toned, deeply dyed. Jesus is crowned with thorns and robed, not radiantly as Cleopatra at her self-immolation, but in the tragic purple of suffering, his cross labelled with the kingship of grief. He breaks the bread and spills the wine of life over the ages to succeed. Though this be a life-vision indeed, its gold-glittering and sparkling nectar is mixed with a bitter substance, as three black crosses are raised against a wrathful and darkening sky, till the heavens themselves thunder at man's act on earth. No book shirks less the horrors of mortal existence. Herein evil is powerful, not a disease but we hear of it, the corpse of Lazarus moulders and 'stinks' in its wrappings. Jesus is crucified on Golgotha, 'the place of a skull': the last stone is added to the architecture of death. And yet there is no truer life-document. It is rich in pain, rich in beauty: a dark, rich wine, offering, not the waters of our fanciful desires, but the richer wine of truth. And the final wisdom is not fearful: for in Jesus' parables we have our central assurance, and they are as grass new-gathered in the paling dawn, all glistening with thrice-consecrated dew, not of paradise, but of earth, warm earth. Against that green foliage, his own story burns, as a dark red rose burns with perfumed life, spreads its life outwards from its heart and fiery centres. There is in this book agony, but it holds within an unutterable peace; we are betrayed, but betrayed with a kiss. The Gospels are like their own loveliest incident. Through them we are washed by the tears that mortal things let fall: these are the tears fallen on Jesus' feet from the penitent, weeping for past blindness. And next, the alabaster box is softly broken, and the perfume rich around us, and we breathe its life.

PART III
PROPHECY

X. IMMORTALITY

SINCE life and death are the main subjects of poetry and prophetic writing generally, and since, moreover, all such literature is primarily concerned with revealing some 'paradise' or 'essential life', it is necessary here to give attention to the concept 'immortality'. My essay, however, is merely an interpretation of what many may know more directly by immediate and intuitive experience. It does not aim, therefore, to prove that immortality exists; still less does it aim to replace any simple belief with one more complicated. I suggest that all readers who have already a powerful immortality conviction may well pass it over. But for many people to-day the intuition of immortality is attacked by a sceptical intellect. Now intellect can never make a belief or prove anything to be true. The word means understanding. When we cannot understand a belief we often distrust it: scepticism is usually lack of understanding. It is negative, not positive. Therefore our difficulty is this: we cannot understand immortality. Here, then, I explain this intuition in intellectual terms, showing how and in what sense we may, if we choose, understand it as much as we understand anything. It will be clear that nothing I say can possibly be supposed to disprove, or supplant, any more concrete sense of victorious life, such as that given by the Christian dogma of resurrection. Indeed, I return to that dogma eventually. My essay will have vaguenesses and contradictions. I aim only to suggest thought-directions which will help us to understand the more visionary statements found in poetry and the Bible.

There is a widespread feeling that man is immortal. There is also a widespread knowledge that men die, that their life comes to an end. It is clear, too, that the poetic and prophetic literature we have been discussing is ever concerned with this very struggle of life against death. In Christianity we have a bodily resurrection; in the Renaissance poets we often find immortality expressed as an immediate experience, such as in *Epipsychidion,* where Shelley sees love and death blended to create a deathless life; a thought recurrent elsewhere, in *Antony and Cleopatra* and Keats. A poet often sees immortality in terms of birth rather than life: Wordsworth, Shelley, Tennyson do this. Death is the end of life, yet man is immortal: which immortality, they seem to say, is something as much of the past as the future. Immortality always has something to do with love. And, rising above all this, there is the weighty fact that life, not death, is our proper concern. Our understanding must take all such thoughts into account.

Our minds are clouded by false associations and illegitimate logic. We must concentrate on realities and refuse scrambling irrelevancies their desired entrance. Consider the word 'immortality'. It signifies 'undeathliness', which, in that it is less soiled by dangerous associations, is perhaps a better term. Now immortality means the opposite of death, which is life; yet it also suggests death, too. It means, then, 'death negated': it is an act rather than a static thing. We may, then, call immortality 'life victorious over death'; and, indeed, no one will understand the poets until he is able to see life victorious, wherever it is so presented, as suggesting immortality, or, conversely, immortality as suggesting not a lengthy duration so much as victorious life. There is to-day a belief that immortality means a kind of ghostly continuance: this is quite wrong.

It is easy to argue not only that immortality can exist but, indeed, that it must exist. For death is only the negative aspect of life. It is parasitic on the life-concept, and itself wholly negative. Birth and death are a sort of framework enclosing an individual human life: they are time-aspects from which we regard it. Now an individual human life is ever an abstraction from the dramatic whole, in fiction, biography, or actual human affairs, and death is then merely a negative aspect, as birth a positive aspect, of an abstraction. Clearly, death holds then but little reality. Any bit of life, any positive and rounded whole, must be, intellectually, victorious over the wraithly line enclosing it. A line is scarcely real: it has length without breadth, as the geometry books say. This may appear an easy proof of immortality. It is, however, perfectly valid. Where, then, lies our difficulty? By isolating an individual life I have simplified our problem. The true difficulty is more complex. I shall now more closely enquire into what we mean by life and death.

Life may mean physical life only: that is, it denotes the working of the machinery which activates a physical organism. But there is psychic life as well as physical life: a man may be very much alive on his death-bed. Our consciousness has variations, some far more vital than others. What I call the imaginative or romantic consciousness pierces further than the lower or intellectual consciousness which blindly feels the contours of realities which the other not only feels, but sees, and hears. The highest life-consciousness is not only mental: it will be physical, too, permeating the body. We are seldom fully conscious of life. We sleep, we unrestfully dream, and the romantic sight is fitful for most of us. Therefore we may have degrees of psychical life, just as there are degrees of physical health. The most perfect state would be, presumably, one where the psychical and physical were both in perfect health: a state rarely found, since the one element tends often to prey upon the other. Indeed, it often seems that neither would endure ill-health apart from such conflict: and that, as all our ills are to be related to such disharmony, we may expect our only good to depend on the corresponding harmony. For man is, at his best, a perfect whole, transcending its constituent parts.

If there are degrees of life, there are necessarily also degrees of death. Death may be physical: we mean then, that the body, whatever may have happened to the mind, is dead. Dead, that is, as part of a human organism: in other respects it is certainly part of the physical universe, and must still be related to life. Our arguments are at every turn rendered hard by the fact that death is unreal: thus the body changes, but cannot die. With the psychic element things are easier. Clearly, there is much psychic death of a sort during physical life; an idea powerful in the poets, in *Hamlet*, Wordsworth's Ode on Immortality, and Tennyson's *Maud*. But neither is this death absolute. An absolute death of the total organism man is always inconceivable. It would mean the utter extinction of the physical body and all psychic qualities. It would include the blotting out of such a man's influence and works in time, his friends' memories and his enemies' dislike, as well as the complete chemical vanishment of his body. Then the universe might be as though that man had never been. This would be absolute death. It is true that, since man is a physical and mental organism, that whole, as a whole, is ended as soon as one part of it is gone or, indeed, out of harmony with any other part; and that it might be objected that this alone constitutes an absolute death. That is defensible, but it is not what we usually mean: for in this sense we are absolutely dead when we have a tooth extracted, or lose our tempers. Such death I prefer to call 'partial': and commonsense will support the term. So, though absolute life is sometimes achievable, absolute death appears inconceivable.

Moreover, if such a state of final extinction were possible, it would be quite desirable. It would be as a mysterious dream, super-natural; a vast, calm sea of unimaginable peace, an exquisite silent harmony with no clash or discord to mar its dark tranquillity. It is not undesirable, since the more we think of it, the more it shapes itself into a symbol of universality, harmony, and peace. It holds no conflict, no unrest. We could not object that to leave our dear ones would be an agony: since the very entrance of dear ones into our conception implies a connexion after death with things of this life, and that we have ruled out by definition. Similarly, we cannot say, this would not matter to me if only my extinction were at stake: but I cannot bear to contemplate those I love so dissolved into nothingness. For here again, if we remember them, they are not so dissolved. Therefore we may say that such death is a philosophical abstraction; that it is quite inconceivable, save to flights of fancy, since death cannot so cut its moorings from the life of created things on which it depends; and that, if it were possible to believe in it, then certainly, in this world where so much partial death, such as sin, sickness, pain, bereavement and misery, has to be endured, such a death would be no evil. Our values would be reversed. Life, so partial, so short, so readily giving place to an eternal nothingness, would be trivial indeed compared with that overpowering infinitude. Though death were nothing, life would immediately be recognized as a minus quantity, less than nothing. This is what happens in Shakespeare's *Timon of Athens.* Timon aspires to such eternity. He sees life as a world of partial death: hence the crimes and physical diseases that impregnate his curses with loathing. Therefore for him absolute death is an ideal. So he speaks:

> Come not to me again, but say to Athens,
> Timon hath made his everlasting mansion
> Upon the beached verge of the salt flood;
> Who once a day with his embossed froth
> The turbulent surge shall cover: thither come;
> And let my grave-stone be your oracle.
> Lips, let sour words go by and language end,
> What is amiss, plague and infection mend!
> Graves only be men's works and death their gain!
> Sun, hide thy beams! Timon hath done his reign.
>
> (*Timon of Athens,* V, i, 217)

Timon wishes all men to die; the sun to go out; indeed, the world to end. And only by such universal ending can any ultimate death be attained by any individual. This is Nirvana, and to Timon the highest good, since life has failed him. But observe that Shakespeare is too excellent a poet to be able to express it: the utter darkness, the vast emptiness and unending age he would suggest are necessarily incarnated in a very lively symbol, the sea. This is Timon's utter death, and in so far as it is possible it becomes a positive splendour in its grandeur, its height and depth and everlasting, unsounded deeps of perpetuity.

But it is not possible. And it is not this that troubles us at all. The varied melodies of absolute life are beautiful; and so, to our imagination, is the silent music of absolute death. Only when the two conflict, we have tempest and discord. And of these two contestants, absolute life and absolute death, one is a reality, the other a dream. But the resulting discord is not a dream; yet, being so closely bound to life, it is not an absolute negation either. Indeed, if the word death is to have its fullest hostile power it must be thought on as partial, or as a life-death relation. We can imagine a living body and psychic death, melancholia or, at an extreme, madness. Whatever form it take, it is, in its degree, horrible. Or we can let our thoughts dwell on a dead body yet a spectral, ghostly, continuance of the spirit; or again, we may consider the material body seemingly half-dead, putrefying but still horribly human, skulls in graveyards. We can imagine the dislocation of a love-contact by death or separation, a dear one gone while lover, parent, or son lives on. Or murder by which a living force thrusts a life into death. And so on. These are all *Hamlet* ideas. We see, then, that death, to be really horrible, must be parasitic on life. The emotions of life must be allowed to come into any discussion: indeed, death is a life-agony always. That is why Hell must be dramatized on the analogy of this world if it is to have any meaning. Death, to be powerful, must be parasitic on life. Try to make it more powerful, a thing in itself, so to speak, and it becomes pleasant. And this is merely an intellectual equivalent to a usual psychic rhythm: awareness of partial death, an almost complete submersion into absolute death, and a sudden recovery to awareness of the glory of life. The moment a negation becomes absolute, it swiftly becomes, next, positive: the only permanently negative force is conflict, disharmony, partial negation. That is why Shakespeare's work, finally, revolves on the tempest-music opposition, not on the life-death conflict, which, though important, is not ultimate.

Death, like evil, is to be seen as an inharmonious relation, not as a thing in itself: observe how death and evil are almost synonymous terms in the Bible and the poets. We must see death dramatically. It is an experience, and since it is an evil experience we find our poets and prophets creating dramas of immortality against it. For immortality will, likewise, be a drama. In Shakespeare we find a powerful immortality vision in *Antony and Cleopatra*. His final plays also dramatize the same theme: a conquest of death by life. We come back, therefore, to our old contention, that individual persons are unreal, that reality is always a relation, or experience. It is always dramatic. Death, or what we usually mean by death, is an experience of disharmony. For we always look at it from the emotional viewpoint of the survivor. In this sense the death-experience is only too real.

I proceed to make some diagrammatic illustrations. First, consider an individual's life cut short by death:

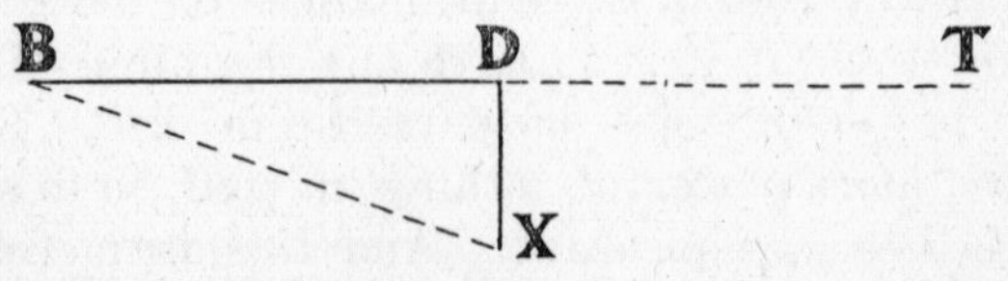

Born at B, he dies at D. His plunge into nothingness is represented by DX. Now this leaves us, his friends, with a sense of disharmony. It is to be noticed that I am not regarding his death, or even his life and death, in cold objectivity. I am visualizing a complex little drama, in which we, in life, have sense of our companion's death. So DB and DX are now two lines meaninglessly and cruelly divergent to us who live. We feel he should be allowed to travel on immortal in time to T, because BDT is a straight line and therefore harmonious. Yet it is hard to see how he can do this. Now one solution I have already clearly indicated. BD is his life, a complete and satisfying whole: there is no plunge to X, D is just the limit of BD. But it is hard for us to feel this. If we have any affection for him, we must think of his death as a big fact: the diagram needs therefore a death-line of its own. We observe that an emotion, our love, forces the creation of DX: DX is an emotional line. To remedy our dualism, I join XB. This line restores harmony and unity by completing the triangle. Incidentally, it also makes two angles, at X and B, which together equal the angle of our disappointment, XDT. Now our disappointment would be removed could we clearly understand the line XB. It may represent reincarnation; or, in that it remedies the mistake of DX, merely a potential higher state of consciousness in ourselves in which we give no reality to death; or an immortality in some way quite outside time. Certainly, it appears that in the line XB, rather than the time-stream DX, the true immortality will exist. So the whole reality of the man who died begins to assume, to us who survive, a triangular shape: it is, indeed, an area rather than a line. And this extra dimension is imparted to it by our emotional experience.

But we do not know how long to make our emotional line DX; and therefore XB, depending on the position of X, is likewise uncertain. The length of DX will, indeed, vary according to our sorrow: utter despair will tend to make it infinitely long.

Therefore, if we imagine that the final truth of the life-death resolution should include all possible positions of X, we have next the accompanying figure.

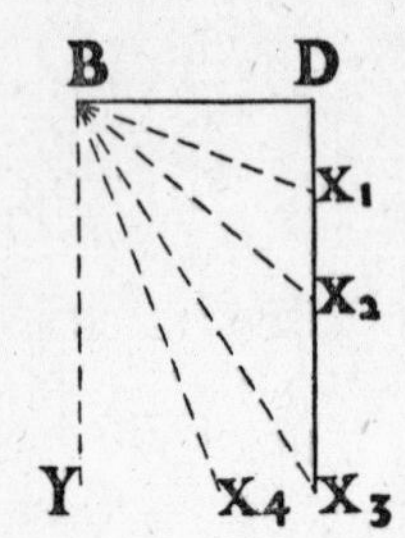

Now, though DX is unreal to the intellect, death being only a negation, our sorrow is clearly real: as an emotional line DX is no illusion. Our answers to these varied dualisms depend, too, on all the BX lines. If our sorrow is very great and the death correspondingly an infinite darkness, then BX can only meet DX at infinity: and, in this limiting case, it will appear as BY, perpendicular to BD. Observe, now, that we are filling up the area of a rectangle of infinite height, drawn on BD. From this, we may begin to see that the immortality of the life BD is not gained by stretching it out along BDT in time, but by completing a rectangle on the base BD. Eternal life is thus not a line at all: it is something less tenuous, an area, an emotional field, of which the time-line BD is only one tenuous section.

This, indeed, fits our facts. For if, in life or a Shakespearian play, we have sense of a time-sequence, we equally have sense of an emotional field, what I have elsewhere called the spatial quality. And this spatial quality may be seen as vertical. It can, of course, be either above or below the time-line, or both. The whole life, so to speak, may be thought on as lifted, generating a spatial area as it moves upward or, if we like, downward. The immortality is thus to be seen properly as vertical, at right angles to the horizontal time-stream. And this is a convenient way of showing ourselves how a single human life may be deathless, even though it ends at death. Its completed wholeness, rounded off by death and birth in time, is bodily lifted up in the other dimension, where it has unlimited freedom. Which other dimension will be seen to represent the world not of time but immediate experience, the mysterious drama in which we are always actors but which we never properly understand; the human drama which is also super-human, needing, as it does, at least an experiencing subject and an experienced object. For our vertical immortality is dependent entirely on some emotional experience. I am all the time showing how a human life is to be considered immortal by a surviving friend or lover, that is, how our past experience of the deceased is vital in eternity. Now this greater life or drama over-arching us like the sky, but yet a sky we often cannot see, is an immortal, deathless life. It is the life of experience in which we are actors from minute to minute but which we seldom see with clarity. Therefore we are not to see persons living on for ever in time: but rather our super-personal experience of them—for all experience is super-personal—from moment to moment, an experience composed of them and of us and transcending both, our greater dramatic life itself, is deathless, upflowering in the other element of eternity. We are the roots, splayed out in time: the flower is in eternity. Or, if we prefer it, our life is submerged in deeps we never guess: like icebergs that meet each other in the ocean and never know that nine-tenths of themselves and their kind are always hidden; and, still less, that it is the force of currents on those nine-tenths that does more to direct their movements than any breeze blowing on their tops.

I have said that our super-personal experience of persons or things is continuous in eternity rather than time. There is nothing distressing in this:

time is a wraithly line, our rectangle is a well spread out area. Time, indeed, is as a thread connecting rich pearls: those pearls are themselves of value, the thread is nothing. So, too, our experiences here on earth are infinitely valuable with a value we cannot always understand: and it is this very value that is suggested by my vertical and emotional eternity. Clearly, too, we have here an illustration fitting many facts. Those theosophical teachings which tell us that the soul dwells, as it were, apart, corresponding to the bodily life but not exactly involved in it, say something similar. Plato's ideal forms of which things mundane are but shadows might also be adduced. And when Jesus says that the children's angels always behold his father, he must mean something similar. But this vertical eternity, corresponding to every event in the time-stream, is not abstract, or unphysical: rather it is concrete, more physical than our usual life. It is itself our usual life in all its physical and mental richness. The very physical love-consciousness opens our minds to it; Shelley's *Epipsychidion* is a vision of it; it makes D. H. Lawrence's intuition of a potential life far richer than that we enjoy. For at any moment in life we may, if our minds and bodies are tuned to understanding, feel our experience developing vertically in the world of significance. Our time-stream is the pallid abstraction: one side only of the rectangle, with length, but no breadth. And when Jesus tells us to see with our bodies, he means that we should open our conscious life to the splendid bodily existence that we live.

The true immortality then is not immortality at all, a term only needed to counteract our death-thinking, but life itself: which life is, however, not at all limited to the time-line with length and no breadth, but has infinite and powerful expansion vertically. Immediate experience is our life, our immortality. And whenever we see anything immediately with some sense of its upward—or downward—reality, we know it, or rather our experience of it, to be immortal. This is what Browning means in *Abt Vogler* when he finely writes, 'There shall never be one lost good.' Such a vision Jesus preëminently possessed. And this faculty is really the same as the space-time vision I discussed in my first chapter. For, though it may not always think in terms of future time, the vertical understanding is invariably creative in time as well as eternity. The prophet at every moment sees life sinking its shaft to the rich centres below, and mines vertically before creating horizontally. Most of us live only on the surface. All such vision, revealing the true life at one point in the time-stream, inevitably affects that whole stream itself. Moreover, sight of the eternal world actually includes in it past, present, and future. Beatrice at one point knows what Dante is about to enquire. She says:

> I speak, nor what thou wouldst enquire, demand;
> For I have marked it, where all time and place
> Are present. (*Paradise*, XXIX, 11)

The eternal world transcends time altogether. Time is one aspect of it, but only that. Elsewhere Dante finely imagines this eternality:

> The celestial love, that spurns
> All envying in its bounty, in itself
> With such effulgence blazeth, as sends forth
> All beauteous things eternal. What distils
> Immediate thence, no end of being knows;
> Bearing its seal immutably impressed.
> Whatever thence immediate falls, is free
> Free wholly, uncontrollable by power
> Of each thing new . . . (*Paradise*, VII, 60)

That is, the immediately apprehended eternity is deathless. It cannot be controlled by 'power of each thing new', that is, time. And yet we must be able to regard the eternal world not as separate from the temporal, but rather inclosing it. The time-stream has, indeed, itself its vertical extension; it, and all that happens in it, is eternal. Time is merely one aspect of eternity. An immediate experience of eternity raises us to a height overlooking time, not turning our backs to it:

> Contingency, whose verge extendeth not
> Beyond the tablet of your mortal mould,
> Is all depictured in the eternal sight.
>
> (*Paradise*, XVII, 37)

All prophetic understanding penetrates to such an eternity. In working direct from the life-source it automatically reveals creative truth about life, and thus appears to foretell the future. The adept in such sight of eternity will be always fruitfully active, creative, in time. For time is never finally distinct from eternity, and any time-section has its vertical significance. Dante once finely imagines time as a root, eternity being the leaves:

> The vase, wherein time's roots are plunged,
> thou seest:
> Look elsewhere for the leaves.
>
> (*Paradise*, XXVII, 112)

Which well suits my vertical diagram.

Now such an understanding as I have outlined will tend to illuminate our poets at every turn: indeed, it is deduced from them. When the poet writes of immortality, for example, he may use the conventional image of a life persisting in time after death: that fits our minds well and is not to be ruled out as always inadequate. But poetry quite as often sees immortality in terms of birth. A short inspection of my first diagram clearly illustrates this. The dotted line represents immortality: it is called in to remedy the sense we have of death, and joins death to life. The immortality line, however, only touches the time-stream at birth. So, when a poet writes of immortality, he is often found, when his more intellectual understanding is working in terms of this figure, to be concentrating on birth, not death or future life. Continually the poets see immortality in terms of vague memory:

> Moreover something is or seems
> That touches me with mystic gleams,
> Like glimpses of forgotten dreams—

So writes Tennyson in *The Two Voices.* These are the 'visions of an antenatal dream' mentioned by Shelley in *Epipsychidion.* Shelley in his *Ode to the West Wind* regrets his divine childhood; so does Goethe in the Prologue in the Theatre of *Faust.* It is a usual complaint. Moreover, Goethe makes his Faust recall child-memories when, on the verge of suicide, he hears the Easter songs and angelic choir. When he was a child 'Heaven's love' floated down on him 'like a kiss', his soul was flushed 'with ecstasy':

> Then did a sweet, mysterious yearning
> Through field and woodland drive me ever on.
> Whilst in mine eyes the tears were burning,
> I felt a world within me dawn.
> My childhood's merry games proclaimed this music golden,
> Spring's free glad feast with it began;
> With childlike feelings now hath memory withholden
> Back from the last grim step, the man.
> Chime on, ye sweet angelic songs that thrall me!
> My tears well forth, to earth again ye call me.
>
> (23)

So the 'Choir of Disciples' is heard chanting how the risen Christ is 'filled with birth-delight'. Childhood is a recurrent theme of paradisal poetry.

Birth and childhood are, indeed, direct immortality impressions in poetry, called in often to oppose death. Here we see how child-thoughts blend with angelic music and how both save Faust. Immortality, as its name suggests, is intellectually a death-opposer. In dramatic action likewise the child or child-thoughts often champion life against death. And, just as birth memories suggest to the poet a diviner world, so the child-symbol is often impregnated with supernatural authority. Hence the child-symbolism throughout *Faust,* in *Macbeth,* and Shakespeare's final plays. In *Macbeth* the conflict is seen clearly as a death-child conflict: my quotation from the Apparition Scene early in this book shows that. In *The Winter's Tale* the Oracle demands that the lost child be found as a condition of averting tragedy; this play and *Pericles* presenting a conflict between evil, death, and tempest on the one side and love, the child, and music on the other. Birth-themes are often important in great literature. There is the divinely born Jesus, next the death-force that would destroy the Holy Child, and finally the resulting Massacre of the Innocents: and all this closely follows the story of Moses. But, like Fleance in *Macbeth,* the protagonist-child escapes. Birth is continually mysterious. Again, we have Macduff's mysterious birth and his accomplished revenge, despite the prophecy that no man 'born of woman' shall harm *Macbeth.* And with Tennsyon's King Arthur we have suggestion both of divine birth and illegitimacy, a twofold direction shadowed also in the Gospels. All these symbols suggest birth to be a mysterious and powerful life-force. And when we have, dramatically, a life-force embattled victoriously against death, therein is explicated an active immortality.

Consider, too, Wordsworth's *Ode on Intimations of Immortality from Recollections of Early Childhood.* This poem does not at all aim at revealing a life after death. Indeed, it says nothing whatsoever about it. It contrasts child-memories and the eternal world that is imagined both to pre-exist birth and enclose the life of a child, indeed all birth-radiance generally, with the death of the intellectual consciousness. Faust, as a child, knew a 'world' within him dawning. Wordsworth says the same. The child-consciousness is supposed to have direct knowledge of eternality, our vertical significances, as opposed to the time-bound thinking to which we are subject later. Such eternality is radiantly expressed here. The earth was then 'apparelled in celestial light', possessing 'the glory and the freshness of a dream'. But a 'glory' has now passed from the earth:

> Whither is fled the visionary gleam?
> Where is it now, the glory and the dream?

In this paradisal birth-vision, Wordsworth tells how the child, new-born from paradise, for awhile knows the paradisal joy. And it is to be observed that in this state it sees earth itself as paradise. The child eventually becomes a pure immortality symbol:

> Mighty Prophet! Seer blest!
> On whom those truths do rest,
> Which we are toiling all our lives to find,
> In darkness lost, the darkness of the grave;
> Thou over whom thy Immortality
> Broods like the Day, a Master o'er a Slave . . .

This is the centre of our ode. So Wordsworth begins by regretting his own lost paradisal child-joy. Next, he describes how the child generally is to be seen as fresh from paradise, 'trailing clouds of glory'. Last, he reaches his magnificent invocation to the Child. I cannot closely analyse the Ode here. But two facts emerge. Wordsworth sees immortality in terms of (1) the Child and (2) this earth transfigured by paradisal vision, the vision primarily of childhood, or manhood in certain blessed moments. This is the true poetic vision: Goethe's allegorical figure of poetry is a 'Boy-charioteer'. We may remember that Jesus tells man to 'become as a little child'. Blake has many correspondences. Indeed, poetry in general is packed with this child-immortality in various forms.

But in so far as the poet reaches back to a prenatal existence, he is doing little better than those who draw dream pictures of a future state. Of course, while he writes in concrete natural and human imagery, it does not much matter where he sets his stage; for he is writing then from immediate life experience. Dante's *Paradiso* is such a poem. And both states, that before birth and that after death, must always be considered creations from immediate experience. Wordsworth's Ode is great because of its imagery, its child-symbol, because it suggests that this earth might be a paradise were our minds awake, because what pre-existence it imagines is vividly depicted in glorious earth-imagery. Therefore our final immortality always becomes an extension, or expansion, of life itself: there can be no other starting point in any profitable analysis. Remember how we saw immortality as the vertical flowerings of a life not limited to the horizontal time-line. Such an immortality is sometimes hard to understand; but so is everything. It is, anyway, as easy to understand as life: indeed, it is life. Most people searching for immortality start by trying to understand death in isolation from life: which is useless. For, since such death is, if it is anything at all, then precisely and exactly nothing, there is clearly nothing to understand.

But our death-line was, emotionally, real enough. After death, there is certainly a sense of loss, a shadow cast by the life we loved. The death-experience known to the survivor thus reflects in the survivor the life of the being that has died. Now it is just this death-experience that is attacked in Shakespeare's greater plays. First, we have a pure tragedy like *Othello*. The hero, through his own sin mainly, loses his wife, and follows her to death. The Lear-Cordelia drama is similar. Then we have *Timon,* where the hero, finding the objects of his love all unworthy, seeks peace in death, seeming to follow his own homeless love into the eternal. Later there is *Antony and Cleopatra,* where the heroine, Cleopatra, loses her lover, and, left alone, first sees him as one with the glorious universe; next, triumphantly follows him. Here we get an immediate immortality intuition beyond the ordinary tragic acceptance. The tragic rhythms suggest that the love-experience is primary: this is what the hero desires. His loved one lost, the love-experience is next equated with death, the emotional death-line is drawn, and next the hero too dies to restore harmony. The chief mourner being dead, there is now no unrest. In *Antony and Cleopatra,* Cleopatra seems to know definitely that she is finding a universal love in death, a love of which Antony is one aspect. Here death is highly charged with positive meaning. Observe, however, that no one person is being considered alone: a disorganized life-death conflict is resolved dramatically, needing at least two persons.

Correspondingly, the later immortality visions, *Pericles* and *The Winter's Tale,* show also such a conflict. The two heroes lose their wives and daughters; endure themselves a period of deathly penitence; and, finally, receive again those they loved. The death-disharmony is conquered by a life-harmony. All these plays reflect the fact that death is a disorganized relation, like evil. Though Leontes has reason to feel that his own sin has brought about his suffering, Pericles, ethically blameless, seems to endure a closely similar penitence. Finally, the harmony is restored, life is victorious. We must see that these final plays present, as it were, an immortality both in eternity and in time. The dead wife is resurrected, the lost daughter found: that is, the love-experience is deathless in eternity and its creation active in time. Moreover, the child is actually born in midst of the tragic conflict: which suggests that the conflict itself is mysteriously creative. Two more points may be observed: the hero himself suffers partial death; and his loved wife is not exactly resurrected, but rather turns out never to have died. From which we may deduce: (1) That to be aware of death is itself a sin and indeed itself a sort of death, a death-experience; and, (2) that the death of a person is not a thing to be remedied and righted by resurrection, but rather a delusion. What seemed dead is really alive; there is no death, there are no dead. These plays present a dramatic explication of the fact that the death-experience is not final, and that life is harmonious. We must conclude that it is eternal with an eternity which in some sense includes time.

Shakespeare's final plays are plotted and woven to expand an intuition that has seen the eternal immortality of things temporal, the deathlessness of time itself or any section of time. They are immortality-visions in that death-suggestion is present, powerfully. But a direct sight of the eternal radiance ignoring death altogether will give us a simple life-vision such as Dante's *Paradiso,* where no death is apprehended. Death being comparatively neglected, this by itself—abstracted from the whole *Divina Commedia*—is not exactly an immortality work at all, but a creation direct from immediate paradisal experience, from the erotic consciousness which sees the earth with Wordsworth's 'vision splendid': hence the dominant part played by Beatrice and the frequent imagery of eyes, smiles, the romantic rose and sense-delight generally. The three divisions of Dante's poem give us, in Mr. T. S. Eliot's phrase, 'different states' of blessedness or damnation. Now these 'states' are 'experiences', and experience is a very earthly thing. Dante thus writes of this life, not another. Though the poem be as universal as anything ever written, the world of living men is not explicitly part of its scheme. And this is not strange, for that world is implicit in every line. So Dante's *Paradiso* may be taken as a prototype of paradisal poetry in general. The paradisal poets reveal essential life, their words are radiant with the life-consciousness. Wherever a poet describes with glistering words a glorious nature or a radiant love, we have such a paradise. This life-vision is the truth to which we aspire. But yet, again, there does in fact exist the death-consciousness. Therefore many great life-works, the New Testament, Shakespeare's final plays, *Romeo and Juliet,* Keats' Odes, are burdened with death-thoughts, and in varied ways seem to reveal, as it were, an overthrow of death: and these, in so far as they do this, are more properly then immortality statements. But in all our poets we find immortality and life finally interdependent: the one depends on an immediate experience of the other. Hence Wordsworth's statement, already quoted, that all our Elysian fields, Paradises, and Heavens express an immediate union with the world around us, a love-intercourse with life itself. Hence, too, the tremendous importance of the love-theme in literature. So Jesus tells us that the Kingdom of Heaven is within us, that our immortality may be possessed here and now. This is Blake's 'eternity in an hour'. No poet will be understood till we can properly be recipient to this immediately known immortality: we must see it wherever his vision sparkles and his words are fiery with delight. All our future paradises are, as Wordsworth says, dream-pictures presenting an aspect of the central, solid whole which is life. But the very essence of life is a present-future dynamism, and all immediate paradisal experience is creative. Therefore a future paradise may be a necessity to us: a reflection in our minds of the onwardness of life, demanding our creative response.

Immortality is then an experience, a life-experience, depending on a living subject. All my examples so far have needed this living subject and, indeed, this is our most important problem: hence, in Shakespeare's final plays, the hero himself does not die, or seem to die. His living experience of death is attacked by life, and conquered. But what of our selves, as subjects? How are we to understand our own impending death? First, we can say simply that such death is a pure fancy. No one can experience dissolution since experience needs a subject and an object: if, as in this imagined death, the subject is destroyed and there is no object, there can be no experience. And if it be replied that I, as a person, will one day certainly seem to others to disappear, I agree: but this brings in the objective aspect I have already discussed. My thoughts of my own death, moreover, are themselves merely drawn from awareness that others die: that awareness once removed, or vitally changed, I shall have no emotional, that is dynamic, consciousness of my own death. It will not be a significant reality. Each problem continually appears as but another aspect of our old drama. Indeed 'my own death' is usually a pallid dream, lacking creative significance. Death-thinking is always inbound with time-thinking, and that alone, being purely intellectual, becomes dangerous if intermixed with the wrong emotions. Certainly, to let emotions overleap the present is evil: Macbeth desires futurity, greedily devours future time or tries to, and this is all related to a death-consciousness and death-activity. So for me to fear my future death is evil, it is an unreal fear. There is, however, room for less emotional forethought. To plan ahead taking the present into account, is legitimate; to feel and think emotionally into the future through present facts is creative; but to fear is always psychically unhealthy. Hence Jesus counsels us both to take no thought for the future and to make plans carefully. Now all this illuminates our discussion: to prepare for my death may be wise, but to fear it anxiously is to fear an unreality. Certainly, the well-ordered life will both think and feel into the future only through the present: and to fear death infringes this law.

But people do in practice quite often think emotionally about their own future deaths, making an illegitimate abstraction from the dramatic interrelations of life-experience, and regarding themselves as solitary adventuring units. They are fear-ing unrealities: but let us suppose them to be justified. I will try to explain what immortality would mean in their terms. It will be directly concerned, not with a future changed existence so much as the life they have already lived. They will find, so to speak, that that life is not finished as they thought, but is still going on in the eternity dimension. Now we have evidences that many poets think somewhat like this. They imagine immortality as union with the best they have known in life. Thus Wordsworth dreams of his happy childhood, Cleopatra dies to meet Antony. That last is significant. To Cleopatra death is as her own life-experience of love and Antony: she goes, so to speak, to find union with the best she has experienced. St. Paul's desire to be 'absorbed by life' and certain ideas in Shelley's *Adonais* are close parallels. Similarly Keats wishes to die during the nightingale's music, to dissolve into it, and again imagines himself dying while enjoying a perfect love-union in his 'Bright Star' sonnet. A high life-experience may well seem to find perpetuation most easily if synchronized with death, and such mystic dying seems to the onlooker, who is here also the subject, to round off and complete life at a perfect moment, so that its wholeness may be the more beautiful in eternity. Faust finds Gretchen in Heaven, Dante Beatrice; and so on. The eternal world is the world we have already known, transfigured, at its best, so to speak. Its best moments give hint of its 'future' immortality; 'futurity' necessarily coming into the discussion through our trying to see ourselves as solitary units adventuring into death. Death is a marriage union:

> Fame, love, and beauty are intense indeed;
> But death intenser: death is life's high meed.

Keats means that death is the final 'experience'. But this is a death which is no negation: rather a consummation of life, a completing of it, the final sealing, stamping and posting of the letter. Such an all-inclusive death we find in Jesus' crucifixion: it sums up, completes, his life, rendering it fit, as a whole, for its eternal existence. Often death may be thus imagined. So much of our life, in the darkened consciousness, seems derelict and lonely. In death there is union. What was partial in life becomes richer in death: the battered nickel currency of time is new-minted in gold. Therefore, the richest joys such as romantic love and marriage are ever powerful in all high vision, in the poets and the New Testament. Eternity, thus known, is not life's end, nor the beginning of an utterly new existence, but rather, as St. Paul continually suggests, the consummation and circumference of all earthly experience and desire. Of this *Antony and Cleopatra* is our most direct expression. What seemed unrealized experience becomes, in that completed whole, final. Browning's *Abt Vogler* and the end of Pompilia's narrative in *The Ring and the Book* are also apposite. In the eternal marriage the blessed face and form is in our arms, our life lost in union with its life.

But an objection may be raised. I have shown how a life to an onlooker may be considered as bodily lifted into eternity; the whole life being immortal. But next, I have said that if we think in personal terms of our own death we may expect to find mainly our better and happier moments; whereas, according to my scheme, we ought to be faced through eternity with our sufferings and sins, and many awkward incidents we had forgotten: a cheerless prospect. But this is where Hell comes in. For, though the whole life must first be considered to persist, yet revelationary documents and common-sense too demand that somehow the good conquer the evil. Certainly, in temporal existence good is, on the whole, victorious: it is unlikely that evil should have equal rights with it in eternity. Now we must not think rigidly in personal terms. Remember that dramatic experiences only are the realities; which experiences have eternal growth. But harmonious experiences must be allowed a richer development than those purely evil: in fact, we would prefer the worst to be utterly destroyed. Therefore we may say that Heaven is the crop and harvest of harmonious and creative experience, whereas evil experience is annihilated in Hell. In so far as we attain union with the life-principle we are thus creating our own paradisal immortality.

In Dante's Earthly Paradise are two streams, Lethe and Eunoe, pouring down on two sides:

> On this, devolved with power to take away
> Remembrance of offence; on that, to bring
> Remembrance back of every good deed done.
>
> (*Purgatory*, XXVIII, 134.)

The taste of Eunoe exceeds 'all flavours else'. Thus the evil is dissolved away, forgotten. Not sinners, but sins, are condemned to eternal Gehenna. In a play where he more closely than elsewhere analyses divine and human justice, Shakespeare has an interestingly analogous thought:

> I have a brother is condemn'd to die:
> I do beseech you, let it be his fault,
> And not my brother.
>
> (*Measure for Measure*, II, ii, 34.)

In this scene Isabella's arguments are all of the sort sanctioned by the play's Christian philosophy: which relates this thought, through Shakespeare, to Jesus. All poetry works in terms of experience: everywhere we are most ill-advised to regard solitary persons as ultimate. Therefore Jesus' words about Gehenna, the destruction vision of Revelations, and Dante's Hell, all ultimately refer, not to people, but evil itself. Evil is banished to outer darkness, all death-experience condemned in some way to utter death. Often in those of Jesus' parables which are here relevant the reference to persons is not explicitly made: hence the truth of parables in general, lending themselves as they do to changing interpretations. But, even when such personal reference is explicit, we may still allow this interpretation, since such statements are ever verbal expressions, narrowed down to personal and dramatic terms, of a profound truth: that death-experience is eventually to die, evil-experience to be banished. It is, however, true that Jesus sometimes seems definitely to threaten actual evil-doers with Gehenna: but this may be the only image adequate to the situation and is to be seen as reflecting and dramatizing Jesus' experience of evil men. We must finally not regard even Jesus as a single oracular authority, but rather as the protagonist of a very complex dramatic art-form. Incidentally, we may note that neither a rigidly personal God nor Gehenna are given high poetic honours or imaginative emphasis in the New Testament. The positive and negative forces are rather life and death; and any imaginative understanding will pay exact regard to such matters of emphasis.

Sin is not, ultimately, part of the real man at all; or we may say that he only attains reality through harmonious experience, creative marriage-experiences of some kind. Hence St. Paul's statement that his 'sin' is not himself. Indeed sin, or any evil, is the enemy of man, not part of his immortality, like Hamlet's madness, which the owner disclaims as his enemy, as not part of his proper self. In Dante's Hell we can note, too, that people are there mostly through associations and experience—their own or Dante's—not only through personal faults. It may even seem that some are there through past suffering only: for to suffer is to partake of evil and partial death. Dante might have met the same personalities in Hell, Purgatory, and Heaven according to their various experiences: and, indeed, we who watch see Dante himself, the protagonist, in all three. His Hell is therefore the reflection in eternity of all evil experience: observe how the persons all are seen as recounting and reliving their earthly experiences. Such reflection, such disharmonious experience, is condemned eternally to darkness, to death. Only in this way can we see how Dante's Hell is a place designed, as he tells us, by a profound and universal love; indeed, it is the final signature of such a love. Certainly, if we think in terms of Heaven we must have a Hell too. Rightly or wrongly we are conscious of evil and suffering: somehow the negative forces—or our consciousness or experience of them, which is the same thing—must be slain. And when Jesus talks of the threshing in eternity by which the true grain is saved and the chaff destroyed; or when in Revelations the New Jerusalem is imagined in splendid triumph while all evil things are relegated to destruction; whenever such pictures are offered to us, we must think in terms not of persons but experience.

New Testament symbolism presents the complete life in a setting which negates causality and death. Jesus, says the Epistle to the Hebrews, may be called

'Melchizedek', that is, 'King of Righteousness', and King of 'Salem' or Peace. Now Melchizedek 'has neither father nor mother nor genealogy, neither a beginning to his days nor an end of his life, but, resembling the Son of God, continues to be priest permanently.' (Hebrews, VII, 3). Thus Melchizedek and Christ have authority, not through sacerdotal genealogy but their intrinsic 'life'. Such is 'one of whom the witness is that he lives' (Hebrews VII, 8). The author goes on to argue that the priesthood and its rules cannot attain to perfection: there is a limit beyond which they are sterile. At this point life itself, the creative principle, asserts its power. What he shows to be true of Melchizedek is even truer of the Christ:

> This becomes all the more plain when another priest emerges resembling Melchizedek, one who has become a priest by the power of an indissoluble Life and not by the Law of an external command . . .
>
> (Hebrews, VII, 15-16)

Observe how this supreme life-authority is related to existence without 'beginning' or 'end', since life-power is invariably to be seen as expressing an eternal reality not limited to our 'genealogies' and surface causalities; as originating not from other life-manifestations but from the heart and centre of all life; and therefore as 'indissoluble.' Only so can we understand, finally, any life, divine or human, or any art-form expressive of the true life. Immortality is thus not a past or future thing: rather something always at hand to be related to the principle of life. St. Paul tells us very clearly that we need not ascend to heaven, nor go down to the abyss, to find Christ: rather the 'word' is in our own hearts (Rom. X, 6). Immortality is not necessarily eschatological, save in poetic creations, where nevertheless it may be often best expressed in such forms. So Jesus has a divine birth and bodily resurrection: and a short inspection of these symbols shows them to fall into line with my other statements here.

Indeed, I have already referred to Jesus' birth, comparing it with other birth-themes in literature. Its divinity certainly recalls the poetic attitude to birth as something sparkling with the dews of paradise, something, too, divinely guarded and impelled. Moreover, Jesus' bodily resurrection is important: it suggests, like so much of St. Paul's imagery, that immortality flowers from physical life. In temporal terms it repeats the substance of my vertical eternity. We have already seen Jesus' life as a powerful life-force: here we note how it is completed at either end. Perfection in life is often in some sort to be seen as a blending of the spiritual and physical —these words being used in a crude sense. Now, whereas we too easily see birth in the false causal chain of the physical alone, we also tend, seeing the body decay in time after death, to imagine immortality as spiritual, since, the physical subtracted, there is little else, it seems, that can be left. Notice, then, how the divine birth and bodily resurrection oppose both faults. If we are to see any life in its wholeness, its every moment must be known as an incarnation, a blending of spirit with the physical; its birth we do well to regard primarily as spiritual; its immortality as physical. Birth and death are falsified in our minds by unjust abstractions: to see them aright, we must have them brought into line with immediate experience, we must see them as concrete and solid positive realities blending the spiritual and physical. Or again, the perfect individual life must be shown as possessing throughout, from start to finish, that positive interlocking with the mesh of all life which is too often lost when we abstract it from its dramatic context in the whole. Such reintegrations the Gospel story gives us. True, they remain mysterious to our darkened minds: a thought that nevertheless argues their necessity. These are universal ideas. Moses was said to have a similar mysterious birth; and Arthur. Resurrections have also been often asserted. Goethe's *Faust* likewise blends into the mysterious and divine at the start and the close. 'Whatsoever has no beginning', writes Sir Thomas Browne, 'may be confident of no end'. Conversely, to understand the origin of anything save in terms of the sacred principle of life is to know its death. Jesus' life-story is thus a true life-revelation throughout. For life itself, properly seen, has neither beginning nor end: it is only known by immediate experience. Thus God is the eternal 'I am'; He is the God of the living, not the dead, of the present and future, not the past. Life is always a present-future dynamism, and the past is only vital as an aspect of the present. So immediate life-knowledge is ever creative: creative in eternity, creative in that aspect of eternity we call time. As union in marriage is a surrender to life creative of life, so any union with our world is likewise a marriage to which we are dedicate from moment to moment. And in that marriage we create our own immortality.

Am I then in this essay denying personal immortality? Not properly. For what do we mean by 'personal'? Surely the word usually conveys only a quaint time-sequence abstracted from its varied dramatic contexts in life, a wraithly series, tenuous and fragile. Is this the real 'I'? Rather my proper self is the experiencing self, engaged from hour to hour in struggle, conflict, attainment, or union in some form or other: ever the more real for its loss in some wider engagement. Not less than personal, but more. If I am 'in love', I myself am lost in a glorious surrender: but I know myself so lost, and enjoy my greater life with full consciousness. Such is the super-personal immortality. Clearly, then, the succession of 'experiences' that make Shakespeare's work tell us not much of the 'personal' Shakespeare, the Shakespeare of long ago that Shakespeare himself would recollect in quiet thought after his retirement. But they are true biographical documents of his immortal, experiencing, self, ever lost in immediate issues, passionately creative, dynamic, in conflict, in love-union. For, to a final understanding, experience of disharmony is itself creative, has itself eternal glory. Our minds, in their darkness, crave for the destruction of destruction, and God, in his kindness, has promised them the Hell they crave. While evil is real to us, we must see it as marked out for death. But Dante's Hell is also a nobly poetic thing, possessing its own grandeur and beauty. So, with awakened sight, we may yet realize that there exists no disharmony, nor ever did, nor any destruction nor death to be destroyed. This is also the way to life. Our various paradoxes are all summed up and resolved in Shakespeare's line: 'And death once dead there's no more dying then'. Therefore all hell-visions, all death-visions are, in great poetic art, themselves creative, which potential glory in evil is reflected in the beauty of the poetry. For, finally, all evil is but an aspect of good, all death but an element of life. Dante's hatred of evil gives birth to his Hell: and that hatred, and therefore that Hell, are, in their degree, good. All great poetry therefore mirrors our experiences, our immortality. For Shakspeare's immortal self is like our own: the poet merely has the technical gift of expressing in words his own and our own life-experiences. It is the same with Dante. Our greater deathless selves are all alike. A poet's life-work is, indeed, always a record of his own, and our own, immortality; and this quality is reflected in the fact that it has in the temporal sequence an immortal persistence and appeal.

XI. EROS

BUT immortality cannot be fully understood save through a heightened consciousness, a purified consciousness. Continually in my book I have suggested that a state is attainable where good and evil are temporarily dissolved in beauty, and that poetry and prophecy both flower from and direct us towards such a state: which recalls the prophetic imagination of my first chapter. But I emphasize no impossible or esoteric experience. We have all known these intuitions. For consider: I am writing about life, and I am describing a life-intuition. Usually, we are but half-awake. Now the experience of 'falling in love' is an awakening such as that to which our poets point us. To the lover, all dualisms within a certain limited field are resolved: a miracle happens wherein there is no tension or antagonism between the ideal and the actual. Suddenly the actual has indeed become the ideal, the divine is incarnated in a human form. A whole universe separates such a sight from our normal clouded vision: it is so simple, there is nothing to explain; so profound, there can be nothing more to learn.

This is the purified consciousness, and from this consciousness, or something very close to it, all poetry is written. The poet, indeed, is always a lover. Dante in Purgatory is asked if he be the author of the poem beginning 'Ladies, ye that con the lore of love', and he answers:

> Count of me but as one,
> Who am the scribe of love; that, when he breathes,
> Take up my pen, and, as he dictates, write.
>
> (*Purgatory*, XXIV, 52)

Shakespeare is as decisive:

Now, for not looking on a woman's face,
You have in that forsworn the use of eyes
And study too, the causer of your vow:
For where is any author in the world,
Teaches such beauty as a woman's eye?
Learning is but an adjunct to ourself,
And where we are our learning likewise is.
Then, when ourselves we see in ladies' eyes,
Do we not likewise see our learning there?
O, we have made a vow to study, lords,
And in that vow we have forsworn our books;
For when would you, my liege, or you, or you,
In leaden contemplation, have found out
Such fiery numbers as the prompting eyes
Of beauty's tutors have enrich'd you with?
Other slow arts entirely keep the brain;
And therefore, finding barren practisers,
Scarce show a harvest of their heavy toil:
But love, first learned in a lady's eyes,
Lives not alone immured in the brain;
But, with the motion of all elements,
Courses as swift as thought in every power,
And gives to every power a double power,
Above their functions and their offices.
It adds a precious seeing to the eye;
A lover's eyes will gaze an eagle blind;
A lover's ear will hear the lowest sound,
When the suspicious head of theft is stopp'd;
Love's feeling is more soft and sensible
Than are the tender horns of cockled snails;
Love's tongue proves dainty Bacchus gross in taste;
For valour, is not Love a Hercules,
Still climbing trees in the Hesperides?
Subtle as Sphinx; as sweet and musical
As bright Apollo's lute, strung with his hair;
And, when Love speaks, the voice of all the gods
Makes heaven drowsy with the harmony.
Never durst poet touch a pen to write,
Until his ink were temper'd with Love's sighs;
O, then his lines would ravish savage ears,
And plant in tyrants mild humility.

From women's eyes this doctrine I derive:
They sparkle still the right Promethean fire;
They are the books, the arts, the academes,
That show, contain and nourish all the world;
Else none at all in aught proves excellent.
Then fools you were these women to forswear;
Or keeping what is sworn, you will prove fools.
For wisdom's sake, a word that all men love;
Or for love's sake, a word that loves all men;
Or for men's sake, the authors of these women;
Or women's sake, by whom we men are men,
Let us once lose our oaths to find ourselves,
Or else we lose ourselves to keep our oaths;
It is religion to be thus forsworn;
For charity itself fulfils the law:
And who can sever love from charity?

(*Love's Labour's Lost*, IV, iii, 309).

All learning, even, is here equated with romantic love and that with 'charity'. Compare, too, the emphasis here on the senses with that in the Gospels. The erotic vision, like poetry, pierces into life itself, its origin and fiery heart. Art and love are thus alike:

Transparent Helena! Nature shows art
That through thy bosom makes me see thy heart.

(*A Midsummer Night's Dream*, II, ii, 103).

Goethe's allegorical figure personifying Poetry is thus naturally described with highly erotic suggestion:

One must avow
Firstly, young and fair art thou,
A half-grown stripling—yet the women's pleasure
Would be to see thee grown to fullest measure.
To me thou dost appear a future wooer,
Frail woman's born and sworn undoer.

(*Faust*, 207).

The great poets very clearly express the love-poetry relation. It is, indeed, obvious. For poetry is creative language: and without a love-union there is no creation.

The poet sees with the romantic vision; he does not, indeed, write while saturated in its fire, but recreates his experiences in passivity. Thus poetry, like a human child, may be seen as resulting from this union, this marriage joy. That is why the poet's view of nature is so important. He sees not the clouded, muffled nature he, or we, usually see in our uninspired moments, but rather nature in its primal nakedness, its paradisal grace. Herein is our paradisal naturalism: something pagan, charged with eroticism, tingling with life. Dante's Purgatory and Paradise are full of such nature. Indeed, his Earthly Paradise is equated by him with the visions of paganism:

> They, whose verse of yore
> The golden age recorded and its bliss,
> On the Parnassian mountain, of this place
> Perhaps had dreamed. Here was man guiltless; here
> Perpetual spring, and every fruit; and this
> The far-famed nectar.
>
> (*Purgatory*, XXVIII, 145).

Goethe's Boy-Charioteer calls himself 'profusion'; 'I am Profusion, Poesy am I'. Profusion, guiltless profusion of all natural delight. To such a view nature appears, to use Wordsworth's phrase, 'apparelled in celestial light', with 'the glory and the freshness of a dream'.

All paradisal visions are thus derived from sight of what Shelley calls 'nature's naked loveliness'. This is the Earth-Spirit of terrible beauty that strikes fear into Faust. And this nature, radiant to these lightning visitations that make poetry, is far from 'nature' as we usually think it; as different, as the lover's bride from all other women; not even, finally, expressed in poetry without a certain loss and limitation. Thus the Earth-Spirit scorns Faust:

> Thou'rt like the Spirit thou graspest with thy mind,
> Thou'rt not like me! (15)

Indeed, there are two primary stages in reality: nature or man as they appear to ordinary consciousness; and nature, or man, as they appear to erotic perception. Between, we have poetry, art, religion, drawing their content from the authentic sight, themselves necessarily less than that primal wonder, aiming, however, to lift our minds towards it. Shakespeare is fond of comparing 'art' and 'nature' and our understanding must often then realize that two natures, the lower and the higher, are involved. Thinking of her dream-Antony, Cleopatra says:

> . . . nature wants stuff
> To vie strange forms with fancy; yet, to imagine
> An Antony, were nature's piece 'gainst fancy,
> Condemning shadows quite.
> (Antony and Cleopatra, V, ii, 97).

That is, 'fancy' is often more gorgeous than the actual: but the actual, illumined by the love-vision, puts all art to shame. Nature, properly understood, includes art. In *The Winter's Tale* Perdita tells how she will not have 'streaked gillyvors' in her garden:

> Polixenes: Wherefore, gentle maiden,
> Do you neglect them?
>
> Perdita: For I have heard it said
> There is an art which in their piedness shares
> With great creating nature.
>
> Polixenes: Say there be;
> Yet nature is made better by no mean
> But nature makes that mean: so, over that art
> Which you say adds to nature, is an art
> That nature makes. You see, sweet maid, we marry
> A gentler scion to the wildest stock,
> And make conceive a bark of baser kind

> By bud of nobler race: this is an art
> Which does mend nature, change it rather, but
> The art itself is nature.
>
> (*The Winter's Tale*, IV, iv, 85).

Throughout our thinking on art, religion, or life we must remember this upward development: the lesser nature, poetry and religion, the greater nature. That greater nature is the divine. Thus our categories represent really the natural, human, and divine. That divine is life: life itself in its profusion and richness, the life known temporarily to the lover. We do not understand our own life: 'Though all men live it, few there be that know it' (*Faust*, 4). Dante more than once compares art with nature. Art, he says, copies nature, whereas nature imitates the Celestial Mind. Thus nature is first, art second, in descent from God; and these two, he says, are, according to 'Creation's holy book', the 'right source of life to man' (*Hell*, XI, 100-113). This is, of course, the higher nature: a thing divinely originated, a paradisal wonder, the wondrous life of which we are part but do not always understand. The poets ever point us toward that nature, that life. And, thus pointing us to life itself, speak continually in terms of the erotic vision.

This vision is more than mental. It is not an attitude to life: it is life itself. To the lower, mental, consciousness the body of man may often seem ugly and unclean, nature herself drab and unpurposeful. This is because one small part cannot enclose the whole; the mind cannot know even its own body. The mental knows the mental, the physical the physical, but life only can know life. That fuller life circumferences both mind and body, its consciousness knows their true stature and their radiant strength. Such is the consciousness of love. And the union of lovers is an act of lightning beauty and resplendent, creative power; for then the life of an individual drinks power from that fount and principle of all life to which our thinking minds are but as sparkling pebbles to the sun. The union of instincts in one human being creates a miraculous knowledge: and this is love, and poetry, and religion. But the union of human lovers creates a yet greater miracle than these: a child. Life itself is greater and more miraculous than any mental or imaginative dynamisms. But poetry, like religion, would awake us to life, to that life and immortality too close for our false long-sightedness to visualize. Thus poetry speaks continually to awake the love-consciousness from which it is itself derived, and the greater Renaissance poets in this matter make a single statement.

Beatrice dominates Dante's *Divina Commedia.* We must notice that Vergil guides Dante through Hell and up the Mount of Purgatory till, in the Earthly Paradise, he meets Beatrice. Henceforth she is his guide. He is now lord of himself, there is no disharmony between his instincts and his will. He is beyond all dualisms. Therefore:

> To distrust thy sense
> Were henceforth error. I invest thee then
> With crown and mitre, sovereign o'er thyself.
> (*Purgatory,* XXVII, 141).

Poetry, and religion, thus lead us to the point where they may be discarded. Poetry itself is but the servitor to this love, and Beatrice, not Vergil, is the final guide to highest vision. Indeed, she originally sends Vergil to save Dante from the 'death' he is enduring on earth (*Hell,* II, 108): so that she is, to Dante, guide and saviour; indeed, she practically takes the place of the Christ. In the Earthly Paradise she appears in a procession, attended by figures symbolizing the Old and the New Testament, in a car drawn by the Gryphon. Now commentary has said that the Gryphon symbolizes the Christ. This may be legitimate. However, it is safer to say that it symbolizes more generally the union of the divine and earthly: Ariel and Caliban. Of course, the supreme example of this union is, to Dante and to Western civilization in general, the figure of the Christ. Whatever our exact interpretation, we see that Beatrice is given the very highest honours, being shown here as the culmination of Biblical revelation. She is greater than all poetry or nature:

> Never didst thou spy,
> In art or nature, aught so passing sweet
> As were the limbs that in their beauteous frame
> Enclosed me, and are scattered now in dust.
> (*Purgatory*, XXXI, 46).

And in her eyes Dante reads the ultimate mystery that he understands once again in the final vision of the circle of light: the mystery of dualisms transcended into unity, the mystery of the Gryphon, half-beast, half-angel:

> And then they led me to the Gryphon's breast,
> Where, turned toward us, Beatrice stood.
> 'Spare not thy vision. We have stationed thee
> Before the emeralds, whence love, erewhile,
> Hath drawn his weapons on thee'. As they spake,
> A thousand fervent wishes riveted
> Mine eyes upon her beaming eyes, that stood,
> Still fixed toward the Gryphon, motionless.
> As the sun strikes a mirror, even thus
> Within those orbs the twyfold being shone;
> For ever varying, in one figure now
> Reflected, now in other. Reader! muse
> How wondrous in my sight it seemed, to mark
> A thing, albeit steadfast in itself,
> Yet in its imaged semblance mutable.
> (*Purgatory*, XXXI, 113).

The *Paradiso* still further glorifies Beatrice—her eyes, her smile, her radiant light. He calls her 'the day-star of mine eyes' (*Paradise,* XXX, 76). His whole Paradise circles round his love for Beatrice. Nor is it any coldly abstract or intellectual love. It is more like a divine flirtation:

> Then by the spirit, that doth never leave
> Its amorous dalliance with my lady's looks,
> Back with redoubled ardour were mine eyes
> Led unto her.
>
> (*Paradise,* XXVII, 83).

Richly he sees and depicts her smile, 'painted on her cheek', her looks of love, her divine sweetness. Her 'laughing eyes' are said to 'scatter' Dante's 'collected mind' with their 'radiance' (*Paradise,* X, 58). In her all mysteries are resolved, all discord harmonized. To Dante the erotic ideal is directly to be equated with the ultimate mystery of the divine: Beatrice is, to him, the Christ.

In Shakespeare, too, love is shown as harmonizing human faculties. This is how Troilus describes his love:

> I take to-day a wife, and my election
> Is led on in the conduct of my will;
> My will enkindled by mine eyes and ears,
> Two traded pilots 'twixt the dangerous shores
> Of will and judgement.
>
> (*Troilus and Cressida,* II, ii, 61).

'Will' means 'passion'. Here the instinctive passion is 'kindled' by the senses and the final harmony, 'judgment', created. Notice that love rises here from 'sight' rather than vision from love. This recalls Dante's:

> Thus happiness hath root
> In seeing, not in loving, which of sight
> Is aftergrowth.
>
> (*Paradise,* XXVIII, 101).

Or again,

> . . . . . the wings
> Of reason, to pursue the senses' flight
> Are short.
>
> (*Paradise*, II, 56).

So keenly do the greater poets dissect the lightnings of intuitive delight. And Shakespeare is one with Dante everywhere in his noble surrender to this love-sight, this 'new nature', as Dante calls it 'knit by pleasure' (*Purgatory*, XVIII, 27). Heroine after heroine witnesses to Shakespeare's ideal. The Sonnets see the Eros in terms both of a fair youth—we may compare Goethe's Boy-Charioteer—and a dark lady. His most wondrous single human figure is Cleopatra. But from Juliet to Miranda and Queen Katharine his heroines are crowned and glorified beyond all other ideals but the divine. Indeed, in Shakespeare this love blends into the divine, as in Dante. The loved one is an 'angel', the place of love 'paradise', its home 'eternity':

> Eternity was in our lips and eyes,
> Bliss in our brows' bent; none our parts so poor,
> But was a race of heaven.
>
> (*Antony and Cleopatra*, I, iii, 35).

Love is the guiding star in life. It

> is an ever-fixed mark
> That looks on tempests and is never shaken;
> It is the star to every wandering bark,
> Whose worth's unknown, although his height be taken.
>
> (Sonnet CXVI)

Throughout Shakespeare love is associated with music and contrasted with all disorders, conflict, discords. Like Beatrice's eyes reflecting the mystic Gryphon, love in Shakespeare induces unity and harmony in a world chaotic with conflict. It is the guiding star in life: it is also the gateway to immortal life-in-death. This, the theme of *Antony and Cleopatra,* is found too in *The Phoenix and The Turtle.* Again, we have a resolution of dualisms:

> So they loved, as love in twain
> Had the essence but in one;
> Two distincts, division none:
> Number there in love was slain.

Shakespeare's world, wherein from the first the music of love was a dream-sweetness, a pastoral delight, at the last finds love the stalwart vanquisher of death. Even had the poet not written his last play *Henry VIII,* we could say, watching the love-victories in the final plays, that Shakespeare's love-intuition at the last was indeed close to, if not identical with, the Christian statement. In both death is put down by a love: which love is in both but an aspect of essential life.

It is the same with Goethe. Love, human, passionate, romantic love, is the very opening of the immortal day-stream, a deathless paradise, a conquering angel of life. Gretchen asks Faust if he believes in God:

> Faust: Thou winsome angel-face, mishear me not!
> Who can name Him?
> Who thus proclaim Him:
> *I believe Him?*
> Who that hath feeling
> His bosom steeling,
> Can say: *I believe Him not?*
> The All-embracing,
> The All-sustaining,
> Clasps and sustains He not
> Thee, me, Himself?
> Springs not the vault of Heaven above us?
> Lieth not Earth firm-stablished neath our feet?
> And with a cheerful twinkling

Climb not eternal stars the sky?
Eye into eye gaze I not upon thee?
Surgeth not all
To head and heart within thee?
And floats in endless mystery
Invisible visible around thee?
Great though it be, fill thou therefrom thine heart,
And when in the feeling wholly blest thou art,
Call it then what thou wilt!
Call it Bliss! Heart! Love! God!
I have no name for it!
Feeling is all in all!
Name is but sound and reek,
A mist round the glow of Heaven!

(*Faust*, 118)

Nowhere can we see more clearly how the poet would reveal life itself; and nowhere is it clearer that such revelation comes most naturally through erotic suggestion and incident. Should anyone desire to know whether the book I am writing urges a belief in a 'personal' divinity, I point to this speech as an exact answer. Observe also how close it is to that of St. Paul at the shrine of the 'unknown God'.

In *Faust,* too, we have the radiant Galatea in processional royalty like Beatrice. Her appearance culminates the whole Homunculus movement of the poem: she is the limit of his quest. His fire irradiates her:

What glows
Round the shell and around Galatea's fair feet,
Now flares out resplendent, now lovely, now sweet,
As if by the pulses of love it were thrilled?

He shatters his life-fire, spills his flame broadcast over his desire:

What fiery marvel transfigures the billows
That sparkling shatter them each on its fellows?
So shines it, so surges, sweeps onward in light,
The bodies they burn on their path through the night,

> And all round about us in fire is embosomed.
> To Eros the empire, whence all things first blossomed!
> Hail the Ocean! Hail the Surge!
> Girt with holy fire its verge.
> Hail the water! Hail the fire!
> Hail the chance that all admire!
>
> (305)

In Goethe's *Faust* the root dualism is that of fire and water. Here the two are blended. Homunculus' fire is spilt over Galatea, sea-goddess gliding in a 'shell-chariot', her attendants on sea-beasts. Galatea in her sea-paradise is irradiated by Homunculus' flame. Fire and water blend in love union, and the paean is raised to Eros, lord of union, of marriage, of birth. And the central piece in the whole of Part II of *Faust* is the *Helena* where the Faust and Helen union is dramatized, symbolizing a wider union to which I shall refer again.

Indeed, the poets one after the other present similar love-dreams, love-dramas. Lyric poetry continually treats of love, and the greater, more inclusive, works follow the tradition so exactly laid by Dante in which the divine is realized through some erotic symbol. Shelley's *Prometheus* is such a poem. The final victory is consummated by the union of Prometheus with Asia: in this union, all discords are harmonized, nature glorified, man and earth alike new-born in peace and joy. Asia corresponds exactly to Beatrice. Like Dante, Shakespeare, and Goethe, Shelley sees the divine in terms of a reunion, reunion with a lost lover; a lover, however, not time-wearied but more wondrous by far in this second discovery. Indeed, all poets tell the same tale. Even Milton's Paradise in *Paradise Lost* is just like all other poetic paradises: there is a sweet and fruitful nature, an unblamed joy, a happy human love.

The whole statement of our poets on this erotic theme is exquisitely repeated in Keats' *Ode to Psyche*. He says himself that he took unusual pains with it. It is, moreover, a poem directly forcing my main argument in this book, for here the poet sees Psyche as a new-throned goddess, receiving honours long-since due:

> O latest born and loveliest vision far
> Of all Olympus' faded hierarchy!
> Fairer than Phoebe's sapphire-regioned star,
> Or Vesper, amorous glow-worm of the sky;
> Fairer than these, though temple thou hast none,
> Nor altar heaped with flowers,
> Nor virgin choir to make delicious moan
> Upon the midnight hours;
> No voice, no lute, no pipe, no incense sweet
> From chain-swung censer teeming,
> No shrine, no grove, no oracle, no heat
> Of pale-mouth'd prophet dreaming.
>
> O brightest! though too late for antique vows,
> Too, too late for the fond believing lyre,
> When holy were the haunted forest boughs,
> Holy the air, the water and the fire;
> Yet even in these days so far retir'd
> From happy pieties, thy lucent fans,
> Fluttering among the faint Olympians,
> I see, and sing, by my own eyes inspir'd.
> So let me be thy choir, and make a moan
> Upon the midnight hours;
> Thy voice, thy lute, thy pipe, thy incense sweet
> From swinged censer teeming,
> Thy shrine, thy grove, thy oracle, thy heat
> Of pale-mouth'd prophet dreaming.

Again, 'eyes'. In all our great poets, 'eyes' are the finest faculty, 'the most pure spirit of sense' in Shakespearian phrase. The child, to Wordsworth, is thus 'an eye among the blind'. It is the same in Blake. And Jesus continually tells us to let the 'eye' be pure. So Keats is inspired by his 'eye'. But it is too late for superstitious reverence, no age for the 'fond believing lyre', 'too late for antique vows'. Not too late, however, for a profounder faith. This is the prophetic message we do well to hear:

> Yes, I will be thy priest, and build a fane
> In some untrodden region of my mind,
> Where branched thoughts, new grown with pleasant pain,
> Instead of pines shall murmur in the wind . . .

'Pleasant pain'. So always in Keats the final beauty does not exclude the darker essences. And this suffering joy brings 'branched thoughts' to luxuriant growth, honouring love, 'warm love' in his own phrase. No sainted ice-cold charity, but a warm, human love; rich, a dark rich wine, a dark rose, red with life.

Keats, in his short poem *On Death*, knows that the future doom of man is to 'awake'. He is the prophet of love: hence, too, the prophet of immortality. And perhaps the most beautiful love-song in our literature is also a death-song and a song of life:

> Bright Star! Would I were steadfast as thou art—
> Not in lone splendour hung aloft the night
> And watching, with eternal lids apart,
> Like nature's patient, sleepless Eremite,
> The moving waters at their priestlike task
> Of pure ablution round earth's human shores,
> Or gazing on the new soft-fallen mask
> Of snow, upon the mountains and the moors—
> No—yet still steadfast, still unchangeable,
> Pillowed upon my fair love's ripening breast,
> To feel forever its soft fall and swell,
> Awake for ever in a sweet unrest;
> Still, still to hear her tender-taken breath,
> And so live ever—or else swoon to death.

This is no tenuous creed of ghostly immortality. Rather a life in death which by including death and blending it with all life, shapes a present actuality, solid and warm and human, a love which is darker than death and more enduring bright than the eternal stars. Love, passionate love, is Keats' Gospel at the last. Like Jesus, he not only writes, but lives for his gospel, perhaps also died for it:

> I have no limit now to my love . . . your note came in just here. I cannot be happier away from you. 'Tis richer than an Argosy of Pearls. Do not threat me even in jest. I have been astonished that men could die martyrs for religion—I have shuddered at it. I shudder no more—I could be martyred for my Religion —Love is my religion—I could die for that. I could die for you. My Creed is Love and you are its only tenet. You have ravished me away by a Power I cannot resist . . .

'Love is my religion', a 'creed of love'. A pagan sentiment?

Our Christian religion to-day stands on the one side; Renaissance poetry on the other. Yet the divine books of our religion are poetic: they use all the usual symbols and imagery characteristic of pure poetry. Crowning these, we have the divine presented in human form, the Christ. Our poets, using similar effects, continually crown their visions with a human form deliberately given the insignia of divinity. The main statement of poetry is life and love, the erotic quest: the main statement in the New Testament is also life and love, universal love. The prophets of the modern world are the poets: they alone have streaked their pages with the sacred fire of life, they only transmit authentic, because original, statements of immortality; for Shelley's *Adonais* repeats no lesson learnt from books, but flowers direct from the origin of life. To-day, despite these convergent similarities, Shakespeare and the Bible, the prophets and poets, are on the one side, our established Christianity on the other.

For the Bible is itself richly poetic. So, though it aims to reveal the ultimate mystery, its natural effects are, as in all poetry, splendidly crowned by the erotic intuition. The Bible also uses, with power and precision, the symbol for full recognition of which I am appealing. The Song of Solomon is a noble paean of praise to love, and the little drama expressed is enclosed among the usual naturalistic suggestions: the child, the sun, harvest, flowers, glittering riches. This is typical:

How neatly you trip it,
  O princess mine,
your thighs are swaying like links of a chain
  that a master-hand has moulded;
your waist is round as a goblet
  (ever be it filled!)
your body a bundle of wheat
  encircled by lilies;
your breasts like a pair of fawns,
  twins of a roe-deer;
your neck like an ivory tower,
  your head on it lofty as Karmel;
your eyes like the pools at Heshbon,
  by the gate of that populous town;
your nose like the tower at Lebânon
  that faces Damascus;
your hair as glossy as purple—
  its tresses hold captive your lord;
'How fair, O my love!' he cries,
  'how delicious for love's delight!
You stand there straight as a palm,
  with breasts like clusters of fruit;
methinks I will climb that palm,
  taking hold of the boughs!
O may your breasts be clusters of fruit,
  and your breath sweet as an apple!
May your kisses be exquisite wine
  that slips so smoothly down,
  gliding over the lips and the teeth.' (VII, 1).

Few modern writers have compassed such spontaneous delight in physical beauty. This is the poetical soil from which Christianity rose. For this poem also sees its love-theme as something of transcendant power, potent as death:

> Wear me as a seal close to your heart,
> wear me like a ring upon your hand;
> for love is strong as death itself,
> and passion masters like the grave,
> its flashes burn like flame,
> true lightning-flashes.
> No floods can ever quench this love,
> no rivers drown it.
> If a man offered all he has for love,
> he would be laughed aside.
>
> (VIII, 6).

A human eroticism here expands and blossoms to a deathless, universal, conquering experience. Love is itself life; and it is the life-fire in such experience that makes man write his Bibles and creeds and systems of poetic fantasy. The usual argument as to whether the love in the Song of Solomon or the love and wine symbols in the work of Omar Khayyam are to be taken literally or symbolically is futile: since all love literature is to be taken both literally and symbolically. Until we understand, indeed, that the terms are synonymous we do not understand poetry; for to receive a poetic effect with due surrender to its fullest content is to see it widening into universal meanings.

In the Old Testament we have both a rich naturalism and a powerful eroticism. Without these, it would not be poetical. It is, indeed, too current an error to regard Israel's Jehovah as a limited personality, a wrathful human deity, hortatory and minatory. He is the god of the seas and winds and gleaming clouds, the fruits of the earth, the birds and trees, god alike of the dove and the leviathan, the cedar and the vine. He is a god of dance and song and human love. He is, too, a god of ethical fervour, exhorting his people to a righteousness demanded by the unswerving righteousness of the universe that surrounds them. This is typical:

> This is the word of the Eternal, who sets the sun to light the day and the moon and stars to light the night, who stirs the sea up till its waters roar, his name the Lord of hosts.
>
> (Jeremiah XXXI, 35).

And again:

> When poor, forlorn folk vainly seek for water,
> with tongues that are parched by thirst,
> I the Eternal will answer them,
> I Israel's God will not forsake them;
> on the bare heights I will open rivers,
> and in the valleys fountains,
> I will make deserts into lakes,
> and dry land into springs of water;
> I will plant cedars in the desert,
> acacias, myrtles, olive-trees;
> I will put fir-trees in the wilderness,
> and planes and cypresses;
> that men may see and understand,
> consider and agree
> that the Eternal's hand has done it,
> that Israel's Majesty has made it all.
>
> (Isaiah XLI, 17).

The Old Testament presents a religion which includes pantheism. Pantheism alone is passive, contemplative, and, if driven too far, sterile. The Old Testament excites to action, presenting an active, dynamic, and comprehensive religion, which includes not only nature but man, his aspirations, his world of good and evil. Thus 'the Eternal' is the god equally of the nesting birds and warring nations; of the ravenous tiger and human charity.

The finest visions of Hebraic prophecy are necessarily often couched in erotic imagery. So Isaiah sees his nation as the bride of the Eternal:

> 'Forsaken' shall no longer be your name,
> your land shall no more be called 'Desolate';
> you shall be 'my Delight',
> your land shall be 'my wedded wife',
> for the Eternal takes delight in you,
> and your land shall again be married.
> As a young man weds a maiden,
> so your Founder marries you,
> and as a bridegroom thrills to his bride,
> so shall your God thrill to you.
>
> (Isaiah LXII, 4).

Do we desire a more electric image? Or could we find a sweeter pathos and gentleness in any other symbol than this:

> The Eternal recalls you like a wife
> broken-hearted by neglect;
> 'But a young wife'—your God asks—
> 'how can she be thrown aside?'
>
> (Isaiah LIV, 6)

In Jeremiah, too, the Lord speaks at length of Israel in erotic terms, and then concludes:

> But as a wife betrays her husband for her lover,
> so you have betrayed me,
> O house of Israel—says the Eternal.
>
> (III, 20).

No poet can write for long without such symbols.

In the New Testament, I have already observed how Jesus continues this tradition, talking continually in terms of the 'marriage-banquet', and considering himself as a 'bridegroom'. The figure, as I have shown, is carried on by St. Paul. It is bright in Revelations. Here God 'has doomed the great Harlot who destroyed earth with her vice' (XIX, 2), but the Holy City is 'the Bride, the wife of the Lamb' (XXI, 9). Therefore,

> Hallelujah! now the Lord our God almighty reigns!
> Let us rejoice and triumph,
> let us give him the glory!
> For now comes the marriage of the Lamb;
> his bride has arrayed herself.
>
> (XIX, 7).

Again,

> And I saw the holy City, the new Jerusalem, descending from God out of heaven, all ready like a bride arrayed for her husband.
>
> (XXI, 2).

Prophet after prophet, poet after poet, asserts a divine betrothal. But there is little erotic suggestion in our organized religion. To-day, novels, theatres, cinemas are charged full with a seething eroticism: a passionate, dissolute, homeless but warmly human eroticism: while our religion, aloof, too often remains cold, chaste, and charitable.

The Old Testament continually presents human propagation as an ideal. 'Be fruitful and multiply'. Hebraic thought ever asserts creation. Creation is an end in itself, and what better thing to create than human beings? But also the prophets see another creativeness: a creativeness in life apart from propagation, a love not limited to sex. Now there are two ways of being thus widely creative: by art and thought, and by action and religious fervour. The Greeks chose the one, the Hebrews the other. But Greek culture ran its course to a conclusion, whereas the Hebraic power was less easily exhausted. It is, indeed, clear that so powerful a super-sexual life-message as Christianity could only come from a race with an excessively developed life-instinct. Christianity is exactly the culmination of the Hebraic ideal of physical propagation. The New Testament definitely supercedes that ideal by urging a new and slightly different creativeness. It is not enough to have children: the world is not yet fit for children. It is not enough to love passionately: the world is not yet fit for passion. Therefore, the love-instinct, the passion-power, must create this world. The New Testament does not repudiate sex as evil: rather, like all poets, it gives human union the highest imaginative honours. But we are urged primarily to rich life, life rich as a lover's, unlimited, passionately strong and deathlessly loving. Sexual love is often as an April day, uncertain, insecure: its obverse, hate, is only too ready for entrance. The love-experience is thus to be channelled, developed, to be allowed to irrigate the whole parched deserts of our lives from birth to death. Too often it is only a dangerous lightning in the midnight storm: rather, it might burn as a star, a dawn-star, herald of a greater sun. We are never urged to be hostile to sex, unsexual: rather, to be supersexual. To love universally, warmly, richly, yet with control: to know the awakened life that comes to the lover, possess it, powerful, invariable, and invincible. All the life-symbols found in the poets are thus found in the Bible.

Indeed, if a conflict has arisen between sex and Christianity, this is not because the two are opposed in essence but because they are so close. To two marriages we may be impelled: the one, as St. Paul suggests, becoming thus a rival to the other. At the birth of Christianity, St. Paul, though himself hating the false intellectual idealisms which denounced marriage as evil, yet counselled celibacy where practicable: so did Jesus, though not strongly. Clearly, that was necessary, if the new marriage was to gain any start in the human consciousness. Moreover, the ascetic ideal at its best has clearly accomplished great things. To-day, celibacy is likewise often advisable. It leads to a certain pressure on the passions, a thwarting and discipline, which may enrich and redirect those passions into high endeavour in art or service of one kind or the other. But, whether expressed in human marriage, social work, or art, the erotic instinct is primary: it is the life-instinct. Calling us to life, Jesus, indeed, is expressly calling us to awaken the very Eros in ourselves which we too often think that he rejects as evil. It is a sorry mistake. But it has, probably, been necessary. For centuries man has had to control and direct passions elsewise curbless: the discipline was needed, and hence asceticism was read into the Christian documents. We see in any great work what we need to find there. And if the past attributing of an exclusive ascetic ideal to Christianity proves its value as a temporary measure, then the clear sight we may have to-day that the New Testament stands for something more exciting than mere repression may argue that we have ceased to need such discipline. Indeed, to-day we must see in Christianity a message positive and assertive; physical as well as mental; exciting to action, exciting to life.

It is true that the problem of sex is not answered for us directly in the New Testament. Indeed, the book is remarkable in its baffling and ingenious indecisiveness. Enlisted for many years in the cause of asceticism, to-day it might be used to support a theory of free love. It refuses to settle the question finally: had it done so, it would have grown out of date. As it is, concentrating only on the essential life, it, like all poetry, is deathless. For poetry, too, likewise wakes us into life, and life is not limited to sex, though sex is one of its noblest, its most miraculous expressions. The Bible and the poets are one in using sexual symbolism to awake us to this life: and the life they would arouse may indeed include sex, but is not at all conditioned by it. Thus Shelley's *Epipsychidion* cannot be immoral. What we might call the corresponding 'action' in 'real life' would probably be immoral, because inexpedient in relation to society as a whole. But the poem is not that action: in that it stands instead of a reckless satisfaction of the life-instinct, it directly reflects self-control. Moreover, like all good art it rouses in us no instincts it does not in the same instant satisfy. It awakes us, and leaves us pleased with our awakening. All erotic symbolism in great art is similarly not only not immoral, but, in its blending of the human and the divine, one with the marriage symbolism in Christianity.

D. H. Lawrence is thus a true prophet, if properly understood. We need, however, to understand him more thoroughly than he understood Christianity. He was a poet of power standing at the threshold of an age that is about to see clearly, for the first time, the relevance of poetry to life. His doctrine, in so far as it is poetry, holds nothing new: he follows the usual symbolisms of Renaissance poetry. His insistence on primal passions, the deep origins of life, his cosmology that would make the sun a vital force, his sympathy with nature, all this is usual. In Shakespeare the sun and moon invariably take part in any scene of vivid life-instincts; Goethe knows all about the primal life-passions; all poets sympathize with nature. D. H. Lawrence was original only in seeing that something was to be done about it. What exactly, he did not understand. He saw a divergence between orthodox Christianity and his poetic intuition: and reiterated his intuitive dislike of conventional doctrines. He is a significant example of the power exercised by associations: he cannot see Christianity straight because it was falsely inculcated, or wrongly received, in his youth. At the last, he falls back on Revelations to supply him with the symbols he wants. That is not really strange, since his doctrines are expressly Christian in essence. His twin ideals of love and power reflect that love and power declared similarly by St. Paul; his hatred of abstract intellectualities when allowed sovereignty is expressly Pauline, and repeats the attitude of Jesus; above all, his assertion of the physical is but a modern reiteration of the Christian principle of incarnation. Moreover, in *Apropos of Lady Chatterley's Lover,* he counsels celibacy as a temporary measure in what he considers our present period of sex impoverishment. Many are 'happiest' if they stay apart—St. Paul's very word. For 'ours is the day of realization rather than action.' Again: 'On the whole it would be better if modern people didn't marry.' Lawrence also makes here a special point of the 'man to man' relationship, which is to be a 'blood-relationship'. Compare with this St. Paul's use of physical imagery to denote the intermesh of life with life in the Christian community. To many people to-day Lawrence should be a direct step towards a proper understanding of St. Paul.

His work is summed up in the exquisite short story, *The Escaped Cock,* or *The Man Who Died.* What he takes to be the Christian ideal is finely set beside the pagan and naturalistic. Jesus, alive after the crucifixion, realizes that he gave men but the ghost of love; and now surrenders to physical love-union with a priestess of Isis. And yet Lawrence here is directly Christian. First, in choosing such a theme, he is, so to speak, recognizing Jesus as the very type and prince of idealistic heroism; and, so doing, is able to drive in his positive doctrine that such idealistic values are not enough. But these are our facts. Jesus asserts that in a world which often negates life-instincts yet life may flower everywhere in all richness, if we but touch the life-centre. Necessarily, himself he shows often as fasting, weary, loveless, without wife or home: in spite of this, he takes pleasure in feasting, in human love and marriage, in domestic joy. All these are good. But man does not live by bread alone; nor marriage; nor even love. Only by life: and even life may at the last be sacrificed in life's cause. To essential life he directs man, and, claiming the key to those rich coffers, he necessarily shows his own life not dependent on any one subsidiary expression. Otherwise, that life would have been invalid as an example and encouragement to the thousands who, suffering in a world of negation, have drawn peace from watching his conquest. But it is true that, in so far as we see his life as shadowed by Calvary, we tend to see too powerful a negation: therefore we are told of his bodily resurrection. Otherwise, death would loom too large, and no negation must be allowed to shadow too darkly so positive a splendour. Jesus' life of sacrifice and final death is not the whole story, and Christian symbolism is one with D. H. Lawrence in asserting this. Now, whatever value we attach to a bodily resurrection, one thing is certain: it does not exclude the richest paradisal and physical actions. What was formerly denied is found more rich: the poets assert this whenever they describe the protagonist's reunion with a lost love. Therefore D. H. Lawrence has but expanded, in realistic narrative, the fact of the Resurrection, and mythically outlines Jesus' personal immortality. His story is a noble, and to-day very necessary, complement to the Gospel narrative.

This is no rash conclusion. For the New Testament is poetry and, being poetry, is close to life itself: and in life there is no grander thing than sex and its law of creative union. Poetry, indeed, can claim a high privilege: modern psychology states, what all poets have long known, that poetry flowers direct from the sex, that is the life, instinct. The Christian religion may likewise claim this honour. Poetry and Christianity, life-born, are life-creative. And, since life itself is ever our final revelation, and that revelation cannot exceed the primal splendour recognized by the lover, therefore poets write continually and necessarily of the Eros.

For Love strikes the human consciousness as a risen sun lights the eye. Melting the opaque darkness, it banishes a thousand phantasmas of death and guilt to take refuge in their own unreality. The former consciousness seems then but a stark and barren land, a rock-strewn desert, greyly corpse-like as some unlitten moon whirling on its loveless track, unknowing, unknown, through aeons of purposeless flight. But the romantic vision dresses all things with the pigments of life. It holds the blue of sky and sea, the green which is the vesture to the earth, the earth's rich brown, the yellow of ripe corn. It is red with the life that mantles a human cheek. Love wears Caesarean purple. It is throned above all other knowledges that man's experience may know, bearing the crown and the sceptre to whose authority all human allegiance unhesitatingly bows. Love needs no tuition. It is the instinctive meeting and mating of life with life. It is life conscious of life, the highest pinnacle of life to which we come, and, being itself life's richest flower, holds the seeds of birth and of creation. In love man is more than human, or, if you will, then only attains humanity. He is then a vessel charged with richest elixirs, and hence love's eyes are as jewels that sparkle with an unimagined joy. You must approach no philosopher nor theologian nor poet to learn the final truth of this: question only one who loves, or, having loved, instates daily in his mind carven memorials to that vision, yet preserving their marbled integrity. But perhaps only one actually indwelling in that radiance and drinking of that deathless rose may speak with valid authority.

Yet, if a writer were to engage under the banner of imperial love in any warfare of words, he might expect an easy victory. For he immediately enlists the deepest and most universal instincts, and can advance a myriad facts to support his argument. Romance is daily afire in a thousand novels, a thousand plays, a thousand films. Those, you may say, are trash: whereas we, of culture, prefer less sentimental themes. But what of our poets; of Dante, Shakespeare, Goethe; of Pope, Browning, Bridges; of the Bible itself? Are not Medieval and Renaissance literature alike dedicate to this Eros? And were not also the ancients? Does it not vitalize Oriental as well as Occidental myth and legend? You cannot wisely play tricks with the instincts of a race, nor

> . . . draw with idle spider's strings
> Most ponderous and substantial things.

To-day, eroticism is rampant, runs to waste, uncontrolled, unrecognized, unblessed by our religion. Tigers of passion, burning bright. A river dammed will surely overflow; so we have dammed, and damned, the divinest fire coursing in the human heart.

I have used the word 'divine' to express this ineffable vision or fact. It is both fact and vision. For in love the fact is afire with visionary meaning, an apocalyptic vision miraculously interfused with fact. This is the marriage of earth and heaven, this the eternal Virgin Birth striking ever a new wonder and a new glory and a rising life across our age-weary world of death; the life-bringing stream from mountains invisible come to irrigate our parched lands. The Christian dogma of the Incarnation directly reflects the erotic and romantic vision. So the Christ himself may become to his chosen lover alight with the plumed splendours of sunrise. Christian mysticism, all mystic experience, is, like the lover's vision, a flooding life, a wine of love. And wherever this Logos of Life is newly incarnated, all theological intellectualisms, all poetic systems, are but tinsel wrappings in that comparison. In the New Jerusalem there is to be no temple. Religion is indeed less than life, a child a greater thing than any creed: the Sabbath was made for man. Yet again, we cannot, or do not, live for ever so charged with vitality: nor would it be readily supportable to us, death-weakened as we are. Love is unruly, unmanageable often. Then again, like a fallen eagle, uneasy in this darkened world, beating fractured wings in agony, soiled and ridiculous; wide wings that late outspread in massive span, to fan the azure steppes and climb with sun-fixed undazzled eye the shimmering paths that upsweep toward the burning zone. Yes, love-sight is an unrest, very often; un-at-home with us here in our twilit world, too tormentingly beautiful, too cruel in its grace. There is no Hell like a fleeting glimpse of Paradise.

And yet I refer not solely to the love of man, nor of God, but remember rather our finer phrase 'to be in love with' God, man, woman, or, indeed, anything whatsoever. That love, not its subject or object, is primary. It is 'to be in life with' someone or something; to be alive and know it and, knowing essential life, to know also immortality. It cannot be further expressed. Words wrong the fire and music of its majesty. If the genius of Dante, of Shakespeare, of Goethe were to combine all three to turn into glittering words one of the thousand romances that thread our country lanes and cinema halls to-night, those words would yet be as gilt paper beside the solid gold they imitate. No art, no religion, is to take precedence of life itself.

The great god Eros to-day moves over us, shadowing our world with his wings, homeless awhile. A great God, searching for incarnation.

XII. THE ETERNAL TRIANGLE

NOW, since reality is to be regarded always as experience it is necessarily super-human. Yet it also quite clearly includes humanity. Experience as we know it is the product of two or more factors, one at least of which is human; and all human experience has an emotional element. Therefore no final statement about reality can be made by logic alone. Either our logic must be presented in words impregnated with emotional power, in which case the logic is far transcended, or some elaborate symbolism is to be employed. Jesus tells us that the Realm of Heaven is like, not a person, but rather a story. 'The Realm of Heaven is like a householder who went out early in the morning . . .' Only by making a story can he include the whole and rounded 'relation' he wishes to express. Reality to Jesus is primarily dramatic rather than personal: hence his use of these miniature dramas to express the divine. Reality exists in relations, in experiences. Drama is perhaps the richest literary art since it so clearly expresses these relations, presenting persons in vivid dynamic interaction. Often direct symbolisms help us to understand the central relation, as in Shakespeare: these simplify the complexity for us. We may have the chorus in a Greek Tragedy or the choric voices in Hardy's *Dynasts* doing much the same. Now, if we agree that in life as in literature reality is a relation, and that elaborate symbolisms are often necessary to simplify complex relations or experiences, we may begin to see how the Christian Trinity is a symbolic art-form, a kind of drama, reflecting and simplifying the complex interactions of our life. It may at first seem irrational; it may seem too elaborate and unrealistic; it may seem all sorts of things. But reality is not simple to our intellects. Remember how Browning chose to tell his tale in *The Ring and the Book* through many different persons, thereby attaining a richer statement than any single narrative, unless heavy with symbolic compensation of some kind, could possibly compass. The Trinity is, if you will, an arbitrary piece of symbolism. Nevertheless, it is drawn legitimately from the New Testament, and simplifies with amazing neatness the chaotic life we live.

It is a commonplace of current religious thought that many earnest minds to-day find no satisfaction in Christian orthodoxy. The average thinking man stumbles at dogma and doctrine. His spokesman, the literary agnostic, from time to time sets forth a volume of religious enquiry and, so far as may be, formulates the beliefs of modern scepticism. This is not wholly negative. There is something of solid and assertive faith left in most of our modern unorthodoxies. Failing all else, we still believe in values. But where a personal god or personal gods are concerned, we hesitate. This is too supernatural: and current scepticism is not supernaturalistic. It believes in nature. Now that is not, by itself, to be condemned: it depends on what we mean by nature. Do we mean the greater universal nature of paradisal poetry and the love-consciousness, or the parochial nature drained of emotional significance and submitted to the dissecting and analytic intellect? If the first, we are right to say that nature is all-inclusive; if the latter, we blunder. And that is where religion and poetic symbolism come in. Addressing themselves to the lower, they aim to induce the higher, consciousness. They assert the universal in terms of the particular; and, in so far as we understand this, we shall begin to understand the Trinity.

For poetic symbolism does not aim to say: 'this is so'. Rather it says, 'look at this if you want to awake'. And how can a coldly intellectual treatise on the evolutionary process and the emergence of human values properly awake the imagination? But, you will say, is Christian symbolism true? I answer that it is. An intellectual statement is true in so far as it is in alignment with the laws of mental reasoning. The human mind, however, is one part only of a greater life, and poetic symbolism is true in so far as it falls into alignment with life itself. Its truth lies thus in its creative power. Our thinking is hampered by our modern instinct to limit the word 'true' to one subsidiary meaning. Consider Wordsworth's lines:

> Type of the wise, who soar but never roam;
> True to the kindred points of Heaven and Home!

That is the sense in which we must read all greater 'truth'. And it is, finally, an inclusive sense; for mental truth too has to produce creative results if it is to survive: which is self-evident. But can our modern rationalist pseudo-philosophies thus qualify for life? Many things have been made the subject of worship in the past: animals, images, natural forces or human creations, the sun, the earth, heroes of history. But it is left to us to sink to the lowest of all superstitions and pay our adoration to a ghostly word such as 'values'.

Intellect and its systems change from generation to generation. The deeper things persist. Man still grieves in his bereavement, just as his forefathers grieved; like them, he falls in love; he endures their fear, their hopes, their disquiet, their passionate achievement. Facing the stars, dare we claim to have read their secret? We are all Chaldeans yet beneath the night skies. And the tiger burning bright in the jungle is to us, as to Blake, a yet fearful thing of mystic creation. These primal experiences endure, and to them our poets and prophets speak. Suppose we offer a realistic interpretation to-day of the Garden of Eden myth in Genesis: will our interpretation be suggesting new meanings a thousand years hence? A paraphrase may be useful but it is not poetry. We may rationalize the New Testament: but is our thesis, like it, immortal? And if not, which holds the profounder truth? Nor is great poetry only emotional. The true imagination circumferences both intellect and emotion: and to the imagination in man are addressed both poetry and Christian orthodoxy. Therefore the defence of Christian symbolism is easy: intellect can only assail it with bullets of cotton-wool.

Let me give a short example. Suppose one of our modern prophets to be writing his treatise to replace Christianity. He rejects all personal gods, and writes about the evolutionary process, man, and his place in nature. 'Man' and 'nature' are presented unpoetically, quite unapparelled in celestial light, so that we are regarding the lower, not the higher, nature, and man as he appears to the ethnologist or barrister, not as he appears to the lover. But, since this prosaic picture clearly leaves out very much, leaves out, for example, the stars and all that we feel about them, leaves out love and ecstasy of any kind, indeed, refuses to communicate the incommunicable, we have a sprinkling of words such as 'values', 'ineffable', 'spirit', and so on. These replace the rich symbolisms found in poetry and religion. But this does not at all dispense with symbolism: for these words are themselves but ghostly symbols, antic shapes parading in foolish pride, parodying the more vital and concrete creations they would replace and from which, if the truth were known, they have been abstracted. Science, by its very nature, refuses to formulate the inexpressible and mysterious: it is a 'knowing', as its name implies. Intellect, as its name implies, is an 'understanding'. But there is much that cannot be known or understood, not because it is too difficult but because it is too large for our minds. The intellect abstracts from experience only what it can understand. But the mysterious and ineffable are exactly the territories of poetry and religious symbolism. All our vague words—'spirit', 'values', 'ineffable'—are by them given local habitation and vital form. Poetry is creation. It explains that inexplicable mystery, life, not by any logical exposition, but by itself creating. For life can only be explained by life: it is incommensurable with pure ratiocination. Poetic creations are thus rounded, solid, radiating power and extra-dimensional to any conceptual abstractions. True, symbolism also falsifies life in varying degrees; but let us be receptive to the best and reject the worst. The word 'values' explains nothing, does nothing, means nothing. It is a dead and negative word. The Christian Trinity is vitally and variously alive: an active drama, a living force. A symbol is not a substitute for something more important: it is rather a dynamic and significant piece of imaginative life, addressed as much to the emotions as to the intellect. Such life, created by poet, prophet, race, or divine being, continues to exert power and suggest meanings: when it ceases to exert power and suggest meanings, it ceases to be an active symbol.

The Trinity is a symbolic art-form abstracted from the New Testament; and, like all art-forms, it discloses new meanings as the centuries revolve. This is the interpretation for our time. God the Father is the creating life, creator of all things, good and evil, beautiful and obscene, inscrutably existing in and beyond our world. He dwells in the enigmatic silences as a mountain crest beetles terrifyingly above the upturned faces of men; dropping his foundations also into those black gorges whither man will not wittingly turn his gaze. In the heights and in the depths he strikes equal awe. But God the Son is the friend of man. He champions man in this mysterious and unfriending universe. He teaches man life and love and suffers in his cause. He is Prometheus, and Jesus the Christ. Now these two persons must yet, in some sense, correspond; in some sense the God beyond good and evil, beyond life and death, must be the God too of human good and human life; the God of nature's cruelty must be also the God of human love. The paradox is asserted: but we reject the dualistic irrationality. Consider the circle, how beautiful its completion and perfected rondure; or the triangle which, however unequally it be drawn, remains yet more graciously beautiful than the most symmetric quadrilateral. Odd numbers are more profoundly mystic than even numbers, each in its indivisibility holding the secret of unity: the three angles of a triangle reduce to the angle of straightness, and for straightness and unity the mazed soul searches, baffled by the dualisms of the even numbers dividedly arrayed against themselves. We imagine time as a straight line and the immortality we desire is an infinite continuance, which we find nevertheless cut short by the precipitous oblique of death: so that experience seems to present to us the two arms of an angle, one stretching back to birth in time, the other slanting into the unknown; and there is no peace in such two-legged incongruities. Therefore the poet has well imaged eternity as a circle, or ring, of light, which eternity might also be imaged as triangular. So, too, we have a Third Person to complete the Trinity and resolve our dualism into geometric unity. This Third Person is the Holy Spirit. What is this 'spirit', this unifier, this peace-maker? The spirit of life, perhaps, inspiring planet and star, earth and sea, the serpent and the butterfly, the trees and grass; and also man and his ideals, his civilization and art. The life-spirit infuses all things, and all things are one as they are seen variously to manifest the one life that burns in creation. Or yet again, we may say that, in the light of this spirit, when filled with richest life, man himself ceases to see the dualism formerly so antagonistic; hearing rather the spheral harmony, knowing himself one with the universal. This life-spirit then has power to rend the veil of the good and the evil and expose the origin of life by love: by its visitation we are brought to recognition.

The Trinity thus dramatizes for us the experience of the race. It is not a statement, not a static picture, but rather cinematographic, a dynamic action, a multiplicity-becoming-unity. It is dramatic. Now, all our thinking depends on conceptions of discord and harmony, diversity and unity. The word 'universe' is significant. We have two sorts of experience: experience of unity, experience of separation; marriage and divorce experiences. Both must be included in a profound symbolism: both, and the dramatic interaction of the two, are found in this Trinity.

Dante's great poem is the supreme vision of harmony in all literature. His whole universe, Hell, Purgatory, and Paradise, the orb of earth, all are circular. Movement is ever circular: we have spirallings, wheelings, rotations and revolutions of all sorts. And, being thus circular, all motion tends to build a static, top-like, solidity, a stillness composed of motion. The final vision, seen first in the circles of Beatrice's eyes, is at the last a circle of light. Now Dante's task is to fit his life experiences into this circular harmony. The ultimate mystery is seen as

> Three Persons in the Godhead, and in one
> Person that nature and the human joined.
>
> (*Paradise*, XIII, 23).

That is, the Trinity and the Incarnation. Both are, of course, finally the same mystery: and, indeed, all dualisms are at root one. He harps ever on this theme:

> How much more
> Must the desire inflame us to behold
> That essence, which discovers by what means
> God and our nature joined!
>
> (*Paradise*, II, 40).

The mystery is profound. In modern phraseology, Dante is wondering how the divine harmony we imagine or have faith in can possibly be reconciled with the sharp dualisms we experience on earth. His poem continually subdues dualisms to unity: hence his circular technique and tri-form structure. But he does not ignore the dualisms; he does not concentrate only on the ineffable music. Somehow earthly experience is part of the divine harmony.

Indeed, all earthly experiences are to him but reflections of the triune drama, as indeed, they must be, unless we say that the triune drama is a simplified refraction of earthly experience: the two are but aspects of the one truth. So he writes:

> That which dies not,
> And that which can die, are but each the beam
> Of that idea, which our Sovereign Sire
> Engendereth loving; for that lively light,
> Which passeth from his splendour, not disjoined
> From him, nor from his love triune with them,
> Doth, through his bounty, congregate itself,
> Mirrored, as 'twere, in new existences;
> Itself unalterable and ever one.
> (*Paradise*, XIII, 48).

'Ever one': Dante stresses the principle of unity. And this 'unity' is here 'mirrored in new existences'. So the ultimate mystery of the Gryphon is perfectly mirrored in Beatrice's eyes:

> Within those orbs the twyfold being shone;
> For ever varying, in one figure now
> Reflected, now in other. Reader! muse
> How wondrous in my sight it seemed, to mark
> A thing, albeit steadfast in itself,
> Yet in its imaged semblance mutable.
> (*Purgatory*, XXXI, 122).

Her eyes are 'motionless', yet reflect the varying mystery. Motion and stillness are blended, division becomes unity. In Beatrice's eyes Dante seeks and finds his mystic resolution.

This, the mystery of the Incarnation, is also the mystery of the Trinity. Here is Dante's creed:

> In three eternal Persons I believe;
> Essence threefold and one; mysterious league
> Of union absolute, which, many a time,
> The word of gospel lore upon my mind
> Imprints: and from this germ, this firstling spark
> The lively flame dilates; and, like heaven's star,
> Doth glitter in me. (*Paradise*, XXIV, 138).

'God' to Dante is ever this triune mystery, this 'union absolute'. He avoids any rigid anthropomorphic image. Variously he finds titles for the supreme being: 'sovereign sire', 'primal mover', 'omnipotent sire', 'celestial mind', and so forth. Thus he uses varied periphrases: Dante never clearly visualises a single human God. Such an image may, however, be useful as a concession to human frailty:

> For no other cause
> The Scripture, condescending graciously
> To your perception, hands and feet to God
> Attributes, nor so means . . .
>
> (*Paradise*, IV, 43).

When Dante would be exact, his God is the 'triune love', or the mystic circle. Here is the ultimate reality, as a circle:

> Here is the goal, whence motion on his race
> Starts: motionless the centre, and the rest
> All moved around. Except the soul divine,
> Place in this heaven is none; the soul divine,
> Wherein the love, which ruleth o'er its orb,
> Is kindled, and the virtue that it sheds:
> One circle, light and love, enclasping it,
> As this doth clasp the others . . .
>
> (*Paradise*, XXVII, 100).

And there is the final vision, wherein the divine circle is mystically harmonised with human experience. Here, too, there is motion, an ever-changing wonder, yet no alteration nor variation, as when a circular disc revolves without visible movement:

> Not that the semblance of the living light
> Was changed (that ever as at first remained),
> But that my vision quickening, in that sole
> Appearance, still new miracles descried,
> And toiled me with the change. In that abyss
> Of radiance, clear and lofty, seemed, methought,

Three orbs of triple hue, clipt in one bound;
And, from another, one reflected seemed,
As rainbow is from rainbow: and the third
Seemed fire, breathed equally from both. O speech!
How feeble and how faint art thou, to give
Conception birth. Yet this to what I saw
Is less than little. O eternal light!
Sole in thyself that dwellest; and of thyself
Sole understood, past, present, or to come;
Thou smiledst, on that circling, which in thee
Seemed as reflected splendour, while I mused;
For I therein, methought, in its own hue
Beheld our image painted: steadfastly
I therefore pored upon the view. As one,
Who versed in geometric lore, would fain
Measure the circle; and, though pondering long
And deeply, that beginning, which he needs,
Finds not: e'en such was I, intent to scan
The novel wonder, and trace out the form,
How to the circle fitted, and therein
How placed: but the flight was not for my wing;
Had not a flash darted athwart my mind,
And, in the spleen, unfolded what it sought.

(*Paradise*, XXXIII, 103)

Dante thus blends the world of human experience with the divine harmony; the form of man with the circle. His whole poem creates a spheral music within whose inclusive love all life has its existence. His harmony is primary, the Circle, so to speak, given from the start. All else has to be fitted to it. Continually he reminds us that all reality radiates from the one heart and core: the mystic circle of the Trinity. All the circles, from Hell to Paradise, are concentric, out-rippling like circles radiating in water. It is important that we see what poetic fire may be struck by Dante from this Triune symbolism, or Circle of Light. And this we shall scarcely do unless we understand how closely these visions of union are in Dante associated directly with Beatrice. Not only is the mystery solved in her eyes before the Paradisal assent: through the guidance of her smile Dante reaches his final vision.

Goethe's *Faust* is a chaotic poem, an untrimmed natural growth. It has the rough turbulence of actual experience. Therefore it is to be contrasted with Dante's circular system. True, the poet knows that poetry itself discloses harmony everywhere, but it is an organic harmony, closer to life itself and therefore also less easy to discover and understand. This is Goethe's poetic philosophy on the matter. The poet, in the prologue, is speaking of his own profession:

> When Nature on her spindle,
> Impassive ever, twists her endless thread,
> When all things clash discordant, and but kindle
> Displeasure in the jarring notes they spread—
> Who with the dull, monotonous flow doth mingle
> Life, and doth mark it off with rhythmic swing?
> Who to the Whole doth consecrate the Single,
> Blended in one sweet harmony to ring? (4)

A very clear statement of the poet's profession. And, finally, the whole *Faust* does not betray this ideal. Yet it remains turbulent. As I have observed, its images are all very active, they rush past, jostling each other: the whole poem seethes and bubbles with disorderly but creative life. Faust, the hero, desires union, creative union. Now the Dantesque ideal of the universal harmony does not satisfy him. He gazes on the sign of the Macrocosm:

> Into the Whole how all things weave,
> One in another work and live!
> What heavenly forces up and down are ranging,
> The golden buckets interchanging,
> With wafted benison winging,
> From Heaven through the Earth are springing,
> All through the All harmonious ringing! (13)

But the sign of the Earth-Spirit appeals more to him: 'Thou, Spirit of Earth, to me art nigher'. He cannot, that is, contemplate union with the vast whole. Henceforth union with earthly life is his aim. Gretchen is a symbol of such union, his life at Court, the raising of Helen, his allegorical marriage with her, his warriorship, his selfless devotion to service, all are earth-unions, of the body or mind. The final perfect union, it is to be noted, is his union with Gretchen, not Helen, in Paradise: Helen being, after all, too allegorical and 'spiritual' a figure for Paradise and not comparable with the vital fleshly life of Gretchen. Paradise, to be Paradise, must hold all the vital warmth of earthly life at its richest. In *Faust,* then, union is reached most vividly through the Eros, just as in Dante the mystery of the Gryphon is reflected in Beatrice's eyes.

But there is much turbulence on the way. The root dualism in Goethe is that of fire and water, and both are turbulent forces. In all systems, we must find first a root dualism: Death and Life in the New Testament, God the Father and God the Son in the later Christian symbolism, the Circle and the Human Form in Dante, Music and Tempest in Shakespeare. Here we have Fire and Water. Both are fine natural forces, but the one, at an extreme, becomes satanic; the other, at an extreme, becomes purely good. Most of the poem balances them fairly equally, since Goethe does not recognize absolute negations at all powerfully. The poem is written around these two symbols; and, at a high point of vision, they are seen as unified. Homunculus, fire-spirit of Medieval aspiration, finishes his water-quest, his search for incarnate life, at the approach of Galatea, the sea-queen, and spills out his life-fire over her. The 'billows' are transfigured by a 'fiery marvel', each wave 'sparkling' shatters itself on its 'fellows'. All is shining, and 'sweeps onward in light'.

> The bodies they burn on their path through the night.

All is 'embosomed' in flame, and a paean is raised to Water and Fire and the Eros that unifies these two (305). I have quoted the passage elsewhere. But notice how our root dualism is unified, fire and water blended, by Eros. Which is repeated, vaguely, when the Chorus of Greek women tell of the 'son of Maia', a young hero here comparable to Homunculus and Euphorion. He steals Ocean's Trident, Ares' sword, Phoebus' bow and Hephaestus' 'pincers'. Water and Fire are well represented. But this child-saviour will not have Zeus' bolt, since to his delicate nature its 'fire' is too fearful. But he overcomes Eros and steals the girdle from Cypria. He is thus to be associated with water; with fire in so far as it is not dangerous; and with Eros and Aphrodite.

Goethe naturally sees the union of fire and water as the highest good. When the Chorus describe one of the many Elysian paradises in this poem, it is clearly, like the Classical Walpurgis Night, a very watery paradise:

> And in gentle wavelets gliding we endearingly will nestle
> To the far-resplendent placid mirror of these rocky walls.
>
> (355)

Again,

> Ever downwards, ever deeper, water we meandrous rolling,
> Now the meadow, now the pastures, then the garden round the house . . .
>
> (355)

And of all the gods Helios is to be most worshipped, 'the sungod first of all' whose fire ripes the vine and fertilizes all life. Air is too spiritual, earth too static, for Goethe: clearly, his dualism must have been the fire-water conflict. When he does draw an earth-paradise, he tends to make it liquid, as here:

> So the pure-born juicy berries' sacred bounty insolently
> Underfoot is trod, and foaming, spirting, foully
> crushed and blent.
>
> (356)

This then is the Trinity of Faust: Fire, Water, Eros. Or we might regard Faust, or mankind in general, as central and set between the fire-principle and the water-principle; at an extreme, between Mephistopheles and pure goodness, a contrast seen in Faust's crime towards Philemon and Baucis, setting their home in flames, and next his noble and altruistic devotion to water-labour at the end of his life. The final reality will, of course, blend fire and water always. As Faust ascends to immortal life, there are mountain-torrents and the dazzling light of Paradise: 'Still dazzles him the new-sprung day' (422). And Gretchen, or the Eros, is here again, as in Dante, the principle of union.

The Shakespearian dualism is seen in terms of tempest and music. Now, since both Goethe's fire and water are dynamic natural forces, these themselves correspond in one sense to Shakespeare's tempests which are, indeed, usually sea-tempests and sometimes also fiery, as in *Julius Caesar* and *The Tempest.* Also music corresponds to Dante's circular harmony. Continually in Dante's Paradise there is paradisal music. Dante's Hell, too, is full of Shakespearian tempests. In *Faust* at high paradisal moments we likewise have music. In Shakespeare, as in Dante, the music is often associated directly with the spheres, and those wider universal realities often shut from earthly sight; Goethe's 'macrocosm'. Thus both Dante and Goethe use Shakespeare's tempest-music opposition, but it is not properly the root dualism of either. For the one most strongly emphasizes harmony, even Hell being part of the whole circular scheme, whereas the other emphasizes turbulence. Or again, Dante concentrates on the divine and tries to fit man into a divine scheme, while Goethe concentrates on nature and tries to fit man into the natural scheme. I have already observed how exquisitely Shakespeare balances these. Tempests are often associated with fierce beasts and are themselves natural phenomena; whereas music is supernatural, the 'music of the spheres', the least earthly art imaginable. Therefore Shakespeare sees his world of men and women set between the natural and the divine, between the world of Goethe and that of Dante.

In Shakespeare, as in Dante and Goethe, the Eros is the maker of harmony. Tempest accompanies tragedy and disunion, music accompanies love and union. This is a consistent symbolism throughout Shakespeare applying to plots political, comical, tragical and metaphysical: discord is set against concord, severance against union. Sonnet VIII gives us a fine example of love-union reminding us of the family reunions in the final plays. And not only is it clear in symbols and plots, and in the Sonnets: in one poem, *The Phoenix and the Turtle,* it is more metaphysically expressed. As in *Antony and Cleopatra,* two lovers are seen to blend in a dying wherein love and death become but aspects of life, or we may say that love is the unifier, life and death the dualism, as in Keats' Bright Star sonnet. So the lovers die to life:

Here the anthem doth commence:
Love and constancy is dead;
Phoenix and the turtle fled
In a mutual flame from hence.

So they loved, as love in twain
Had the essence but in one;
Two distincts, division none:
Number there in love was slain.

Hearts remote, yet not asunder;
Distance, and no space was seen
'Twixt the turtle and his queen;
But in them it were a wonder.

So between them love did shine,
That the turtle saw his right
Flaming in the phoenix' sight:
Either was the other's mine.

Property was thus appalled,
That the self was not the same;
Single nature's double name
Neither two nor one was called.

Reason, in itself confounded,
Saw division grow together,
To themselves yet either neither,
Simple were so well compounded,

That it cried, How true a twain
Seemeth this concordant one!
Love hath reason, reason none,
If what parts can so remain.

This is a remarkably clear and direct expression in and of that higher mode to which I have elsewhere referred when using terms such as the 'prophetic imagination', the 'body-soul continuum', the super-human world of 'experience'. And it is here beautifully and exactly related to the Eros: the Eros in our poets continually appearing as the unifier. In this poem division becomes unity. 'Number' is slain in 'love'. But indeed, neither duality nor unity, both being 'numbers', exist. For here we see not merely a transcending of duality: rather the duality-unity dualism is itself transcended. Division is now unity, unity division, indeed the self is no more the self and reason the only irrationality. Here not only does tempest become music; the tempest-music distinction is resolved.

In *Antony and Cleopatra* likewise we find a similar statement. Tempests are stilled and music accompanies an apocalyptic tragedy. Throughout Shakespeare love and music are principles of union and harmony: in *The Phoenix and the Turtle* and *Antony and Cleopatra* the Eros actually unifies the profounder dualism of duality and unity; the tempest-music opposition is itself dissolved in music. And, indeed, these are but particularly striking examples of a universal poetic process, since all Shakespeare's tempests are likewise finally but an aspect of poetry's resolving music.

In any great work we can similarly expect a root dualism, and the unifying principle in literature is nearly always the Eros. Certainly in Dante, Goethe, and Shakespeare the Eros is the usual principle of harmony. It will be clear how I am leading direct to our understanding of the Christian Trinity. But first, I would point to Shelley's *Prometheus.* It is most interesting here, since Shelley evolves a theology in personal terms, and thereby challenges more direct comparison with Christianity. His poem, indeed, helps us to understand the Trinity. Shelley here dramatizes a universal conflict. Prometheus is mankind, or mankind's champion: it is the same thing, and often we must think of God the Son as likewise personifying humanity. Prometheus is noble, courageous, good. He suffers under Jupiter, a god cruel, stupid, and evil. This is so far an easy symbolism to understand. Prometheus corresponds to God the Son, and Jupiter to God the Father in so far as he is in conflict with the Son. We must always remember that the First Person tends to include evil as well as good; yet, as we shall see, Jupiter is not himself finally the real God. Now, faced by this absurd dualism of the good Prometheus being tormented by a stupid Jupiter, Prometheus' adherents, including his separated love, Asia, go to Demogorgon, to ask what and when the solution may be. Demogorgon is a strange spirit. He is darkly mysterious but kindly on the whole, and corresponds more or less to the human imagination: this is stated for us. Now, exactly as Faust has to descend to the Mothers, and also get help from the learned Wagner before reaching Helen; and as Dante has to go through Hell with Vergil before ascending Paradise with Beatrice; as all great poets have to burn through their satanic visions and intellectual agonies before creating their resplendent paradises; as, too, the intellectual reign of the Law and sin preceded the freer life announced by St. Paul; so, before Prometheus and Asia are joined in happy love, there is this descent to Demogorgon, creature of dark thought and consciousness of evil. He is said to know all things. Questioned on various ills, he answers, that they are due to the one who 'reigns', that is Jupiter. Behind Jupiter, however, there is 'Almighty God'. Although he is supposed to be all-wise Demogorgon cannot answer the problem of evil completely, but he can foretell the fall of Jupiter. Jupiter, the medium through which evil works, begins to appear insignificant. The time comes, he is thrown into the abyss. Prometheus steps free, and all nature joins in a paean of joy as he wins his long-lost bride, Asia. She is transfigured, music breaks out to honour the reunion and the new radiant life to be.

The marriage union of Asia and Prometheus is our Paradise. It is not properly eschatological: rather a heaven entwined with earth, an earth irradiated with fire-dew of the divine. It depicts, like Revelations, the establishment of the Kingdom of Heaven. And Shelley's theology is close to the Christian symbolism. Prometheus is the Christ, or mankind at its best; Jupiter corresponds to Satan, or the Satanic attributes of the Father; and 'Almighty God', who is suggested to be ultimately responsible for Jupiter's evil, is definitely God the Father. Now Demogorgon only exists while Jupiter rules. He represents the dark imaginations of man, probing evil, willing its end, inspirer of satanic visions. He is explicity related, like Goethe's Mothers, to a stern and grim eternity. And he goes into the abyss with Jupiter. He is therefore to be equated vaguely with Goethe's Wagner in his gloomy medieval room, more directly with Vergil in Dante. He is the Third Person of the Trinity blackened by the dislocation of the Father-Son harmony. When Jupiter gives place to 'Almighty God'—who does not appear, but must be allowed to cover all things and the final paradise—and Prometheus and the universe are at peace, Demogorgon exists no more, vanished into the abyss. And Asia now assumes new glory. She is transfigured at the final apocalypse, the symbol of love and beauty and union.

I have said that God the Father must be allowed to include evil. This is only partly true. If we are to see evil in a single theological person, it must be in the Father, since Satan is not personified in the Trinity. But the truer solution is to be found in terms of the Father-Son relation. The Holy Spirit cannot exist in its bright splendour when the Father-Son relation is starkly out-of-joint: it is then Demogorgon, a dark agony, a lonely progress in the imaginative world. But it is always trying to assert unity: like all poetry it would unify the Father-Son dualism, and hence Demogorgon's interest in Jupiter's downfall. Jupiter is finally unreal, only a false aspect of Almighty God as he appears while the God-Prometheus relation is disorganized. Conversely, when there is perfect harmony, Asia may be best allowed to represent the Holy Spirit, now incarnated in love. All our erotic symbols, Beatrice, Cleopatra, Gretchen and Helen, Asia, all are unifiers. All correspond to the Holy Spirit: they are incarnations of that spirit. The divine life is incarnated in these marriage unions, and in the new elixir flooding and tingling through all nature when the poet creates his paradise. And in this way we must always regard the Trinity: it is a drama, like *Prometheus*, of disunion-becoming-union. Satan is not part of this ultimate reality; he is not personified; not real, as a unit. Rather he only exists in so far as the Father-Son relation is out-of-joint, often seeming to usurp then the place of either the Father or the Holy Spirit. Or, better, we can say that the Holy Spirit is itself but an aspect or condition of a Father-Son harmony, becoming at once the Evil Spirit whenever the Father and Son are in conflict. Just as death is finally to be seen as an inharmonious relation of life-elements, so evil is a dislocation of things good: no negations have any individual strength. Remember, too, how in the poets' symbolisms all evil satanisms are usually to be related to a distorted and obscene sex-desecration, all harmony to a glorified sex-love. Such evil is ever seen as a homeless, unincarnated desire. Thus the Holy Spirit, until incarnated in some union, is itself in part evil: only in incarnation is it 'Holy'. And to-day for us it is far too wraithly, too 'spiritual', a reality. But the Eros we understand, we know its power, in poetry, in life. The Holy Spirit is thus to be directly equated with the Eros.

In the poets evil is related to severance, loneliness, and darkness; it originates in some mysterious sex-desecration; and it is associated with unrestful aspiration, unruly desire. In the Bible sin likewise originates in close association with sex. Throughout the Old Testament the God-man relation is out-of-joint and the world darkened by evil. The Hebrew prophets, and indeed their whole nation, endure a lonely quest. In the Old Testament, too, is the profound myth of Babel: through unruly aspiration, man is divided against man, there is error, misunderstanding, severance. Men speak henceforth in various tongues. Now, just as in the poets misunderstandings, errors and all evils are finally resolved by a paradisal union with a victory for the resplendent and fiery-bright Eros, so in the New Testament the tragedy of Babel is reversed. At the coming of the Divine Life-fire at Pentecost, differences are levelled, man with man is unified, difficulties of language and all barriers to communion mystically removed. Ever in the poets the Eros corresponds to the Holy Spirit, or, in better phrase suggesting incarnation, the Sacred Life. Further, when we see that the poets ascend from life-effects generally through the Eros to the divine, whereas Christianity moves from the same life-effects, including erotic suggestion, to a more universal love, and so on to divinity, the necessity of our equation becomes patent.

This Eros will cover the whole domain of art. Art and the Sacred Life are one. Hence Goethe aptly shows his Boy-Charioteer, an Eros figure personifying poetry, as dispensing Pentecostal flames to the chosen poets:

> A flamelet that my hand hath sped
> Glows upon this and yonder head,
> From one unto the other skips,
> Fastens on this, from that one slips;
> It flames up rarely like a plume
> And swiftly gleams in briefest bloom,
> Yet oft without acknowledgment
> It burns out sadly and is spent.
>
> (210)

To the poets, art and the Eros are one, and both are always unifiers and makers of harmony. Moreover, Goethe writes of 'holy Poesy' (350), for both poetry and the Eros are also one with the Holy Spirit or Sacred Life. Nor will this understanding be dangerous on ethical grounds. I have already shown that art and high symbolism are not to be too rashly impugned by ethic: elsewise we risk crucifying every saviour in turn. The erotic instinct is both the gate to evil and the way to paradise. We need not to neglect it, but see rather its own potential excellence and sanctity. So in Revelations we have the Harlot set beside the Holy Bride. Therefore Christian Orthodoxy lacks an essential understanding of its own symbolism. It fails to channel the erotic instinct. Vast areas of misery to-day are to be directly related to our refusal to recognize the royalty due to this passionate God of Love.

A symbol is no slight thing. It is a Sun whose attraction drinks the Ocean on which it burns. In its passivity and mystery it yet draws adoration from thousands, centres their hearts on it so that those hearts find therein a serene freedom and joy, absolving and absorbing all guilt, channelling the passional instincts, purging, purifying, healing. We want this health-bringing life-symbol to oppose alike our shallow cynicisms and neurotic sanctities. The Eros in man to-day is doubly-portcullised in dark bondage and, crying for liberation, it finds no champion for its cause save in poetry and the arts. But were such a divine Eros, in beauty of eye and limb, to replace in our visionary thinking that third spectral figure in our Trinity, untold millions, their inmost souls hungering for a warm and human, not a ghostly, love, would have found release there, and happiness. It is, indeed, no unknown spirit, no ghost however holy, that reconciles us to that tremendous dualism of the unknown God beyond good and evil and his children and their God of Love who strive for good alone. This dualism is resolved by the Eros in man, by this only. The sacred life of art, born from desire and love, has alone this visionary quality whereby we see the Good and the Evil slain together on the altar of Beauty: which vision is always a life-bringing and creative thing, leading, not to evil, but good. This indeed is, and must be, included in our understanding of the third Divine Person, since this Eros alone, in life or art, habitually resolves our dualism. This is our surest approach, following as it does Renaissance poetry and the nature of man, to contemplative understanding of the Triune Godhead.

I know that many sincere Christians find their resolutions in Church teaching, and are satisfied; for all I urge is already implicit in Christianity. But it is not widely recognized, nor are its implications always followed in practice. It is still possible to think Shelley an unchristian poet; or Keats.

It is still possible to think that the erotic theme of a cinematograph romance has nothing whatsoever to do with Christianity. I ask then that Christianity sanctify the Eros and all great art at least, allowing all this to be, at its best, included within the third Person of its Trinity. And I ask that we cease to betray the Christian law of Incarnation by continuing to refer to the 'Holy Spirit', or, worse still, the 'Holy Ghost'. 'Spirit', to-day, suggests a pallid spiritualism rather than the warm breath of life; 'ghost' suggests not life but death, and therefore evil. Words are dynamic things, and mean what they mean, whether they should or not: the organic life of language caring no whit for derivations. Let us lay this ghost and incarnate this spirit. This is the New Incarnation. I ask that we recognize the Sacred Life alike in poetry, and Christianity, and human love.

Then once more we shall see the Triune Godhead reassume the blaze and grandeur it held for Dante. We do ill to wrong its majesty with our sorry understanding. For this is the noblest piece of symbolism the race has produced. Our Church too often tries to defend its belief in a personal God: it does not, however, or should not believe in any such God, but something far more complex: the Mystic Trinity. Nor is this to be unfaithful to Jesus' intuition: for it is for us to believe not directly in Jesus' God, but rather in Jesus' belief in, and experience of, his God, and the Sacred Life it has created in St. Paul and other Christians. God, Jesus, and the divine life-stream and love-stream welling from that fountain; this is our Trinity. The Trinity is, indeed, a necessary complement to the New Testament, which alone would seem, to our darkened minds, to lack that philosophic and intellectual design possessed by our other poetic systems. And the meanings of this Trinity are infinite. Call it a time-succession. God the Father is then the Creator God known vaguely to primitive peoples; the Son is Jesus the Christ, bringing in the Christian era; and the Divine Life of the Christian Renaissance I herald in this book. So we have the Creation, the Incarnation, the New Incarnation, or Renaissance. In the Shakespearian system this corresponds to Tempests, Mankind, and Music; the natural, human, and divine; Goethe, Shakespeare, Dante. It may likewise suggest the absolutes of the True, the Good, and the Beautiful: or we may reverse the order. But we can go on indefinitely finding new and ever new meanings.

For this is more than a picture-language: it is dramatic. Reality only exists in experience and experience can only be expressed in drama. Now not only is the Trinity a mystic drama of differentiation-becoming-unity, but all drama tends to create a mystic trinity: the hero, his desire, and some impedimenting force. So we have Faust, Gretchen, and Mephistopheles; for Goethe's Devil helps to prevent the perfect love to which Faust aspires, and at the last tries to drag Faust from union with that love. Or again, in Shakespeare, Othello, Desdemona, Iago; Hamlet, the good he loves, and the wicked world which denies his aspirations; Leontes, Hermione, and Leontes' tortured memory of sin and death. And so on. Hence our term, 'the eternal triangle'. Triangularity is eternal, eternity best imaged in circular or triangular form. Three is a divine and mystic number. And it is mystic because it is rooted in the drama of our ordinary lives. There are three persons in our grammar: myself, yourself, and the rest; and Greek nouns had three numbers: singular, dual, and plural. Now all drama tries to build harmony from this triangular scheme: either by a happy ending, or a tragic grandeur. So the Trinity is both one and three, three and one. It asserts the dynamic interaction of unity and multiplicity. All our experiences may be divided into those of union and those of severance; marriage and divorce experiences. We live in alternation from one to the other. When we, the sons of God, are severed from our father and the sacred life, there are three gods in the Trinity; but, again, we find union and there is created a new harmony, there is then a oneness transcending theology, for a while. The Trinity is thus creative: and indeed the number three is the number of creation: two elements are blended, married, to create a third newness. Hence the three dominating persons, husband, wife and child, in *Pericles* and *The Winter's Tale,* plays which are, as it were, pure myths of creation. Hence Jesus and his God, that is Jesus' experience of God's fatherhood, the Jesus-God union, creates the Sacred Life of the Christian World.

Indeed, this symbolism is universally valid. For we are distraught continually by the dualisms of experience. All great literature has its root dualisms: without them there could be no dramatic action. So in our lives, within our horizon are rich plains and sun-glittering peaks, towering eagle-flights and melodies of air and water; yet also dark abysms, in whose slimy depths serpents coil their inhuman hatefulness, creatures whose existence is, it would appear, an obscenity and disgrace to creation. From these our baffled gaze returns perplexed and searches inwardly for resolution. Though banished for awhile by metaphysical argument, by love or faith, yet the good and evil remorselessly return, plaguing us with ambiguity, and the boa-constrictor drinks the same air fanned by the royal eagle's wings. But love or mystic sight or simple joy of any kind is the resolver; a spark leaping antagonistic poles, ablaze in the dark; lightning that hovers and is gone. When such dualistic pain and such resolution ceases to hold meaning for us, then the Trinity may appear but an insubstantial dream, and some other symbolism of East or West dethrone the Triune Majesty. But till then this unfitting and unnatural differing between what is, or seems, and what should and must be, this consummate artistry yet inextricably twined with so inscrutable an inconscience in creation, is more real, more daily part of our experience than any one person we know or any sight we see. The Trinity is a sublime poetic abstraction from racial experience in the past, a sublime foreshadowing of its futurity. Like all fine abstractions, it has a permanency denied to phenomena, but it also shares with poetry the vesture and rounded completion of dramatic symbol. Being dramatic, it is presented in human terms: for we know no nobler nor any more significant shape than that into which life has chiselled the mind and body of man. Humanity alone can tap the deeps of humanity, and that is why Shakespeare is so transcendent a poet. But yet the Christian Church does not believe in a 'personal God', save for purposes of prayer, wherein nevertheless it generally and rightly includes the name of the Christ. It believes in the New Testament, that is, in Jesus' experience of God; or in the Trinity, that is, a superpersonal relation, something complex, dramatic, and dynamic. The Trinity reflects the fact that drama is the only perfect statement and that experience is the only reality.

The Trinity is thus the most sublime simplification of human destiny ever imagined. Current agnostic speculation is often but a paraphrase of this eternal triangularity. Who will prefer a paraphrase to poetry? Moreover, all Western religious poetry is herein crystallized. The polytheistic symbolism of Hellenic religion blends with the monotheism of the Jews. In the Trinity, the Three in One and One in Three, the Olympian and Sinaitic hierarchies meet.

This Triune symbolism is a reflection cast by human existence, as it were, on to the heavens above, that we may there observe the eternal essence of that Life in whose drama we are actors; uplifted, as the Greek heroes are uplifted, to blazon with jewelled constellations the heroic arch of night. This is the eternal drama of Good, Evil, and Reconciliation; or, put otherwise, Life, Death, Resurrection; divinely and mysteriously set over us, like some majestic Southern Cross hung athwart our darkened seas. By contemplation, we are here to understand the drama of our existence. Like all high dramatic art, it tunes our minds to consciousness of the life we live and suggests an awakening to us while we sleep. But when, by its own activity, by love, or any ecstatic experience, we indeed awake, the Trinity, as formulated by intellect, may cease to have meaning. There is a point where symbolism is known to be provisional only. The symbols of religion and poetry are thus not addressed to that consciousness which it is their aim to awaken, but rather to the consciousness they would expel: all religious dogma is as a match to light a blaze in which its own illumination is lost. Symbolism is dynamic, and in its proper activity functions as a gear-change from the secondary to the primary consciousness. This is how and why all poetry and symbolism is dynamic and creative. Therefore, in our intellectual and unawakened life, this symbolism is, and must remain, valid. No enlightened discussion of this, or any other profound matter, can proceed save in terms of variable consciousness: indeed, the assumption, or rather recognition, of these twin modes is the root dualism of my book. When humanity, in all its activities, in sorrow and pain and fear, can yet preserve a radiant peace in knowledge of its own sacred life, then perhaps the Trinity will be dead; its dramatic persons dissolved in the one blaze they have created. There will be then no philosophy, no theology, no poetry. At the hour of that flaming apocalypse when the Kingdom of Heaven is finally established on Earth or Earth ascended into Heaven, neither will Heaven be Heaven, nor Earth, in that music, be any longer Earth. These things, however, are beyond words, and vain.

XIII. THE SACRED BIRTH

THE final reality is Life and beyond this we may search no farther. That is why 'life', not 'God' or even 'love', is the key-word to the New Testament and the poets. Jesus' 'God', at the last, forsook him. But the great principle of Life, the 'living God' of the New Testament, has ratified his sacrifice. Jesus' Mother was made pregnant by this Sacred Power; Jesus himself, the Son of Man, being thus also the Son of Life. There is no sin comparable to blasphemy against the 'holy Spirit', that is, against the sanctity of Life (Matthew XII, 31-32): hence Jesus' condemnation of all who wrong children, and St. Paul's denunciation of any sin against the physical body. Life is likewise the origin and purpose of its manifestations. But we recognize many enemies to life: evil, fear, death. Against these are enlisted our sciences, philosophies, and theologies, and all religious and poetic symbolism. They are all right and none wrong: or, conversely, all wrong and none right. Their values vary from age to age and place to place. Life is right and Death is wrong; so all fertile thought, and especially religious and poetic symbolisms, are mainly right, being creative, life essences. But no logical statement can be, by its logic alone, either right or wrong save at the cost of being both: its worth lies in its vitality. Hence the paradoxes that characterize prophecy and poetry. And yet intellectual formulation is useful, indeed of the very greatest importance, provided we do not expect it to prove or to create. It may be very powerful when serving the higher visions, but only in such service will it be truly confident and safe from its own inherent contradictoriness. In this book, for example, there are, no doubt, many minor and surface contradictions. You find them bristling unashamedly in St. Paul's Epistles. They are not to be feared, however. For, since all the important statements here are as lines radiating from one centre to a circumference, there can be no intersection. Any contradiction could, therefore, be readily shown as apparent rather than final. But, in writing of poetry and religion it is, indeed, most urgent that we recognize this interpretative function of intellect. Properly used, intellect is always interpretative: hence its derivation. It is a means to understanding, and never itself creative unless blended with emotion, vision, instinct, or whatever we choose to call those richer qualities that vitalize our literatures and religions.

Now, since important statements on these big matters must never fall any further than is absolutely necessary below the higher realities of poetic creation, love, and life, it will be clear that as many of our concepts as possible should suggest life-realities and life-processes. That is why I have built this book on such terms. At the start, I treated poetry as a blending, or 'marriage' of essences, showing it to be thus as an 'incarnation', and therefore a 'creation'. I analysed its newness, its 'virgin birth'. Poetry has been shown, also, to be closely related to the sex or romantic instinct, a true flower of purest life. The poetic substance, too, has been seen ever as a life-statement, crammed with life-suggestions, a creation splendid with created and creative imagery and symbols: the death-visions being, of course, but the obverse of these. I have shown that the main themes in poetry are related to the erotic experience, the marriage-experience. And reality itself I have continually asserted to exist only in some 'experience' or 'relation', a blending and marriage, or, oppositely, an antagonism and divorce, of two units. Never must we for too long regard individuals in lonely chastity. In the mental as in the physical world creation and life exists only by continual unions. Love, it is said, makes the world go round. And our life on earth, whether physically married or single, is clearly but a succession of marriage or divorce experiences: interests and antagonisms, friendships and enmities, creation and destruction.

And all this that is true of poetry applies equally to the Bible. It also, and our interpretations of it, are to be known by reference to these life-suggestions. The New Testament asserts not any rule of behaviour, but rather a radiant life. So all poets and prophets are similar in their main statements, they are winged messengers from Paradise foretelling and inducing our heritage of richest life, descending to fire our hearts with immortal possessions. In this book I have abstracted certain dominating symbols. But that should in no sense suggest that the New Testament or our poetic visions are, in their mass, mainly irrelevant. All vitalized imagery, metaphors and symbols, all richly inlaid imaginations, are everywhere significant. And from all these we find emerging a radiant nature, a glorified humanity. That humanity, at its finest transfigured by poetic vision and erotic perception, blends into other mysterious symbols, angels, seraphs, God. The romantic perception of life is the heart alike of Christianity and poetry.

I have tried to show the relevance of poetry to Christianity and the relevance of both to life. And in my assertion that the poets' imagery is everywhere vitally significant, aiming to awake and direct us, I only follow the New Testament. It cannot be wrong to say that pure poetry, however pagan, has something that may enrich our Christianity, since Jesus' teaching is unique in this very respect: that he does not so much lay down a code of ethics, or a rigid theological belief, but rather himself aims at enriching human life with poetry. His ethic is paradoxical, and his theology vague: but his imagery and symbolism is consistent, and on that he bases his teaching. He is, indeed, ever making that transference from the poetic to the actual world which D. H. Lawrence aimed to perform; thus, in Johannine phrase, representing the incarnation of the divine Logos in human life. And every true poetic interpretation has a similar purpose. Jesus' disciples ask him why he always speaks in parables; and he answers, as might a modern poet asked to interpret his own work, that he aims to let those see who can, but does not even wish to be clear to those who have eyes, but do not see. This is not only irritability, though there may be an element of that in it: rather it is sound psychology. In any case, it is better for Jesus' hearers to remember his story without seeing the interpretation, than to remember the interpretation while forgetting the story: for poetry is more important than any paraphrase. We must see Jesus, then, as preaching not merely a poetical doctrine, but rather a doctrine of poetry, telling man to live the poetic world, to contemplate the birds, the vine, the harvest, the luxuriant growth of the seed, the quiet but gigantic powers of natural law. He urges us to creative life, like that we find in a poet's imagery. A mustard seed's faith can thus move mountains: for a mustard seed grows by the mighty strength of that same life which not only plants and overturns mountains, but sets the planets in their courses, and makes the stars to flame.

Jesus thus channels the whole realm of the sacred imagination and relates it to life. The poet makes metaphors. The true Christian lives them, his thoughts and acts unfurling into leaf with the ease and unhindered strength of spontaneous life. All of us know the wonder and delight that can be experienced through a heightened consciousness, stimulated by drink, by erotic fervour, by art or religious mysticism. These all, in their different ways, draw the curtain and display the life-drama in all its excellence, its colour, its song and music. But they are all, in their degrees, difficult; some are usually inexpedient, all may become dangerous. Religious ecstasy may be immoral as drunkenness. Life is what we all desire: but we must beware how we grasp at it. An authentic experience may, in its suddenness and transience and consequent reaction, prove destructive; lacking solidity, permanence, and creative power. Now all poetry incarnates these life-instincts along creative rhythms, and hence its dominant theme is the Eros. It displays it before us in action, in success or failure, relating it to affairs in general. Poetry aims to channel and direct the erotic life-instinct. But poetry is not enough. Next, poetry itself must be incarnated in action, given gradual development and expression, out-flowering in the whole life, not limited to the sudden and short-lived blaze and lightning dangers that too often characterize the erotic experience, nor only a thing of poetic understanding, an inward and meditative act unrelated to outward affairs. True art and true morality both are as creative, natural growths. The poets all seem to regard their work in this way. Shakespeare compares poetry to vegetable life:

> Our poesy is as a gum which oozes
> From whence 'tis nourish'd; the fire i' the flint
> Shows not till it be struck; our gentle flame
> Provokes itself, and like the current flies
> Each bound it chafes.
>
> (*Timon of Athens*, I, i, 21)

Poetry flowers organically. It is thus here said to be more like water, the 'current', than the sudden 'fire': a comparison to be related to Goethe's fire-water opposition. It is a 'gentle flame'. And Keats tells us that poetry must come naturally as 'the leaves to the tree'. In his *Defence of Poetry* Shelley compares poetry to the first 'acorn', which 'contained all oaks potentially'. So, too, Jesus sees the divine truth as growing plant-wise: as a seed destined to become a vast tree, as a harvest crop, as a growth brought about by God, not man, the plant springing up in the night, 'no man knows how'. Erotic experience in life is a sudden blaze: but poetry, Christianity, and my assertion that the Eros is to be equated with the Divine Life, all these point, not so much to any riotous and blazing extravagance, but something creative, a 'gentle flame', an organic growth. Symbolism and poetry, dealing in essences so bright with splendour that they may be dangerous and difficult when too rashly expressed in action, are not themselves those actions: indeed, they are our only safeguard against rash life-expressions. For they stand in their stead, universalising and directing what were else a selfish and limited satisfaction; reminding us ever that we only attain reality in relation to the dramatic whole of life. Poetry and all high art induce harmony, they do not lead to immorality: they raise no desires they do not in the same act satisfy. And the actions which correspond truly to the rhythms of art are properly creative, not rash; wise, not destructive; enduring and powerful and good.

So Jesus speaks in poetry. 'Without a parable spoke he not unto them'. And he plants his teaching, leaving it to grow organically. Not by man's endeavour but by God's. And he was right. It has done so. This is what Jesus says:

> The Realm of Heaven, he said, is like a grain of mustard-seed which a man takes and sows in his field. It is less than any seed on earth, but when it grows up it is larger than any plant, it becomes a tree, so large that the wild birds come and roost in its branches.
>
> (Matthew XIII, 31).

Again:

> It is with the Realm of God as when a man has sown seed on earth; he sleeps at night and rises by day, and the seed sprouts and shoots up—he knows not how.
>
> (Mark IV, 26)

The great God of Life makes the seed grow, as He thinks best; and all growth is miraculous. Jesus' words here are exactly similar to Shelley's description of the functions of poetry: which is not at all strange. For consider our Renaissance poets. They are the prophets of the modern world. I have shown that the New Testament is throughout poetical, and that poetry itself is ever an incarnation. Poetry and Christianity can therefore never be distinct, and no Christian prophet can properly be independent of the poetic world. The Realm of God can thus scarcely be considered to have flourished wholly, or even mainly, on unpoetical soil. Moreover, if we regard our greater Renaissance poets, Dante, Shakespeare, Goethe, Keats, Shelley, for example, we shall find that, even though they may not always outwardly subscribe to Christian doctrine, and often are definitely antagonistic to the Church, they all are throughout impregnated with Christian feeling, and are, by virtue of this and their own intrinsic poetry, prophets of that greater poetic Christianity to which the Church, with all its Christian doctrine and symbolism, is likewise pointing us. This, indeed, they appear often to realize, their latest work being often remarkably Christian in point of surface detail: I am thinking of *Henry VIII*, the conclusion to *Faust*, Shelley's *Prometheus*, and Wordsworth's alterations to the *Prelude*. There is here no analogy in Keats, but his poetry is so purely and spontaneously in the tradition of Jesus' poetry that one would scarcely wish it mixed with anything but its own perfection. Therefore we find the great world of poetic vision to hold one of the two keys to the Realm of Life. The Christian Church holds the other. And this poetic Christianity, or Christian poetry, has grown organically, without pressure or effort, often itself thinking to be cut adrift from Christian teaching. Jesus' prophecy has been remarkably fulfilled. We can see a Christian Renaissance rising in the near future. God has made the seed to grow after his own wisdom: and a mighty harvest awaits us to-day. But no celestial avatar need be expected. The time for miracles is past: it always was. The Kingdom of Heaven is at hand: that too has been so before. Only our poetry awaits our understanding. The branches of the fig-tree are softening and putting out leaves and the summer is at hand.

Renaissance poetry is Christian on two separate counts. First, it is Christian because it is poetry, and Christianity properly understood is not only a poetical religion but a religion whose central dogma, like the teachings of its central figure, is precisely Poetry or Incarnation. Thus pre-Christian poets too are properly complementary to our faith. The New Testament rises over former and subsequent visions, the heart of all poetry, its life pulsing equally in Hellenic and Renaissance literature: for we must sometimes try to see all literature laid out, as an area, all contemporaneous, all supplementing and drawing life from the central origin and heart of life. While we isolate the New Testament, comparing it with no other poetry, we shall fail to understand its proper authority. All poetry is Christian. Secondly, all literature of the Christian era must be especially impregnated with Christian feeling. Its death-visions and life-visions pursue closely the Biblical rhythms: poet after poet writes his Old and New Testament. Consider how our Renaissance poets stress union and love and an awakened life; a death-conquest, a freedom from evil: all this is close to Christian doctrine. In both worlds death and evil are interdependent concepts. In our poets, the origin of evil is often given expression similar to that in the Old Testament: and the conquest of evil, as in St. Paul, is always reached by love. Necessarily, many of our great and so-called pagan poets become specifically Christian in their latest work. Such has been the organic growth of the Realm of God.

But this rich poetic life has not been properly united with Christianity. The Provencal troubadours, blending the erotic ideal with the Virgin symbol, started a betrothal which has never been consummated in marriage. The Renaissance was well-named. A splendid rebirth, it vitalized our poetry with many Hellenic excellences, but failed to integrate the new poetry with Christianity. That integration awaits us to-day. This is no new and extravagant suggestion. Christianity itself was born from a marriage of East and West, Hebraism and Hellenism: without a marriage there is no birth, nor continued life. Jesus himself was a Jew, of Judaic training, St. Paul by education and intellectual sympathy, partly at least, Greek. St. John is likewise somewhat of an Hellenic philosopher. Jesus spoke in Aramaic, the New Testament was written in the Greek language. The stage of this first act was aptly Judaea, at the meeting of the two worlds, Eastern and Western. Now for centuries of Christianity the Hebraic and ethical element preponderated, rightly and with necessity, over the Hellenic. But, at the Renaissance, a new influx from Hellenic power-sources created a splendid blaze, a new life. Spenser's poetry shows for a while a blending of Christianity and the Renaissance imagination comparable with Dante's: and it is a rich thing. But there was no lasting union, and to-day poetry and religion are absurdly separated: two separated pursuits of the same kind, pointing, it would seem, diversely, and simultaneously honoured by our distraught and paradoxical civilization. If the Churches are failing to-day, that is not through any intellectual and scientific advance: but because two gods, the Eros and the Christ, are contending in our hearts for sovereignty.

Our great prophet in this matter is Goethe. In Part I of his *Faust* he points the danger of the life-instinct allowed precipitate expression. In Part II he dramatizes the Renaissance ideal of an absolute Beauty not conflicting with actual life. Starting with court entertainment introducing Hellenic and rustic personages, mythical and realistic, men and gods, he passes from entertainment, through the highly erotic but fleeting vision of Helen and Paris, to a serious, indeed a profoundly significant, quest: that of Faust for Helen. I have already shown how this is helped by Wagner, the medieval student, who succeeds in the alchemist's ambition to create life. Homunculus is made: at least, all but made. He is still in his 'glass', not yet incarnated, not free from the laboratory, till he meets Galatea, and spills his flame in love-union with her. So Goethe sees the Medieval science as on the brink of a great new life, pointing to it, and this life is something beautiful, something Hellenic. So Medieval science loses itself in the Renaissance, a Renaissance it has itself created, and the stage is free for Faust to unite with Helen.

The whole *Helena* deserves close attention. It is profoundly significant. Exquisite indeed are the Medieval descriptions given to Helen, telling her of the brave new world she is to enter. The marriage is not one-sided: Faust offers her as much as she can offer him. Here is the grand ceremony:

> Faust, after the pages and esquires have descended in a long train, appears above in the staircase in medieval knightly court-costume, and descends with stately dignity.

Faust addresses her with courtly chivalry. Helen, late in danger from Menelaus, is in a new world of chivalry: Greece herself knew not how to honour the living beauty of woman. But Christianity, and the birth of romance literature, stand between Menelaus and Faust: so Faust is gentle, chivalrously noble. He reproaches Lynceus for not announcing Helen's arrival. Lynceus is

> the man
> With rarest eyebeam, from the lofty tower

> To gaze around appointed, Heaven's abyss
> And Earth's expanse keenly to over eye . . .
>
> (329)

Is he the Christian Church? Yet his name is Greek. Consider him rather to represent the Medieval intellect at its highest. Anyway, he is quickly subdued to the wondrous lady. Praise after praise he pours on her:

> We wandered from the Rising Sun,
> And straightway was the West undone!
>
> (331)

And Faust prepares for splendid life:

> Paradises
> That nothing lack of life but life prepare.
>
> (333)

There is the exquisite dialogue where Faust speaks in rhyme unknown to ancient Greece, and Helen asks the sweet secret of this novel speech:

> Faust: 'Tis easy, so but from the heart it rise;
> And when the breast with yearning doth o'erflow,
> You look around and ask—
> Helen: Who shares the glow?
>
> (334)

So the game goes on. This is no retrogression to a past age: rather a dynamic and immediate union leading to new birth. Old legends of Greece are dead, since their meaning is lost: that is, lost until recreated by new understanding, and that new understanding will transform the old myth:

> Hear ye tones most sweetly golden!
> Free yourselves from fables! Lo,
> Overworn the medley olden
> Of your gods is. Let them go!
>
> None your meaning recognizes;
> Now we claim a higher toll!

> What from out the heart arises
> Can alone the heart control.
>
> (344)

The grim Phorkyas speaks these lines; but Phorkyas is changed in this Renaissance joy. The Greek Chorus wonder at it all:

> Hath the witching strain outpoured,
> Fearful Being, charmed thine ears,
> We, as new to health restored,
> Feel us touched to joy of tears.
>
> Quenchéd be the sun's high splendour,
> In the soul if day hath shined!
> What the whole world would not render,
> That in our own heart we find.
>
> (344)

'The Kingdom of Heaven is within you'.

By this Hellenic and Erotic Renaissance, our Renaissance poets attain to Christian grace. Have Dante, Shakespeare, Goethe, been blundering in the dark? And is our Christianity, as preached to-day, all sufficient? Now Goethe sees Euphorion, that is Byron or Shelley, the Romantic Age, born of Faust and Helen and therefore child of the Renaissance, yet failing through over-aspiration. So Shelley and D. H. Lawrence fail: in life, though not in art. Goethe presses on to a more tangible gospel of creative action and service to man, and a Christian immortality. He creates the Hellenic splendour, next returns to practical problems and his gospel of creative work. And this complements, but does not invalidate, the prophetic glory of the *Helena;* just as the *Helena* complements, but does not invalidate, the love-mysticism of Part I. And all is finally unified when Gretchen, the primal love-force in the poem—since she has an actuality over and above Helen—receives Faust into a Christian Paradise.

Goethe is a noble prophet. Most noble, perhaps, in his expression of the sanctity of the human heart:

> What from out the heart arises,
> Can alone the heart control.

That is why a true prophet must be a poet: and to a true prophet, all poetry is easy:

> 'Tis easy
> So but from the heart it rise.

'From the heart'. Has our religious literature since the Renaissance always risen 'from the heart'? Or has it not had something in it of a forced growth, a hothouse plant, exotic, unnatural, when set beside the splendid outspoken statements of the poets? The Realm of God is a tree that refuses to be enclosed in conservatories: it has taken its own way, growing in fertile soil.

But the Renaissance is not yet over. It has, indeed, not yet properly begun. From the first shock and kiss of that contact poetry and Christianity have reeled asunder, in amaze, embarrassment, fear. To-day again they approach each other: and we are all weak in our fear and pale-spirited anxiety. Life's richness eludes us, and no heaven compensates for our impoverishment on earth. But the poets sing to battle and can yet array our weakened minds in the glistering armour of truth. A long succession of richest prophecy is ours. By our own wilfulness, or the will of God, it has been clasped in books sealed impenetrably to our understanding. But those treasures are no longer closed to us: they can now awake our unsettled dreams to a daylight sanity and Christian strength.

For the world to-day is in a sorry case. On the one side, we have a weakened Christianity, irrelevantly defending itself against a science that has ceased to attack it; on the other, a chaotic art, in its popular expressions erotic to the point of immorality. Two joints of one limb are horribly dislocated, and our civilization writhes in pain. While the Churches lose power, we see that dances, the radio, cinematographs, the revue stage, romantic novels, all draw men and women in multitudes, speaking direct to their hearts. Clearly a significant unity pervades these attractions, lying somewhere between the limits of sexual desire and a sense of ideal beauty. Romance, actual or imagined, in dances, jazz-music, in entertainment of all kinds, relieves the tension of a sterile existence, its restraint, monotony, and slow pain. These are, in part, valuable, being at least, active, assertive things, enthroning the positive powers. And in comparison our Christianity is too often dark and threatening; or, worse, pallid and fearful, diluting the rich wine of its poetic heritage with the waters of scientific rationalism. At its best, it offers too much that is negative, minatory, awe-inspiring, alienating rather than channelling the erotic instincts: it is not in any sense alluring. We are still afraid of Israel's Jehovah, forgetting the Christ.

It is not possible to condemn popular eroticism as superficial; still less as, in essence, vicious. For in the best literature, as in the worst, eroticism is powerful. We need often to forget distinctions of artistic merit, for such blur our sight from universal significances. Just as it is fatal to make any too rigid technical distinctions between one great poet and another, so it is ultimately fatal to distinguish finally between the life-blood beating in *Wuthering Heights* and *The Rosary*. Certainly the popular novel of to-day, the works, say, of Miss Ruby Ayres, or Miss Berta Ruck, though not intellectually profound, are usually true enough to the main purpose of romantic narrative, the awaking and directing of the erotic perceptions, and the relation of these to the world-order of frustration and death. It is the same with our cinemas. They are usually not immoral: they are not, anyway, addressed to the intellectual minority. For consider. Is it not right that masses, of varying culture, should take pleasure in seeing youth, virtue, and beauty continually triumphant over middle-age, ugliness, and evil? Our sentimental films regularly assert life's sovereignty over death. So our more popular art is, however weakly, in the tradition of great poetry. For youth and love are universal ideals: we do not paint our angels on crutches.

And all this is true, too, of the drama. And yet, to-day, the drama endures an indecisive and baffling transition. We have a realistic drama which aims to present typical, though crucial, scenes with as much similarity to 'real life' as possible: and yet such is not life at all but only the husk or shell passing for reality to a hasty and unconsidering eye. It is photographic and colourless, lacking the richer qualities which the drama at its best includes: the surges of emotion, rhythm in gesture, verbal melody, colour, grouping, and design. Photographic drama is a corpse whose life-blood is drained. Yet these richer elements are found elsewhere, rioting in meaningless extravagance, without co-ordination or control or any relevance to human life, and therefore dangerously divorced from ethic. So we have violent and mechanical dances, drenching limelights of hectic colour, jazz-music unvaried and misapplied. Nakedness, by itself quite legitimate in service to the true Eros, is often so employed as to raise sexual desire without any corresponding artistic satisfaction. So a thousand insubstantial emotions are jumbled together in a hashed medley of cheap vulgarity. And yet it is here, rather than in the intellectualized problem play, that we find those appeals to colour, erotic emotion, rhythm and music, from which Dante builds his Paradise.

Our refusal as Christians to recognize and direct the vast powers of erotic instinct within man is indeed dangerous. For, cut adrift from all issues but titillating amusement, the Eros is truly vindictive; and rightly. All art, all Christianity, at its best, is this ever and this only: a means to direct the life-instinct, to relate it to its own fulfilment in vision, ethic, and creative action; to awake man to his immortality, his heritage of richest life. At present, we have a popular drama awaking sex-instincts, and leaving them undirected; while our Church concentrates on the anger or peace of God, yet leaving its statements quite divorced from those richer instincts through which only it can be truly creative. Christianity must include, not reject, the Eros; for Eros is a great god, jealous as Jehovah, and quite as powerful. Our cloistered palaces of devotion cast but a dim religious light across the stone floors of our minds, too sickly a pallor for a world so darkened by incertitude. How can this religion, concentrating on reproof, discipline, and sacrifice, challenge with its ghostly canticles the lithe grace and laughing eyes of our as yet unrecognized Eros? But is this Christianity, or merely the ghost of it? Is this the radiant poetry of life, the freedom from the Law, envisaged, experienced, and announced by St. Paul? Where is the living water promised by Jesus? Where, to-day, the resurrected and triumphant Christ? It is significant that Dante sees condemned souls as solemnly moving with a motion that suggests Church ritual:

Earnest I looked
Into the depth, that opened to my view,
Moistened with tears of anguish, and beheld
A tribe, that came along the hollow vale,
In silence weeping: such their step as walk
Choirs, chanting solemn litanies, on earth.
(*Hell*, XX, 4).

But his Paradise is a place of dance and song, smiles and laughing eyes, a place of 'amorous dalliance' (*Paradise*, XXVII, 84), of 'laughter unblamed, and ever-new delight' (*Purgatory*, XXVIII, 98). Nor do I suggest that death-experience and that solemnity it creates be erased altogether from divine ceremony. That ritual must take note of death, yet never forgetting that its primary aim is to raise us to life. To-day there is all too little life-splendour in the ecclesiastical imagination, and paradisal hopes have deserted our pulpits. So we prison the very Script of Life in solemn black, and the priests of the living God are aptly uniformed in mourning.

Never in the world's history have poetry and religion, drama and divine worship, been so cruelly divorced. And until that separation becomes again union, our pain shall inevitably endure. Poetry and religion since the Renaissance have been as two splendid coupled horses curveting and prancing aside from their direction, fighting the one against the other: one fiery and of sparkling eye, impatient of restraint; the other noble in dignity but darkly suspicious of its companion, angry that its natural and unhurrying pace be disturbed. So the twin imaginative forces inspiring our Western civilization have been mutually hindered, and the chariot they would lift onwards and upwards now rumbles from its path, all but overturned, among boulders and watercourses and mud. We need to-day, as Christians, to face our Renaissance, our poetic heritage, accepting and ratifying this marriage union with all its implications and all its splendour of life. Half-life is safe, but life itself in its deathless naked beauty is a terror to us, squint-eyed, and veiling our understanding from the sun. Nor, when this marriage is consummated in a true union, will Christianity be one whit impoverished. As a man takes a wife and finds, or should find were these things more happily arranged, his own self enriched and empowered by the other self he loves, its very difference a joy and a wonder and a liberation releasing an unguessed strength, so will our Christian revelation be found only the more splendid for the new truth it encloses and transcends; its own dogmas most strangely revitalized; its own prophecies most miraculously fulfilled. Then, indeed, our Church will cease to send missionaries to far countries; rather those countries will send their legates to us, as they have done already in matters of scientific learning, searching in our Christianity for the secret of our life. But while the Church refuses to recognize its own children in inspiration, it denies that very life it cherishes.

Only a Christian Renaissance can fulfil the derelict purposes of the modern world: and birth is conditional on marriage and union. It is indeed most significant that our finest and most representative English poet, Mr. T. S. Eliot, has to-day written his positive life-visions in terms both of Christianity and Shakespeare's most exquisite paradisal play, *Pericles*. To both Shakespeare and Christianity we must look for guidance. And to other poets also. For all art will be sanctified by our enlightened religious understanding. We may therefore expect a new Christianized literature and a newly-poetic Christianity. Neither religion as it is to-day, nor poetry as it is to-day, will survive. Yet, again, our Christian faith, our Shakespeare, our poets, will indeed live, but not as they have lived before. They will pass, they are already passing, toward the greater life of our new-born recognition. Dogma and symbol, though no longer rigid strictures on our worship, will be known as the very language of the ineffable, the richest currency of truth. They will be seen to exist in order to extend, not to limit, our understanding. So a new poetry will arise, and a new drama; and all our arts and our religion will alike recognize that each and all serve the one great purpose of their existence: the refraction itself of life, or immortality.

A new drama must necessarily accompany our revitalized theology. The two are, indeed, interdependent. This dramatic art, as yet unwritten and only dimly conceived, will respect the prompting instincts and diverse aspirations of man. It will be, like Shakespeare's work, both erotic and visionary; and, finally, more deeply Christian even than his. It will distil the rich essences of human emotion, human desire and failure, life and death and that immortality enclosing both. The representation will often appear as an idealized representation: since, to express essentials, we must employ poetry of speech and grace of movement, effects of colour and grouping, and accompaniment often of music. In this drama man will be, as it were, transfigured by poetry, a creature of compelling life whether he be, in the fiction, criminal, lord, or lover. Such poetry has deserted our stage. But there will be a renaissance. The bastard forms may continue for awhile: the advent of the true cannot for long be delayed. The theatre is, indeed, no place for trivialities. Its orchestration can, and should, release the varied harmonies of the life we live, revealing those extra dimensions in our psychic experience, which we, our sight surface-bound, seldom observe. In great drama we know our life as it is, those deeper seas into which it sinks and which its movement cleaves, those sun-arrows glistening on its topmost peaks. And such profound knowledge reveals always not sordid but noble qualities, riches of emotion, whether of tragedy or romance, vast forces of Christ-like good and Satanic evil, contesting powers of life and death. Every great drama is a branch on the Tree of Life. It crystallizes for us that meaning and fine purpose in human existence to which we are too often blind. It is dynamic and points towards futurity, since only by learning what we truly are do we simultaneously learn what we may become. Drama is creative of life. We are all alive, but seldom know it. By knowing our life we expand and enrich it until, becoming one with Life itself, we attain our immortality. The drama, like the religious symbolism from which it has grown, awakes us to ourselves. Addressing its meaning first to our unawakened consciousness, speaking in terms of disunion and disharmony, next, these antinomies resolved in the whole, it creates and recreates our life.

Such a drama depends on our understanding of symbolism. Drama at its highest is intensely symbolic. And therefore the advent of a new poetic drama is one with the advent of a newly vitalized theology. In the world of symbolism no rigid distinctions must be made between the human and the divine. The divine is symbolized in the human, is, indeed, in art or life, one with humanity. Poetic drama is throughout humanistic, yet mystic, creating a greater humanity whilst it reveals us to ourselves. Christianity likewise has been extravagantly humanistic, showing the brows of man himself ablaze with the fire-gold laurels of the divine. This is the fine hyperbole whereby, through the Incarnation, the splendours of poetry are inbound with a perfect human life in the present order of darkness and illusion. And our Christian Trinity is, as I have shown, but a simplification in human terms of all drama, the one dramatic architype and pattern to which all drama and all life, in Dantesque metaphor, are as concentric circles out-radiating, out-furling, out-flowering.

But all this we cannot understand while we think a symbol is a savage and idolatrous thing; nor while we fear its mystery, and resent any attempt to exploit its meaning. Such attitudes characterize, indeed, only those to whom symbolic speech is dead. But, when once we recognize the fluidity and elasticity of symbolic utterance, its height and depth, its solid statement, its variation within unity, its modernity, above all, its creative power, we shall know symbolism to be, indeed, the very way to life. We shall then find truth in all high prophecy, questioning less as to whether its reference to future events be earthly or eschatological: usually, indeed, we do well to regard it as both. For both are projections into futurity of an immediate and creative idea. Unless so projected, such statements lose their creative power: they are thus creatively true, and to see their meaning we must first believe; their very truth being conditional on our belief and creative response. Symbolism is a live, not a dead thing; dynamic and creative, not repressive; originating from the future to which it points, not to be understood in relation to the past from which its face is turned.

To-day we have scant insight into these things. So, though organized Christianity satisfies some, it repels many others. It leaves a great number, devout and anxious, unsatisfied, baffled, without direction or hope; because symbolism is a dead thing to us, and also because the legitimate and natural emotional appeals are repressed, ignored, or denounced. We desire liberation and are loaded with fetters; we ask for life, and are too often only reminded of death; we need to be awakened, and are given narcotics. Long past humanity first ate of the Tree of the Knowledge of Good and Evil. We have fed long on that knowledge and the taste is bitter. We are yet in the dreamland of good and evil, and our eyes but fitfully focus the eternal Beauty which is our star. In that Eden there was also the Tree of Life, which had power to confer immortality and make gods of men: its fruit is now swiftly ripening. The race of man to-day stirs unrestfully in his fevered sleep, hearing across his world of chaotic dreams the voice of ancient Greece, the poetry of Renaissance Europe. Let but the Church recognize the inclusive splendours of her Revelation. She is as a mother who, afraid that her child cannot safely preserve his own individuality, tries to hold him from dangerous contact with the world. Christianity has nothing to fear, save fear itself. It holds greater treasures than any poet can create, and indeed, if all the pens that ever poets held were to unite to recreate the Christian drama, they would find one wonder at the least undigested in their art. But the poets, and all they stand for, are necessary to us, just as Christianity is necessary to them. Through union only will there be any further creative life. And if it be asked how exactly this renascent life-force is to be brought to Earth, it is, indeed, quite possible to name the first step we, as Christians, must take. We may remember that 'spirit' in our theological metaphysic has been always, until incarnated, evil. The Holy Ghost or Spirit, in so far as it is not incarnated in our hearts, our lives, our actions or our art, is directly equivalent to Death, not Life: only in incarnation is it a life-force. No ghost is good: but incarnate life is good. Therefore the New Incarnation and Christian Renaissance must see the embodiment in art, in ceremony, in our lives, of the Holy Eros and Sacred Life to which our Renaissance prophets direct us. This is the necessary fulfilment of our Trinity. This only, the relating of the third person of the Trinity to the erotic vision, and the consequent recognition of all poetry's sacred life. From that, all that we need will follow. Poetry alone can awake the heart of the Western world at the dawn of the white fire of Christ.

I must not conclude in a blaze of light. Both religion and poetry, as practised and understood to-day, will pass. They will pass, when the time is ripe, to bring to birth a greater thing than either, a new Life, splendorously paling those twin candles that have stood before its altar. There is much talk to-day of a return to Christianity; but rather we must advance towards it, grow up to it, measuring our understanding to its true stature. Now throughout this book we have seen that the purest and richest visions are quiet, not extravagant; richly coloured, but not dazzling. Jesus, Shakespeare, and Keats are the great masters of the perfect speech. But our light-poets are necessary too, St. Paul, Dante, Shelley, for we dwell mostly in realms of night. And yet, again, we may remember how in Dante's final vision the triple Godhead was seen blazing outward from a human form. Our religious literature, ceremonial, and music, should awake us to life: there is all too much death already. We need a fiery star to glitter in our hearts and before our eyes, illumining our darkness: but human existence, richer often for sacrifice than for self-assertion, for sorrow than for joy, will go on as before. The eye altering all; it is we who must first change, not our existence. We must create a finer life, or rather let that life create itself in us. Already we have done so, and the world of men grows better hour by hour. The noblest wine will still often be crushed from humanity by pain and thwarted longing; but within the coarse texture of material things is woven a richer thread, a coloured pattern unexposed, foretold in dreams, in sleep, most exquisite and rich. No fevered flush, nor dazzling blaze, but a warmth, an embrace, a rich happiness. Our future poetry must see our city streets tipped with that pentecostal flame; but those cities will for long be areas still heavy with suffering, with darkness, illusion, and death. These themselves must pulse with life; through these we must burn our way, in spite of these know our freedom, because of these create our hope.

Nobly indeed the Christian Church, in all its branches, has worked, and is yet working, to alleviate this suffering. It is easy to blame it for all the thousand ills our mortal flesh inherits; to ignore both its leavening influence throughout the centuries and its activity to-day. It is easy, all too easy, to forget the arduous labours the parish priest performs the while the poet makes his dreams. But again, our Church is itself the body given to a dream once lived in Judea; and we neglect the vital power-sources at our peril. We have long obeyed and respected a father-god. But another desire is poignant to-day: one which suggests not separation but union. I ask that we receive the Holy Eros and divine comforter, whose silent kiss and invisible embrace holds warmth and joy without which we starve. Though our days be darkly embroidered with suffering, our pain is not unheeded; and however grim the forces of death may seem to us, life is always marshalling new myriads to drive that death finally into the hell from which it first arose. For life, not death, has the victory: this is the message alike of poet and prophet. But indeed, the poet is the prophet. We must henceforth see all great poetry as truly prophetic, so that Shelley's words may be fulfilled in all their splendour:

> Poets are the hierophants of an unapprehended inspiration; the mirrors of the gigantic shadows which futurity casts upon the present; the words which express what they understand not; the trumpets which sing to battle and feel not what they inspire; the influence which is moved not, but moves. Poets are the unacknowledged legislators of the world.

And Jesus, as Carlyle tells us, is the greatest of all poets.

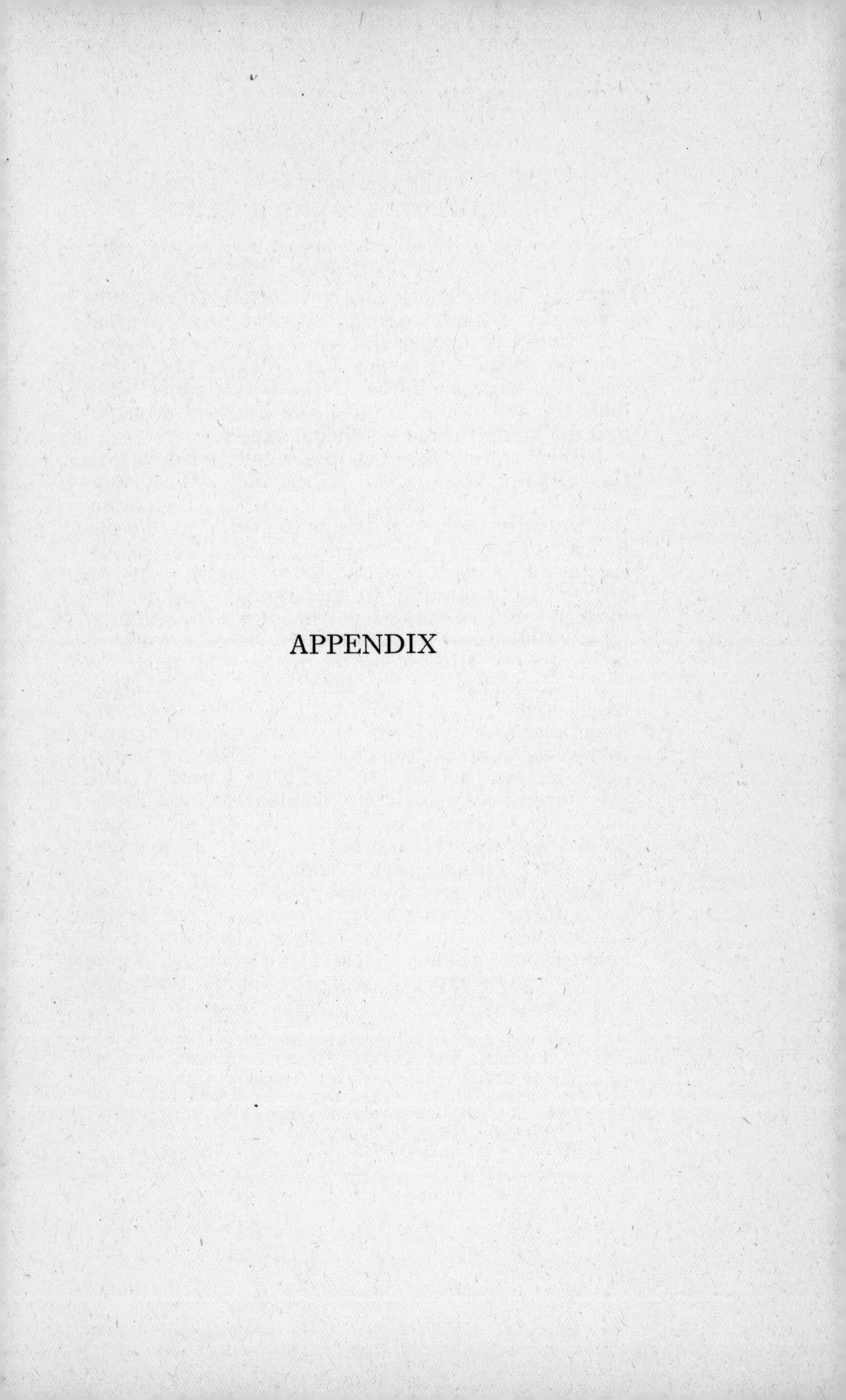

APPENDIX

A NOTE ON THE POETRY OF T. S. ELIOT

(Composed for the radio, and delivered from the University of Toronto, February, 1932)

THE best modern poetry is often difficult. To say in its defence that this is true of all great work is to shirk the issue, since recent poetry is clearly difficult in a new way. Taking Mr. Eliot's poetry as representative of the best that is being done to-day, I shall try to make clear its direction and the kind of thing we should expect.

Hitherto poets have, on the whole, tried to give their imaginations some appearance of common-sense, in plot, in sentence-structure, in punctuation. But the most important things in poetry were never primarily these, but rather consisted of colour, suggestion, association, and word magic. This we are to-day beginning to understand, and so the modern poet sometimes tends to cut out the starting-point of logic and plunge straight into the world of imagination. Himself on the roof-top of vision, he carelessly kicks away the ladder, and so makes it a little difficult for others to join him. And yet something is gained: we are in no danger of mistaking the surface for the essence. Modern poetry often has no surface. In Mr. Eliot's work I shall therefore notice shortly his imaginative associations and colourings rather than expect any exact philosophy: and this is what we should always first do in interpreting a poet's vision.

His earlier poems are pessimistic. Often we find some form of present-day sordidness put beside bright images of legend or history. Drabness is set against vivid colour. Here is an example, where 'eagles' and 'trumpets' are used to suggest the heroic and romantic:

> The red-eyed scavengers are creeping
> From Kentish Town to Golder's Green;
> Where are the eagles and the trumpets?
> Buried beneath some snow-deep Alps.
> Over buttered scones and crumpets
> Weeping, weeping multitudes
> Droop in a hundred A.B.C.'s.

The contrast is the more powerful left just like that. So often in Mr. Eliot's work a scarecrow is set to droop its rain-soaked rags beside a Greek statue. And this poetic act is very interesting. The world's history is bright with romantic splendour. Heroes of myth stride colossal and divine across the ancestry of our race, and Christianity is the culmination of a necessary and universal instinct. It would be rash to call such stories false. They keep alive our romantic faith, when romance is, at first sight, hard to discover in the present. Yet it must be there, too, if anywhere.

> Where are the eagles and the trumpets?

The answer is that they are to be found somewhere very close to the 'butter'd scones and crumpets'. To know this is easy, to feel it is often, but not always, impossible.

Mr. Eliot's poetry thus has very deep meanings. His longest single work is one called *The Waste Land*. It is a difficult poem, but again there is a starkly cruel contrast of past romance with present reality. We wonder whether it is we who to-day are blind, or whether the racial memory has false-painted history with a harlot's art. And one with this jostling of the centuries is the poet's frequent use of time-honoured literary quotations left to sprout and flame exotically in their grim contexts. At one moment we have

> I think we are in rat's alley
> Where the dead men lost their bones

and, soon after, a line from *The Tempest*:

> Those are pearls that were his eyes . . .

The Waste Land is chaotic. But the gaps in its logic may be said to serve a purpose since to fill them in would show a sequence and relation where the poem would point rather to the absence of any such relation. No earlier poet has so emphasized the illogical chaos of things in this world. Thus, at this extreme of despair, we necessarily see all history as unreal. Here is a passage from *The Waste Land:*

What is that sound high in the air
Murmur of maternal lamentation
Who are those hooded hordes swarming
Over endless plains, stumbling in cracked earth
Ringed by the flat horizon only
What is the city over the mountains
Cracks and reforms and bursts in the violet air
Falling towers
Jerusalem Athens Alexandria
Vienna London
Unreal.

Notice how the Celestial City towers over the desert pilgrimage of time, dissolving, reforming, bursting—and the fallen pieces are as the broken pieces of the cities of this world.

This is, therefore, poetry of essential death, and Mr. Eliot's sombre work is finely consummated in the death-vision of the poem called *The Hollow Men.* Here we have a choking darkness, blindness, strangling impressions of 'light', 'sight', 'stars' which would dimly penetrate the murk:

This is the dead land
This is cactus land
Here the stone images
Are raised, here they receive
The supplication of a dead man's hand
Under the twinkle of a fading star.

* * * * *

The eyes are not here
There are no eyes here
In this valley of dying stars
In this hollow valley
This broken jaw of our lost kingdoms . . .

The poem concludes with a struggle between the cynical and distorting intellect with its dark army of complications and the breaking light of a Christian dawn. But cynicism wins.

Yet its victory is not final. Mr. Eliot's later poems advance with varying assurance toward visions of light and life. These are mostly sought in terms of Christianity. This new style gives us *Ash Wednesday,* a series of religious poems reflecting our present religious incertitudes in a subtle poetic technique made of delicate assonances, alliteration, internal rhyme, a delightful texture of inwoven sound and meaning:

Where shall the word be found, where will the word
Resound? Not here, there is not enough silence
Not on the sea or on the islands, not
On the mainland, in the desert or the rain land,
For those who walk in darkness
Both in the day time and in the night time
The right time and the right place are not here . . .

Mr. Eliot's present work thus marks an advance in vision, and, after the death valleys of *The Waste Land* and *The Hollow Men,* we find images of life and hope—the 'veiled sister', the 'children at the gate', and so on. We have the brilliant immortality line:

While jewelled unicorns draw by the gilded hearse . . .

And in *Animula* we find a study of childhood reminding us of Wordsworth's great Ode.

But perhaps the finest of Mr. Eliot's recent poems is *Marina,* closely related to Shakespeare's *Pericles.* Two themes are blended: a wearied ship piercing through the fog toward the bird-music of some magic island; and the death of death, as the wanderer wakes into some new mode of life, and recognition, and love. Here all who make rumour of death

Are become unsubstantial, reduced by a wind,
A breath of pine, and the woodsong fog
By this grace dissolved in place
What is this face, less clear and clearer
The pulse in the arm, less strong and stronger—
Given or lent? More distant than stars and nearer
than the eye
Whispers and small laughter between leaves and
hurrying feet
Under sleep, where all the waters meet.

The poem ends on a note of expectancy:

What seas what shores what granite islands towards
my timbers
And woodthrush calling through the fog
My daughter.

Again we have children—the 'small laughter' and 'hurrying feet'—and the idea of the child in 'my daughter'. This interweaving of child-symbolism, the ship, the sea, and a magic shore, reminds us variously of *The Tempest* and Wordsworth's Ode. The whole poem is, as it were, breathless with adoration and expectancy, on the brink of an impossible awakening, an undreamed joy.

These poems are typical of our generation. Typical of its despair, its sense of futility. But typical, too, of the stirring which to-day heralds a revival to dispel our consciousness of death. That Mr. Eliot's more positive poetic statements should be presented in terms of Christian Orthodoxy is extremely significant. It is equally significant that his most recent, and perhaps his most exquisite, happy poem should be directly related to one of Shakespeare's supreme acts of paradisal vision.

Mr. Eliot's work has all the characteristics of enduring literature. His most powerful imaginative effects are not private and personal, but rather repeat the traditional colourings of the Bible, Dante, Shakespeare, Goethe, Shelley, Tennyson. We must attend always in studying poetry to these—the symbols, the impressions of life and death, the riches of imaginative statement, not to inessential differences of technique between poet and poet. Then all poetry will become more easy, and far more important. Moreover, if we regard Mr. Eliot's work as a whole, we find a small, but intense, poetic world of the same quality as Shakespeare's and Dante's. It has its visions of darkness; its progress towards paradisal radiance. Starting from the Old Testament of cynicism and death, it moves towards the New Testament of victorious life.

P.S. Since writing this note I have been shown an essay by Prince D. S. Mirsky which draws attention to Mr. Eliot's use of water and fire in *The Waste Land;* which recalls my interpretation of Goethe's *Faust*. Mr. Eliot's poem is full of these and other such naturalistic and fertility symbolisms. On such all good poetry must to a large extent depend; and probably *The Waste Land*—its title is significant—is far closer to such a work as *Faust* than is usually supposed.

All poetry celebrates a divine creation by marriage of humanity and nature.